THE ADVENTURE GUIDE TO COSTA RICA

Harry S. Pariser

MPC
HUNTER
PUBLISHING INC

Hunter Publishing, Inc.
300 Raritan Center Parkway
Edison NJ 08818
(201) 225 1900

ISBN 1–55650–456–X

Published in the UK by:
Moorland Publishing Co. Ltd.
Moor Farm Road, Airfield Estate
Ashbourne, Derbyshire DE6 1HD
England

ISBN (UK) 0 86190 427 3

ACKNOWLEDGMENTS

Thanks go out to my publisher Michael Hunter and his staff, my mapmaker, Joyce Huber, Serge Volio, Waldon P. McDonald Jr., Xavier Saunders, Barbara, Michelle, Natalie Ewing, Howard Solomón, Sergio Miranda T., Rodrigo Quiros F., Maria Pinagel, Bob Grey, Amos Bien, Katsuo Fujii, Susie Poulelis, Carl Parkes, Gordon Slack, Linda Holland, Max Barnett, Meg White, Dave Henson, Lisa, and to many others.

Photo Credits

All photographs by author, except as indicated.
Cover: sloth, along the waterway to Tortuguero.

CONTENTS

LIST OF MAPS

ABOUT THE AUTHOR

Harry S. Pariser was born in Pittsburgh and grew up in a small town in southwestern Pennsylvania. After graduating from Boston University with a B.S. in Public Communications in 1975, Harry hitched and camped his way through Europe, traveled down the Nile by steamer, and by train through Sudan. After visiting Uganda, Rwanda, and Tanzania, he traveled by passenger ship from Mombasa to Bombay, and then on through South and Southeast Asia before settling down in Kyoto, Japan, where he studied Japanese and ceramics while supporting himself by teaching English to everyone from tiny tots to Buddhist priests. Using Japan as a base, he returned to other parts of Asia: trekking to the vicinity of Mt. Everest in Nepal, taking tramp steamers to remote Indonesian islands like Adonara, Timor, Sulawesi, and Ternate, and visiting rural areas in China. He returned to the United States in 1984 from Kanazawa, Japan, via the Caribbean where he did research for two travel guides: Guide to Jamaica and Guide to Puerto Rico and the Virgin Islands, the first editions of which were published in 1986. Returning to Japan in 1986, he lived in the city of Kagoshima—a city at the southern tip of Kyushu which lies across the bay from an active volcano. During that year and part of the next, he taught English and wrote numerous articles for *The Japan Times.* He currently lives in San Francisco. Besides traveling and writing, his other pursuits include printmaking, painting, cooking, hiking, photography, reading, and listening to music—especially jazz.

Other guides from Hunter Publishing by Harry Pariser: ADVENTURE GUIDE TO BELIZE; ADVENTURE GUIDE TO BARBADOS; ADVENTURE GUIDE TO PUERTO RICO; ADVENTURE GUIDE TO THE VIRGIN ISLANDS; JAMAICA, A VISITOR'S GUIDE.

HELP US KEEP THIS GUIDE UP-TO-DATE

In today's world, things change so rapidly that it's impossible for one person to keep up with everything happening in any one place. This is particularly true in Central America, where situations are always in flux. Travel books are like automobiles: they require fine tuning and frequent overhauls to keep in shape. Help us keep this book in shape! We require input from our readers so that we can continue to provide the best, most current information available. Please write to let us know about any inaccuracies, new information, or misleading suggestions. Although we try to make our maps as accurate as possible, errors do occur. If you have any suggestions for improvement or places that should be included, please let us know about it.

We especially appreciate letters from female travelers, visiting expatriates, local residents, and hikers and outdoor enthusiasts. We also like hearing from experts in the field as well as from local hotel owners and individuals wishing to accommodate visitors from abroad.

INTRODUCTION

Encompassing an area half the size of Ireland, the nation of Costa Rica brings together pronounced geographical extremes—from spectacular beaches to majestic volcanoes, from swampy lowlands with swarms of birds to highlands which turn frigid at night. Although smaller than most US states and Canadian provinces, it is larger than Holland, Denmark, Belgium, and Switzerland. In addition to traditional Tico hospitality, Costa Rica offers hiking and water sports, casinos and discos, and a wealth of wildlife which makes it a paradise for naturalists and birdwatchers.

THE LAND

the big picture: The Central American isthmus is the only region in the world which is both interoceanic and intercontinental. Bordered by Mexico to the N and Colombia to the S, the region comprises seven nations: Belize, Guatemala, El Salvador, Honduras, Nicaragua, Costa Rica, and Panama. As all of the nations except Belize are former members of the Spanish Empire, although some contain large Indian populations, they share a similar culture base which includes the Spanish language and the Catholic religion. Despite their surface simi-

Costa Rica

Peñas Blancas
La Cruz
GUANACASTE
SANTA ELENA
Upa
RINCON
GOLFO DE PAPAGAYO
Liberia
El Coco
Bagaces
Tamarindo
Santa Cruz
Cañas
PALO VERDE
Nicoya
NICOYA PENINSULA
Nosara
Sámara
Paquera
Mo
ISLA DEL COCO
PAC

U.S.A.
Atlantic Ocean
Mexico
Caribbean Sea
Pacific Ocean
Nicaragua
COSTA RICA→
Panama
South America

larities, each has evolved its own national character, making union unlikely. To the region's N lies Mexico; to its S lies the continent of South America to which the region is connected at Colombia.

geography: Covering 19,653 sq. mi. Costa Rica lies on a NW-SE axis between Nicaragua to the N and Panama to the S. It extends 288 mi. N to S and 170 m. E to W, and no part of the country is more than 300 mi. from the sea. A series of *cordilleras* (mountain ranges), ridges, and valleys traverse its length. Its unofficial border with Nicaragua, accepted provisionally by both sides, extends for 186 mi. along the N. Definitively delineated only in 1941 after a century-long dispute, its S border with Panama covers 226 mi.

mountains: The nation has four principal mountain ranges. The Cordillera de Guanacaste lies in the far NW; to the S rises the lower and smaller Cordillera de Tílaran. Farther S still are the Cordillera Central followed by the Cordillera de Talamanca. Although the first two are non-volcanic origin, the latter two sets of ranges contain several volcanoes. Two, Poás and Arenal in the Cordillera Central, are active. The Cordillera de Talamanca has 10 peaks over 10,000 ft. including 12,500-ft. Cerro Chirripó, the nation's highest point, located inside the national park of the same name. A geographical continuation of the plains (*llano*) found in Nicaragua, lowland covers most of the N and stretches along the Caribbean coast.

rivers: Innumerable rivers and streams originate in the interior highlands and flow either to the Pacific or the Caribbean. The Río San Juan collects water from streams in the northern lowlands and then flows through Nicaragua until it reaches its mouth, a delta region formed in conjunction with the Río Colorado, which lies almost entirely within Costa Rica. The Río Tortuguero flows directly to the Tortuguero waterway which parallels the Caribbean coast, stretching from the mouth of the Río Colorado to a point just N of Limón. The rivers that empty into the Pacific Ocean are fewer, shorter, and steeper.

valleys: Nestled in the Central Highlands and situated in a temperate area 3,280–4,920 ft. in elevation, the Meseta Central, comprising the major part of the Valle Central, consists of two basins separated by low hills. Taken together, these encompass an area of nearly 3,861 sq. mi. As well as being rainier and more humid than its San José neighbor to the W, the Cartago Basin to the E is smaller and higher (4,920 ft.). Situated between the Cordillera de Talamanca and the mountains bordering the Pacific, the low lying Valle de General lies to the S. Settlement began here only in the 1920s.

the coasts: Marked by steep cliffs and numerous narrow beaches, the Pacific coast stretches 631 mi. and contains three peninsulas: Buriya, Osa, and Nicoya. Although it is not entirely continuous—being separated in stretches by low-lying coastal mountains—a narrow alluvial coastal plain extends from the Peninsula de Osa in the S up to the port of Puntarenas where it widens, merging with the Valle de Tempisque. The Palmer lowland complex to the SW includes rainforests. Widest along the Nicaraguan border, the swampy, heavily forested Caribbean lowland comprises about 20% of the land area. Received after a boundary dispute with Panama was settled in 1900, the 9.3 sq. mi. Isla de Coco, situated 200 mi. SW of the Peninsula de Osa, is a national park.

CLIMATE

As holds true for the rest of Central America, Costa Rica has a delightful climate, especially in its highland areas. Its mild, subtropical weather varies little throughout the year; most of the variation in temperatures comes from differences in elevation. The E and SE coasts cool down delightfully at night during the winter. Rain, which usually consists of short showers, is most likely to occur from July through the end of November; the driest months are February and March. Although the average rainfall is about 150–200 inches annual precipitation totals actually vary from 59 inches in the NW to 197 inches in the S. Although no area is drought stricken, there is a considerable variety in both rainfall and the length of the dry and wet seasons. Winds prevail from the N during the winter and early spring months and come in from the SE during the rest of the year. Receiving the heaviest rainfall, the Caribbean coast has no dry season, and its mean annual total exceeds 79 inches everywhere. During the rainy season along the drier NW coast, rain falls in late afternoon or evening.

seasons: What residents of the northern temperate zones know as "summer" and "winter" are reversed for the Costa Ricans. As arriving Spaniards acclimatized, they associated their Mediterranean regimen of hot, dry summers and cool, wet winters with their new abode, disregarding the time frame difference. Thus, while *verano* (summer) refers to the dry season between Dec. and May, *invierno* (winter) refers to the wet season which, running from May through Nov., corresponds with the northern hemisphere summer and fall. In some years the Pacific coast has a third period, *veranillo* (little summer)— a short dry season which sometimes emerges during July and August. Temporary rainstorms of short duration which cover a small area are known as *aguaceros;* less intense storms, of wider distribution and of longer duration are known as *temporales. Temporales del Atlantico* and *temporales de Pacifico* are the two types. Both are the result of laterally moving air masses reaching mountains, rising, and cooling. More and more, as a result of widespread deforestation, *temporales* result in flooding. March showers are known as *"aquacero de los cafetaleros"* (the coffee grower's shower), and the mid-Dec. rains are known as *"las lagrimas de Mary"* (Mary's tears). Between Nov. and Jan. *nortes*—cold polar air fronts channeled southward between North American mountain ranges—reach Costa Rica, one of the few places in the world where polar air travels so close to the equator. When it blows inland from the Pacific Ocean this wind brings fine weather to the Pacific coast where it is known as *papagayo*.

climatic zones: Costa Rica has three. The *tierra caliente* (torrid zone) encompasses the two coastal plains which rise up to 1500 ft. with a corresponding temperature range of 85–90 °F. The *tierra templada* contains the Meseta Central as well as other regions between 1,500 and 5,000 ft. with temperatures from 75° to 80 °F. The *tierra fria* (frigid zone) includes areas over 5,000 ft. with temperatures ranging from 41 °F to 59 °F. On lower slopes and intermontane depressions, mean annual temperatures range from 52° to 78 °F. Up in the higher regions of the Cordillera de Talamanca and the Cordillera Central, the annual average is less than 52 °F, and the temperature may reach 32 °F on occasion. Variation in temperatures is greatest during the dry season when the nights are cool in the highlands.

earthquakes: Other than crazy drivers, the major environmental hazards are volcanic eruptions and earthquakes. Most of Cartago was destroyed by a volcanic eruption in 1910; it was also devastated by others in 1620 and 1841. Limón was heavily damaged in 1935. Three of the most recent earthquakes were in 1973 in Tilarán and two in 1983 when an April quake off the tip of Osa Peninsula left one dead and 500 homeless, and a second quake in July, based 60 km S of San José, left 3,000 homeless, two dead, and 13 seriously injured. The latest quake, measuring 5.5 on the Richter scale, struck on Mar. 25, 1990, causing landslides on the San Juan-Atlantic Coast Highway and extensive damage in Puntarenas. A series of frequent, smaller tremors followed during the ensuing months. Positioned atop a number of faults, Costa Rica is second only to Guatemala in Central America as a center of seismic activity. But Costa Rica has not experienced quakes as catastrophic as those affecting Nicaragua in 1972, Guatemala in 1976, and El Salvador in 1986. If you should experience tremors during your visit, just remember that they have been going on for millions of years and will continue until the planet's final demise. If a major tremor should occur, don't rush outside. Get to a doorway, an inside corner wall, or climb under a desk or table for protection.

FLORA AND FAUNA

Although it straddles an area from 8° to 11° N of the equator, Costa Rica has an unusually varied ecosystem. Its high, rugged, and youthful *cordilleras* contain a complex ecological mosaic as do its plains, rivers, and coasts—an ecological diversity paralleled in Central America only by Guatemala. As defined by L. R. Holdridge, there are 12 life zones in Costa Rica which are based on combining rainfall and temperature with their seasonal distribution and variation. There are four major zones (tropical dry, moist, wet, and rainforest) each with premontane and lower montane divisions; there's also the tropical subalpine rain *páramo,* or cold region.

nature watching: The land seems very much alive, and nature abounds outside of crowded and polluted San José. Many species are nocturnal, but tend to gather in early evening or morning at water holes. Tours can get you where the animals are. See "nature tours" under "practicalities." Orchid lovers can visit the University of Costa Rica's Lankester Gardens (see San José travel section). If you're visiting on your own, don't be disappointed if you fail to see any animals; the dense underbrush frequently makes viewing difficult. Many of the smaller animals are strictly nocturnal and others are wary of humans.

PLANT LIFE

Costa Rica has a phantasmagorical variety of flora. There are over 800 species of ferns, 1,200 species of orchids, and 2,000 varieties of trees. To appreciate what still exists and understand today's problems, it's necessary to examine the past.

what once was: Arriving Spaniards found a covering of virgin forest, most of which was rain forest largely made up of broadleaf evergreens. Deciduous forests abounded in the NW;

mangrove forests lined the coasts. A dense growth of palms stretched along the Caribbean coast from Puerto Limón N to the Nicaraguan border. Although the indigenous people had practiced slash-and-burn cultivation, they were so comparatively few in number that they had little impact. During the 19th C, much land was stripped of its primeval growth in the Meseta Central to be used for agriculture and, along the Caribbean coast, for bananas. Due to the dearth of sawmills and the lack of transportation, nearly all of the timber was either burned or left to rot on the ground—a process that virtually exterminated a number of species. By the 1940s only scattered stands of timber remained in the Meseta Central. However, it was estimated that 78% of Costa Rica was still covered by largely virgin growth forest as of 1942. The opening of the Costa Rican segment of the Inter-American Highway opened up the valley area of the Río General along with other areas for cultivation. The expansion of agriculture in general and cattle ranching in particular also took its toll. From 1950 to 1960 an estimated 108,000 acres were cut annually, a figure that increased to more than 148,000 acres in the 1961–67 period. The forests were viewed simply as impediments to economic progress. Also, by cutting down the trees, the *campesino* earned squatter's rights because he had "improved" the acreage. According to government figures, as of 1977 some 12,000 sq. mi.—or about 39% of the total land area—was wooded. Despite the protection afforded by the government, the remaining forests are threatened by the estimated 100–200,000 *precarista* (squatter) families and by the estimated 200,000 refugees in the country to whom forest reserves and private forested tracts are idle lands waiting to be claimed. In their eyes, although farmland is easier to squat initially, forested land appears a better long term bet. A study of satellite photos taken in 1983 showed only 17% of the country was still covered by virgin forest. Ironically, owing to the nature of its soil composition and topography, more than half of the land is judged unsuitable for growing anything other than trees. Although the nation contains a dozen ecological zones and 8–12,000 species of plants, its forests are still falling at a rate nine times faster than Brazil's.

1. Poás National Park
2. Braulio Carrillo National Park
3. Lankester Gardens
4. Irazú National Park
5. Tapantí National Wildlife Reserve
6. Turrialba Volcano
7. Guayabo National Monument
8. Rara Avis
9. La Selva/Selva Verde/El Gavilan
10. Monteverde Reserve
11. Lake Arenal
12. Arenal Volcano/Arenal Observatory
13. Finca La Pacifica
14. Lomas Barbudal Biological Reserve
15. Las Imágenes Biological Station
16. Rincón de la Vieja National Park
17. Santa Rosa National Park
18. Guanacaste National Park
19. Isla Boñanos Wildlife Refuge
20. Caño Negro National Wildlife Refuge
21. Tamarindo National Wildlife Refuge
22. Oistonal National Wildlife Refuge
23. Barra Honda National Park
24. Palo Verde National Park
25. Curú National Wildlife Refuge
26. Cabo Blanco Absolute Nature Reserve
27. Peñas Blancas Natural Refuge
28. Guayabo, Negritos, and Pajaros Biological Reserves
29. Carara Biological Reserve
30. Manuel Antonio National Park
31. Uvita Marine National Park
32. Golfito Wildlife Reserve
33. Wilson Botanical Gardens
34. Corcovado National Park
35. Marenco and Drake's Bay
36. Isla del Coco National Park
37. Isla del Caño National Park
38. La Amistad International Park
39. Chirippó National Park
40. Tortuguero National Park
41. Barra del Colorado National Wildlife Refuge
42. Hitoy-Cerere Biological Reserve
43. Cahuita National Park
44. Gandoca-Manzanillo National Park

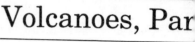

Volcanoes, Par

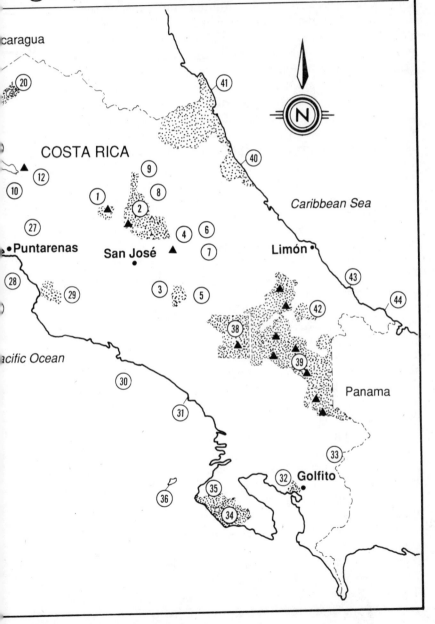

fuges, Reserves, and Gardens

caragua

COSTA RICA

Caribbean Sea

Pacific Ocean

Puntarenas

San José

Limón

Panama

Golfito

N

rainforests: Containing the planet's most complex ecosystem, rainforests have a richer animal and plant life than any other type of forest. Unlike other areas in which living organisms face conflict with a hostile climate, in the rainforest organisms struggle for survival against each other. Since the climate has been stable here for some 60 million years, each being—whether plant, animal, insect, or microbe—has been able to develop its specialized niche. Rainforests occur in regions without marked seasonal variations and which commonly receive more than 70 in. of rain annually. When seen from the air, the canopy appears uneven because there are trees of varied species and stages of development. Life in the rainforest is highly stratified in vertical layers. The upper canopy layer contains animals which are mainly herbaceous and, in Costa Rica, have prehensile tails. They rarely descend to earth. The next lower layer is filled with small trees, lianas, and epiphytes. Some are parasitic, others use trees solely for support purposes. The ground surface layer is littered with branches, twigs, and foliage. Most animals here live on insects and fruit; others are carnivorous. Contrary to popular opinion the ground cover is thick only where sunlight penetrates sufficiently to allow thick vegetation; secondary forest growth is generally much more impenetrable. Most of the nutrients are regenerated via the ecosystem: the extensive root system of the trees and associated fungi form a thick mat which holds thin topsoils in place when it rains. If these are cut, the soil will wash away: the steeper the slope, the faster the rate of runoff. The type of rainforest common in Costa Rica is the subtropical forest which ranges from 10° N to 10° S. Others include equatorial and monsoon rainforests. Mangrove forests are found along the coasts. Cloud forest is another name for montane rainforest, which is characterized by heavy rainfall and persistent condensation due to the upward deflection of moisture-laden air currents by mountains. Trees here are typically short and gnarled. The so-called elfin woodland or forest contains extremely stunted moss-covered trees. Tropical dry forests once covered Pacific coastal lowlands stretching from Panama to Mexico, comprising an area the size of France. Today, they have shrunk to 2% with a mere 200 sq. mi. under protection in Costa Rica, Mexico, and Panama.

trees: The tropical dry forest contains more than 30 species of hardwood. Found only in the NW, two of the three species of *caoba* (mahogany) are indigenous. Attempts to grow the hardwood commercially have been stymied by the mahogany shootborer which thrives in mahogany groves. Another giant which thrives in Guanacaste, the deciduous *cenízero*'s English name of raintree derives from the antshrikes who, residing in its branches, extract large quantities of sap. After they drain it of nitrogen-rich compounds, the birds defecate diligently. Growing up to 128 ft. in height, the *fruta dorada* (wild nutmeg) abounds in moist forests. One of the largest trees, the deciduous *calyptrogyne* or "dovetail" tree possesses a well-formed straight and smooth trunk. Commonly seen on coffee plantations, the *puro* tree's function is not only to shade coffee but also to fix nitrogen into the soil; its prunings provide feed for animals as well as firewood.

forbidden fruit: Small, with a short trunk and numerous branches, the machineel (*manzanillo*) grows near the sea. Its elliptical-shaped leaves have a strange bright green sheen. The machineel secretes an acid which may be deadly. Said to be the original apple in the Garden of Eden, this innocuous-looking yet highly poisonous fruit will cause your mouth to burn and your tongue to swell up. In fact, all parts of this tree are potentially deadly. Cattle, standing under the tree after a torrential tropical downpour, have been said to lose their hides as drops fall from leaves. Other tales tell of people going blind after a leaf touched an eye. Slaves (in the Virgin Islands to the NE) wishing to do away with a particularly despicable master would insert minute quantities of juice into an uncooked potato. Cooked, these small doses were undetectable but always fatal if served to the victim over a long period of time. If you should spot one of these trees—which are particularly prevalent along Manuel Antonio's beaches—stay well away!

epiphytes, climbers, and stranglers: Costa Rica's extraordinary natural wealth also includes 247 species of epiphytes (from a Greek work meaning "upon plants") and 1,200 varieties of *orquídaes* (orchids), the grandest collection in all of Central America. Although they grow all over the country orchids are most diverse in the 2,625–6,562 ft. humid forests. An epiphytic, tree-dwelling cactus, the *pitahaya silvestre* thrives in the NW. Its flowers, some 11.8 inches long and weighing up to 4 oz, are among the world's largest. Opening only at night, they release a potent, moth-attracting, jasmine-like fragrance which may be sniffed as far as 1,000 ft. downwind. Tiny epiphytes living on leaf surfaces, epiphylls (algae, liverworts, lichens, and mosses) are generally found on lower plants. Bromeliads are ground-dwelling epiphytes, the most famous of which is the *piña* (pineapple). One of the species of bromeliad typically found in Guanacaste, *piñuelas* are equipped with large (39–55 inches), skinny, and jagged, aloe vera-like leaves. Woody (vines, lianas, and bush ropes) and herbacious climbers are rainforest landmarks. One of the most remarkable of these is the *uña de gato* (cat-claw bigone), a species of liana which, in its juvenile form, grows leaves and tendrils bearing a remarkable, almost haunting resemblance to cat claws. It appears almost as if the plant could walk! Beginning life as epiphytes, some species of *Ficus* and *Clusia* send down woody, clasping roots that wind themselves around the trunk as they extend down into the earth. These "strangler figs" most likely kill the tree not through strangulation but by robbing it of canopy space.

unique natives: The *pejibaye* palm is well known for its fruit and edible palm heart. Found mainly in dry forest environments, *Indio desnudo* (naked Indian) utilizes chloroplasts under its orange bark in order to continue to synthesize during the months from Nov. to May when it is leafless. Noted for its eye-catching "plank" root buttresses, the *ceiba* or kapok tree has conical spines on its trunk. The silky quality of the fibers surrounding the seed in its fruit have given it the English name of silk cotton tree. The *guanacaste* or ear fruit receives its English name from the unique shape of its fruits. Although it gives the province of Guanacaste its name, these trees may well be extinct in the area within 100 years since they need an enclosed tropical forest filled with noncompetitive species in order to thrive. The *encino* or *roble* (oak) is distinguished by a hard-covered dark bark and acorns which may take two growing seasons to mature. Another variety is the *roble encino,* an evergreen which thrives in upland dry forest. While some palms have adapted to brackish tidal swamps and dune swales, the coconut palm (*coco*) is the only one that makes these areas its sole habitat. It may have originated in the Indian Ocean. While those on the Pacific coast are related to Asian varieties, the ones on the Caribbean side are of the Jamaican tall variety found in W Africa and in the W Indian Ocean. Producing a resin that, when fossilized, is the source of amber, the *guapinol* (stinking toe) tree bears large, toe-shaped pods. A cousin of the tree which produces the Brazil nut, the *jicaro* (monkey pot) bears large woody fruits which hang upside down. Upon ripening the lid drops off, revealing 20–50 seeds which are favored by hungry bats. Lightest of the commercial woods, *balsa* is native to humid subtropical and tropical areas; Spanish for "raft," it has had a variety of uses through the centuries. The latest is to deter supertankers from building up static charges owing to wave action which can result in explosions. Large, symmetrical, strong, and stout, the sandbox tree's (*jabillo's*) English name comes from its fruit; the ribbed peel, when de-seeded and flattened, was used to sprinkle sand used for blotting ink spilt on parchment.

others: Vegetation that makes an impression on the imagination of most visitors, tree ferns abound in the high-rainfall forests. In Costa Rica, they are labeled *rabo de mica* ("monkey tail") ferns in reference to their uncurling young fronds. Often called "living fossils," *zamia* (cycads) superficially resemble small palms and have conelike flowers which emerge from the base of their fronds. A free-floating aquatic perennial, the *jacinto de agua* (water hyacinth) has spread during this century from its South American homeland to become one of the most troublesome and widespread aquatic weeds. Members of the three species present can be seen everywhere from Carara to Tortuguero. The red spots on the underside of the green leaves belonging to the *sangre de Cristo* ("blood of Christ") plant resemble stained glass windows. Of African origin, *jaraguá* is the commonest cultivated pasture grass, and it is especially abundant in Guanacaste where, owing to its remarkable regenerative abilities after a fire, it has been supplanting other indigenous grasses. Represented in Costa Rica by some 30 species, the *platanillo* (heliconia), famous worldwide as an ornamental, lends an infusion of bizarre color and shape to the tropical landscape. Rendered distinctive through its large (up to 6.5 ft.) leaves, the *sombrilla de pobre* ("poor person's umbrella") is common in verdant, elevated areas; locals cut them down for use as umbrellas. By producing nectar both deep in their flowers (for bees and hummingbirds) and also at nectaries on petals, stems, and leaves (for aggressive ants and wasps), passion flowers provide themselves with both pollination and protection. Unforgettable residents of the rainforest, *labios ardientes* ("ardent lips") or *labios de puta* ("hooker's lips") lend a bit of local color to the rainforest landscape.

mangroves: Found only along the coasts and banks of rivers, these water-rooted trees serve as a marine habitat which shelters sponges, corals, oysters, and the like around its roots—organisms which, in turn, attract a variety of other sealife. Aboveground, they shelter seabirds. The five species found are red, black, white, tea, and buttonwood.

ANIMAL LIFE

As with the plants, the Animal Kingdom is also wonderfully diverse. Many of the indigenous species are in danger of extinction, largely from loss of their traditional habitats through deforestation. Sea turtles, though, are threatened by overhunting and beach development. The panoply of species includes manatees, ocelots, sloths, deer, coatimundis, coyotes, jaguars, marguays, peccaries, tapirs, plus squirrel, capuchin, and spider monkeys.

domesticated animals: Today's barnyard animals—cows, pigs, horses, donkeys, goats, and chickens—come from a lineage stretching back to the 1560–70s when the *conquistadores* brought them in from Nicaragua. There are also fine but few examples of the Paso Fino and Andalusian (a special favorite) horse breeds, and a herd of water buffalo which was imported from Trinidad in 1975 and lives near Limón.

Mammals

primates: Actually sounding more like a "growler" than a howler, the sounds of the mantled howler monkey (*mono congo*) reverberate up to several miles away. Living in groups of up to 20 led by a senior male, they dine on flowers, fruits, and tender leaves. Moving rapidly through the trees, the black-handed spider monkey (*mono araña, mono colorado*) has a very complex language and lives in bands of about 20 which frequently subdivide into smaller groupings. Dining on fruit and insects, the white-faced capuchin (*mono cara blanca*) has white shoulders, upper chest, and face. Its name comes from the resemblance of its head and shoulder covering to a monk's hood. Both extremely curious and agile, it lives in groups of five to 15; its varied diet includes birds, fruits, tender leaves, eggs, and honey. The squirrel monkey (*mono titi*) dwells only in the SW corner of the country.

carnivores: Omnivorous, solitary, nocturnal, crafty, and clean, the raccoon (*mapache*) will dine on anything from frogs and fish to fruit and vegetables. Nimble, omnivorous, and solitary in old age, its cousin, the mischievous and sociable coati (*pizote*), hunts at dawn and dusk—resting in treetops or in hollow trunks the rest of the time. The term coati-mundi refers only to solitary coatis, adult males over two years old. Mainly nocturnal, the gregarious kinkajou (*martilla*) dines on small animals, birds, eggs, and honey. An unusual relative of the panda, it has short and wooly fur, large eyes but small ears, and a long prehensile tale. Smaller and lacking the prehensile tail, the *olingo* or pale-faced kinkajou is a close relative. With attractive, short and thick but soft fur, the weasel's (*comadreja's*) slim frame allows it to slither into the burrows of mice. Perhaps the nation's least popular mammal, the skunk (*zorro hediondo*) is probably better left unseen and unsmelled. An excellent swimmer, the otter (*nutrio, perro de agua*) eats fish, shrimp, and turtles. Resembling a lanky mink with a lengthy long-haired tail, the *tayra* or *tolumuco* feeds on grubs, bird nests, fruit, eggs, fruit, and chicken and goat meat. It lives in an underground burrow.

cats: The graceful, nocturnal "king of the tropical rainforest," the jaguar (*tigre*) is this hemisphere's largest cat; it may reach over six ft. in length and 36 inches in height at shoulder level. It dines on peccaries, deer, monkeys, sloths, and even fish. Sometimes called a cougar or mountain lion, the *puma* ranks second in terms of size. Slightly smaller than a jaguar, it has an unspotted tan or dark brown hide; a leaner, more low-slung frame; and a longer, thicker tail. Resembling a miniaturized jaguar, the ocelot (*manigordo*) feeds on anything from rabbits to insects. A smaller, similar version of the ocelot, the tiger cat (*tigrillo*) has a combination of spots and stripes. Rarely sighted, it survives in the Tortuguero, Santa Rosa, and Corcovado national parks, the Reserva Forestal Río Macho, and on the lower slopes of the Cordillera Talamanca. More solitary and nocturnal than the ocelot, the margay (*tigrillo, caucel*) is the size of a large house cat. It has a somewhat bushy tail which runs well over half the extended length of its head and black-spotted body. Once widespread and now endangered more by habitat loss than by hunting, this majestic and magnificent feline abounds now only in Corcovado and Santa Rosa. With unspotted blackish-brown or chestnut to red fur the jaguarundi (*león breñero*) has a small flattened head with short round head, long sleek body, short legs—all of which make it appear to be a cross between a cat and a weasel.

marsupials: The three species of opposum (*zorro*) are called four-eyed, woody, and regular. Born only eight days after fertilization, opposum infants follow a trail of their mothers saliva from the cloaca to her pouch where they secure themselves to their mother's nipples for the next 60 days. Arboreal, omnivorous, and nocturnal, the *zorro* is a nocturnal omnivore.

edentatas: Indigenous to the Americas, the name of the order which includes anteaters, sloths, and armadillos refers to the few teeth found in the latter two and their complete absence in the anteaters. Sloths and anteaters are both arboreal, soft-furred creatures. Living in the highest tops of trees and eating plants and leaves, the three-toed sloth (*perezoso de tries, dedos*) is camouflaged by the blue-green and green algae which grows on it fur. Cecropia (*guarumo*) trees provide the best view. They descend once a week to defecate; one hypothesis for their descent, which exposes them to predators, is that the decomposition of their feces at the tree's base might provide them with a higher quality food supply. Beetles, moths, and mites live on sloths and deposit their eggs in the sloth's dung. The two-toed sloth is also present but is rarer. Possessing a prehensile tail and a long retractile tongue, the strictly nocturnal silky anteater (*tapacara, serafín de planar*) breaks open ant and termite nests to feed. The best way to find one is to gaze into clumps of lianas up to 33 ft. above the jungle floor for something resembling a golden tennis ball, which is in reality a sleeping anteater. Another species is the banded or lesser anteater (*oso jaceta, oso hormiguero*), distinguished by the black V-shaped mark across its back, resembling a vest worn backwards. The nine-banded armadillo (*cusuco*) dines on beetles, ants, termites, fungi, berries, slugs, centipedes, millipedes, and other such exotic cuisine.

tapirs and peccaries: This group (the perisodactyles), which includes the African and Asian rhinoceroses, is characterized by two unmatched or unequal hoof-covered toes. One of the Americas' most corpulent mammals, the tapir (*danto, danta*) weighs as much as 550 lbs. and may grow six feet long and up to 36 inches high. Dining on seeds, leaves, twigs, and fruit, its excellent hearing and sense of smell compensate for the ungainly creature's poor eyesight. Solitary, nocturnal, and marsh-dwelling, it bolts when frightened—flattening everything in its wake! Resembling a gigantic pig, the collared peccary (*saino*) lives in a group of two to 15, whose members recognize each other by their pungent, musky body odor. Another species is the *cariblanco* or white-lipped peccary.

rodents: Living near rivers, the edgy brown-colored agouti (*guatusa*) dines on tender shoots, fruits, and seeds. Living in a burrow its cousin, the nocturnal paca (*tepezcuintle*) is larger and twice as heavy with horizontal rows of cream colored spots along the flanks. A clumsy vegetarian covered with short, strong, and rigid quills, the skinny prehensile-tailed porcupine (*puercoespín*) forages at night for fruits and seeds. Dwelling in thickets and forests, cottontail rabbits (*conejo*) eat grass and tree bark; they may have up to five litters per year.

bats: Costa Rica has over 100 species, as compared to only 40 in the US. Hiding out in caves in harems guarded by a single male, the short-tailed fruit bat (*murciélago*) flies out at night. The infamous vampire bat (*vampiro*) lives in Costa Rica. Landing on a horse or cow, it makes an incision, a process which may take up to 20 minutes. Exuding an anticoagulant, it proceeds to lap up the blood. Its feces contain a fungus which causes histoplasmosis, a dehabilitating disease. Other species include nectar bats, the Jamaican fruit bat, the lesser short-tailed fruit bat, the black myotis, the fishing bulldog bat, the sac-winged bat, and false vampire.

other mammals: With a total of 205 mammals, Costa Rica has a seemingly endless variety. Coyotes thrive in Guanacaste. The white-tailed deer (*venado, venado cola blanco*) was almost exterminated during the 1940s when the harvest of 10,000–40,000 animals was used for leather goods manufacture and for dog food. They are identical but smaller than the white-tailed deer found in the US. Another variety is the brocket deer or *cabra de monte*. The red-tailed squirrel (*ardilla roja, ardilla chisa*) is widespread in some parts and may commonly be observed scurrying up a tree. Popularly known as the sea cow, the manatee (*manatí*) has been sighted in Tortuguero on rare occasions.

Reptiles and Amphibians

turtles: There are a large variety. Smaller turtles include the *tortuga bocado* or snapping turtle and the semiaquatic *tortuga jicóte* or mud turtle. Medium-sized with a total length of about 40 inches and weighing 180–480 lbs., the large finned, herbivorous *tortuga blanca* or *tortuga verde* (green turtle) lays eggs every two to three years, storming the beaches in massive groups termed *barricadas*. It has a short rounded head and occurs on both coasts. One of the smallest sea turtles at 35 inches or less in length, the *tortuga carey* (hawksbill) has a spindle shaped shell and weighs around 220 lbs. Because of its tortoise shell—a brown translucent layer of corneous gelatin that covers it and peels off the shell when processed—it has been pursued and slaughtered throughout the world. It dines largely on sponges and seaweed. Worldwide demand for its shell, which sells for a fortune in Japan, appears to have condemned it to extinction. With a head twice the size of the green turtle's and narrow and bird-jawed, the short-finned *tortuga cabezona* (loggerhead turtle) is rarely longer than 46 inches. It dines on sea urchins, jellyfish, starfish, and crabs. It is threatened with extinction by coastal development, egg gathering, and from hunting by raccoons. Black with very narrow fins, the leatherback's name comes from the leathery hide which covers its back in lieu of a shell. Reaching up to six feet in length and weighing up to 1,600 lbs., the leatherback's chief predator is the poacher. In Costa Rica, poachers traditionally lie in wait for the turtles. Flipping the latest arrival on her back, they stab it with long knives, slicing down to the lower shell which is torn off. After extracting the calipee, which is used to make turtle soup, a poacher will run off to the next turtle—leaving his victim helplessly flailing with her intestines exposed. Arriving the next morning, vultures circle the still living turtle and then descend to feast on her entrails. Most abundant but least understood of the sea turtles, the Pacific ridley (*lora, carpintera*) is endangered by its nesting habits. Although restrictions have been put in force since then, in 1968 alone the Mexicans slaughtered over a million for use in the leather industry. And as beachside development continues worldwide, their future appears in doubt. A final species is the *tortuga negra* (Pacific green turtle) which, like the green, hawksbill, and leatherback, are found on both coasts. The ridley is found only on the Pacific side. While the loggerhead is found mainly in the Caribbean, it is occasionally seen in the Pacific.

nesting sites and times: Green turtles generally nest at Tortuguero and Barra de Matina during early July into Oct., peaking in Aug. Leatherbacks nest from Feb. to July, peaking in April and May, at Barra de Matina and from Oct. to Mar. at Playa Grande. They also nest at Nacite and Playa Naranjo. Pacific ridley arrive in *barricadas* of up to 120,000 to lay eggs on Playa Nancite and in Oistonal along the Pacific side during periods of four to eight days from July to Dec. Pacific greens nest at Nancite and Playa Naranjo; hawksbills nest on both coasts all year round, but they can be seen most easily at Tortuguero from July to Oct. For information on egglaying, see the description in the Tortuguero section.

frogs and toads: The glands of the marine toad (*bufo marinus*) contain toxins. Don't try to pick one up: it'll urinate on you! The predominantly nocturnal marine toad exercises control over its paratoid gland, and it directs its poison in a fine spray, one that can prove fatal to dogs and cats which pick it up in their mouths. If you carry it around, it will be likely to defend itself by urinating. An equal-opportunity eater, it will dine on anything from wasps to dog and cat food set out for pets. Second only in size to marine toads, the aggressive *rana tenero* (smoky frog) grows to at least six inches and has been known to eat snakes up to 20 inches long. Resembling an amorphous blob of jelly, the *sapo borracho* (burrowing toad) dries up completely while underground; when disturbed, it excretes a sticky white substance which causes an acute allergic reaction in some humans. So translucent that it barely casts a shadow, the small *ranita de vidrio* (glass frog) has green veins and a visible red vein leading to its heart. Smooth skinned and lacking warts, the poisonous true toad (*sapo*) dwells in mid-elevation wet forests. With bright, leaf-green back, creamy-white throat and belly, orange hands and feet, dark blue side markings, and blood-red irises, *rana calzonudo*, the gaudy leaf frog, is Central America's most colorful. Named after its sharp call, so incredibly powerful for one less than one inch long, the tink frog (*martillito*) exercises remarkable agility and can run like a mouse on its stubby legs.

the golden toad: Aside from the quetzal, the nation's most famous living creature is the golden toad, found only in Monteverde's rainforest preserve. In 1983, University of Miami researcher Marc Hayes spotted hundreds; none have been spotted since 1987. This is part of a worldwide decline of amphibians (also encompassing glass frogs and rain frogs), and no one knows what the cause is. Some think that acid rain and airborne pesticides may be to blame. Some scientists maintain that amphibians may be like canaries in a coal mine, portents of coming ecological disaster. Others connect this depletion with a concommitant increase in lawyers, politicians, and advertising account executives.

poison dart frogs: Dendrobatids are the genus of poison dart frogs (*ranita roja, ranita venerosa*) which are aspomatic—possessing a warning coloration which advertises their toxicity. Their natural Danskins, coming in bright red and blue decorator colors, broadcast a message geared chiefly towards predatory birds. Many other frogs also possess these "flash" colors, primary coloring on the undersides and groins which are flashed at predators, causing confusion. The frog's English name refers to Colombia's Chocó tribesmen who extracted an alkaloid-based poison from the skin glands which they used on the tips of their blowgun darts. The frogs are harmless to handle as long as your skin is unbroken; putting them in your mouth is not recommended. Males perch in mushrooms, calling out for a mate. After a female arrives, he scouts for the proper site. When she lags behind, he calls and waits. The female rubs the male's head and chin with her head. Facing back to back, she lays a few eggs which the male fertilizes and guards for a two-week period after which the female returns. Taking one of the newly hatched tadpoles on her back, the female deposits it in a suitably isolated pool of water (which is often the leaf axil of a bromeliad). As the water lacks nutrients, the female returns later and lays an unfertilized egg which the embryo feeds on.

lizards: The basilisk or "Jesus Christ lizard" is so named because while fleeing predators or pursuing prey it may dart across the surface of a stream, balancing itself with its tail. They resemble miniature sailfin dinosaurs and you'll undoubtedly see these lowland dwellers scurrying across your path. There are also a wide variety of anoles, small sit-and-wait predators that North Americans mistakenly call chameleons. The territorial, primarily vegetarian *garobo* and *iguana negra* (ctenosaur) occur in the drier lowlands. The iguana is distinguished from its cousin by a large scale on the side of the head slightly below and behind the rear angle of the lower jaw, green coloration, and a longer tail. Other lizards include the skink and the spiny lizard. The two species of crocodillians are the occasionally cannibalistic caiman, which grows up to eight feet, residing in many lowland swamps and slow-moving streams, and the larger, coastal-dwelling crocodile.

snakes: Despite what you may think, there is a *much* greater chance of your dying crossing the street in San José than from receiving a poisonous snakebite! Of the 162 species, 22 are poisonous. Most infamous is the *terciopelo* (fer-de-lance, velvet snake) which is olive green to dark brown with yellow, V-shaped markings along the sides. Reaching lengths of six feet or more, this lowland-dwelling snake dines on mammals, especially opossums with an occasional bird thrown in for variety. Its natural foe is the snake-feeding *zopilota* which is immune to its venom. Another similar variety, but stockier, aggressive, and with an upturned nose is the *mano de piedra* ("stone fist," hognose viper, *bothreicheis nasutus*). The small (20 inches), strictly arboreal *bocaracá* (eyelash viper) is quite poisonous as is *la coral* (coral snake) which does not bother humans unless handled. There's also the *cascabel,* the tropical rattler. The harmless *sabanera* (grassnake) has a dull brown color and a distinctive red or orange underbelly. There's also the *bejuquilla* ("little vine"), a vine snake living in arid areas. Climber par excellence, the large, nonvenomous *boa* (boa constrictor) devours everything from lizards to dogs. After striking its prey, the *boa* coils around it, then after its death locates the head and swallows it whole. The most frightening snake is the pelagic sea snake (*culebra del mar*), for which there is no serum available; it's found from one to 12 miles off the Pacific

Strawberry poison dart frog, Tortuguero (Costa Rica Expeditions)

Author and "poor man's umbrella" (Price Deratzian)

coast from California to Chile. Fortunately, only 10 people have been bitten by it during the past decade.

Birds

There are over 850 species of birds here, more than in all of North American N of Mexico—a population which includes brightly colored wild parakeets, a wild assortment of trogons and macaws, hummingbirds, pelicans, antshrikes, swallows, wrens, thrushes, warblers, ovenbirds, cuckoos, hawks, swifts, owls, egrets, and others.

where to find birds: One of the reasons birdwatchers flock to Costa Rica is the number and variety of its species. Even if you aren't a diehard, be sure to bring binoculars. Everyone has a favorite spot. It may be around your hotel or at a nature preserve. The parks and reserves are sure bets, and one of Costa Rica's great outdoor aviaries is the area surrounding the mouth of the Río Tempisque inside the Palo Verde National Park. Birdwatchers will want to pick up a copy of *The Birds of Costa Rica* by F. Gary Stiles and Alexander Skutch, the most authoritative guide available.

seasonal migrants: A winter resident, the small yellow-throated vireo is commonly found in the countryside as is the *sargento* or scarlet-rumped tanager, and the red winged black-bird (*tordo sargento*), the sanderling, and the Tennessee warbler.

birds with character: First arriving in the New World from Africa around 1877, the cattle egret or common white heron (*garcilla bueyara*) follows cattle and dines on insects disturbed as they move about. Thriving in deforested territory, the sedentary roadside hawk (*gavilán*) abounds in Guanacaste, preying on lizards, snakes, rodents, and large insects. The enormous *rey de zopilote* (king buzzard) has creamy white and black on its wings, and a red and orange head. Found in the waters near Puntarenas, the nearly jet black frigate bird (*rabi-*

horcado mango) swoops ominously overhead, occasionally veering down to the water to make a capture. Dark colored antbirds or ovenbirds (*hormigueros*) are best seen on solitary excursions. Related to the oriole and the grackle, the omnivorous *oropendolo* is mostly black with yellow outer tail feathers. The female constructs her sagging saclike nests on the ends of tree branches. "Motmot, motmot" is the cry of the turquoise-browed motmot (*pajaro bobo*) which numbers among the most beautiful of the birds. The chestnut-mandibled toucan (*dios tede*) is the largest in Central America. One of the forest's largest fruit eaters, its piercing call and brown and yellow bill are its trademarks. The *perico* (orange-chinned parakeet) is bright green with an orange patch just below its bill.

the scarlet macaw: Residing on the Pacific side, this spectacularly-plumaged parrot is perhaps the nation's most beautiful bird. You are likely to see it flying overhead and sounding raucously. Its bright red-orange plumage has touches of yellow and blue and does not vary with age or between sexes. Scarlet macaws (*loras*) mate for life which is one reason they are in danger of extinction. Another is their blackmarket value—up to $500 per bird.

the quetzal: Residing in the cool cloud forests of Monteverde, Braulio Carrillo, and Chirripó among other places, the resplendent quetzal is simply the nation's most famous animal. Costa Rica is the easiest place to see a quetzal, and the place to find them is in damp, epiphyte-laden mountain forests between 4,000 and 10,000 feet, particularly along edges and canopies. The bird usually keeps the highest profile during breeding season between March and June when it nests in high hollows of decaying tree trunks. Because it subsists on fruit and insects, the easiest place to spot them is around fruiting trees. Males and females take turns sitting on the blue eggs. It is readily identifiable by its red underbelly, iridescent green back, and trailing green plumes. Usually found solitary or in pairs, it sounds with a sharp cackling "perwicka" when disturbed or taking off. The male sounds a strikingly melodious or whining "keow kowee keow k'loo keow k'loo keeloo." It also cries "very good, very good" in rising display flight. The tall lengths range from 14 to 25 inches for a male's streamers. Only the male of the species grows a long tail. The Aztecs borrowed the bird's image for Quetzalcoatl, their feathered serpent god, and its name is derived from *quetzalli,* an early Aztec world for its tail feathers, also meaning "precious" or "beautiful." Native American kings and priests used the bird's feathers for adornment. Decreed sacred, males were caught, plucked, and released. Nine other species of trogons, the group to which the quetzal belongs, also live in Costa Rica.

hummingbirds: Bold and strikingly beautiful, the fiery-throated hummingbird (*colibri garganta de fuego*) hovers above flowers. Colored a glossy green, it has iridescent patterning which is only visible from above and at close range. Its dull-colored relative is the long-tailed hermit (*ermitaño colilargo*).

others: Other indigenous species of note include the Muscovy duck, an assortment of woodpeckers, the rufous-necked hen, the turkey vulture and its relatives, the long-tailed manakin, the green kingfisher, the boat-billed heron, the bananaquit, the great curassow, the groove-billed ani, all five species of tinamou, the homely brown jay, the chestnut-collared swift, the rufous-tailed jacamar, the ruddy quail dove, the laughing falcon, the mangrove swallow, the jacana, the ochre-bellied fly-catcher, the white-fronted nunbird, the pauraque, the tropical screech owl, the spotted barbtail, the great-tailed grackle, western and spotted sandpipers, variable seedeater, ruddy-tailed and common-tody flycatchers, the barred antshrike, the tropical kingbird, the wrenthrush, and the rufous-colored sparrow.

Insects and Marine Life

Insect life is both varied and abundant. In the 89,000 acres of Corcovado National Park, there are at least 220 species of butterflies. In mountainous Chirippó, only 43 miles away, there are 30 species with less than 5% overlap. The total number of cicada species is greater than all those found E of the Mississippi River in the US. Lest you be tempted to view insects as uninteresting, remember that they have been around for at least 400 million years and butterflies are believed to have evolved around 200 million years ago during the Triassic.

butterflies: All told there are 1,239 species. Possibly the world's most beautiful butterfly, the morpho (*celeste común*) is common in forests from sea level to 4,500 feet. The more colorful of the two forms found, which has almost completely iridescent blue upper wings, is most plentiful on the Caribbean coast. The cream owl butterfly (*buhito pardo*) has two glaring eyes on its underside. These may serve as mimicry to suggest a vertebrate or large distasteful tree frog and ward off attacks, or as target spots for predators which allow the butterfly to escape relatively unscathed. Other species of note include the common calico, the zebra, and Saturnias, skippers, *hecale, orión,* giant swallowtail, and the orange-barred sulfur.

memorable viewing: The pencil-thin helicopter damselfly (*gallito azul*) beats each of its four wings independently, resembling a slow-motion windmill. Its wing movement renders it invisible to spiders, upon whom it launches a single attack burst, snipping and capturing the succulent abdomen as the rest falls. The pit-making ant lion (*hormiga león*) is actually the larval form of a beautiful fly similar to a damselfly. It spends its childhood digging a pit, heaping up loosened particles on its head and tossing them clear. Then burying itself— only its jaws project—it awaits its prey. Any captured game has its contents sucked out and empty skin tossed out of the pit. After it has stored up enough food to support its next incarnation, it enters a cocoon and then re-emerges as a sexually mature adult. A pretty good handful, the male rhinocerous beetle (*cornizuelo*) sports a long upward-curved horn, but the females are hornless. They are endangered by habitat destruction. The most conspicuous moth larva found in Guanacaste, the frangipani sphinx (*oruga, falso coral*) appears to mimic the coral snake, both with its bright yellow coloring and red orange head and in the way it thrashes back and forth when touched as does the coral. It also bites viciously! With a color that harmonizes perfectly with the large branches and logs on which they rest, the *machaca* (peanut-head bug, lantern fly) is one of Latin America's best known insects. Its enormous hind wing eye spots and lizard-shaped head are probably designed to confuse predators. If pestered it will release a fetid skunk-like spray or drum its head against a tree trunk. A popular Latin American folk saying maintains that if a young girl is stung by a *machaca* she must have sex with her boyfriend within 24 hours or die. Other intriguing bugs include a tarantula, paper wasp, the local version of the praying mantis, and the Guanacaste stick insect (*palito andando*).

ants and termites: Commonly seen marching along a forest trail holding aloft cut pieces of leaves and flowers, leaf-cutting or farmer ants (*zompopas*) cut leaves into shreds, and carry them off to their nests where they then chew the plant material, mixing it with a combination of saliva and excrement, in order to cultivate a spongy, breadlike fungus on which they dine. Joined in a symbolic relationship with the acacia tree, the acacia-ant (*hormiga de cornizuelo*) wards off herbivores while the tree supplies the ants with nectar, protein and protection in return. The ants produce an alarm pheromone which may be smelled several yards downwind. The rarely seen red-colored trapdoor ant thrusts her abdomen forward, injecting venom with her stinger. Other major species include army ants, giant tropical ants, and Azteca or cecropia ants. Resembling gigantic wasp nests and found on trees, dark brown or black termite nests are a frequent feature of the forested landscape. Made of "carton," wood chewed up by workers and cemented with fecal "glue," the nest has a single reproductive king and queen commanding hordes of up to 100,000 attending workers and soldiers. Camouflaging itself with bits and pieces of termite nest, the assassin bug (*reduvio*) preys at the entrance.

loathed by humans: Nearly invisible, chiggers (*coloradillas*) thrive in locations ranging from lowland cattle pastures to rainforests. A form of mite larva that inserts the tips of its well-developed mouthparts into your skin, it loves to squeeze into protected places such as bra and belt lines and the genital area, where it bites and deposits a histamine which makes the surrounding region itch like hell! Small gnats which favor the tender skin of the ears and neck, *purrujas* (no-see-ums, biting midges) are almost invisible and are most active on warm days and windless evenings. Only the females bite humans. In the forest, you'll also find an abundance of *garrapatas* (ticks). Horseflies are an annoyance during May at 2,000–5,000 feet, and another biting fly is the hardy but hunchbacked black fly (*mosca de café*). Coming in a number of species, the mosquito (*zancudo*) needs no introduction, nor does the giant cockroach (*cucaracha*). With 20 body segments, the forest-floor millipede (*milpies*) is readily identifiable both by its movements and its dull whitish-yellow color. Its ability to curl up in a spiral and expel violently a solution of hydrogen cyanide and benzaldehyde as far as a foot away discourages predators. An interesting phenomenon is the male practice of "riding" the larger females (28–39 in. long) for periods of five days or longer. Unescorted females are rare in millipedal society, but bachelor millipedes may remain sexually unfulfilled for long periods. Since copulation generally occurs within the first few hours, it is thought that the natural selective purpose of this "riding" behavior is to discourage the females from mating again. As the sperm is utilized only after ovoposition and a female will mate with many others if left alone, rivalry among sperm would result. If faced with a sexual competitor, the male will flex the rear of his body in order to force a female's head and rear over her genital openings, thus barring access. Finally, although they should not be a problem for visitors, Africanized "killer" bees are proving a menace; since their arrival in 1983, they have attacked more than 500 people, resulting in nine deaths.

sealife: Avoid trampling on that armed knight of the underwater sand dunes, the sea urchin. Another marine creature to keep away from is the floating Portuguese Man-of-War which is mainly found on the Atlantic side. Actually a colony of marine organisms, its stinging tentacles can be extended or retracted; worldwide, there have been reports of trailing tentacles reaching 50 feet. The ghost crab abounds on the beaches, tunneling down beneath the sand.

coral reefs: Corals produce the calcium carbonate responsible for the buildup of most of the offlying cays and islets as well as most of the sand on the beaches. Bearing the brunt of waves, they also conserve the shoreline. Although reefs were formed millenniums ago, they are in a constant state of flux. Seemingly solid, they actually depend upon a delicate ecological balance to survive. Deforestation, dredging, temperature change, an increase or decrease in salinity, or sewage discharge may kill them. Because temperature ranges must remain between 68° and 95°F, they are only found in the tropics. Acting more like plants than animals, reefs survive through photosynthesis: the algae inside the coral polyps do the work while the polyps themselves secrete calcium carbonate and stick together for protection from waves and boring sponges. Reefs originate as the polyps die, forming a base for the next generation. Closely related to the sea anenomes, they may be divided into three groups. The hard or stony corals (such as staghorn, brain, star, or rose) secrete a limey skeleton. The horny corals (for example sea plumes, sea whips, sea fans, and gorgonians) have a supporting skeleton-like structure known as a gorgonin (after the head of Medusa). The last category consists of the soft corals. Nocturnal, corals snack at night by steering plankton into their mouths with their tentacles. The coral appear to be able to survive in such packed surroundings through their symbiotic relationship with the algae present in their tissues: Coral exhale carbon dioxide and the algae consume it, producing needed oxygen. Not prone to celibacy or sexual prudery, corals reproduce sexually and asexually through budding.

Costa Rican reefs: The nation's largest coral reef is found off of Cahuita on the Atlantic coast. Much smaller ones are found off the Pacific coast and in the Gandoca-Manzanillo Reserve.

HISTORY

the start: The area now known as the nation of Costa Rica was, before the Spaniards' arrival, a sparsely settled chunk of the extended isthmus linking two enormous continents—a region where the northern Mesoamerican cultures met the southern Andean cultures. Arriving in the 16th C, Spaniards estimated there to be 25,000 indigenous people, divided into five major tribal groups. Living in the Peninsula de Nicoya, the Mayan Chorotegas accounted for half the total number. They had arrived from Chiapas, Mexico around the 13th C. The warlike, nomadic Caribs roamed the Caribbean coast. Dwelling in fortified villages comprised of enormous cone-shaped huts, which could contain up to several hundred people, the fierce Boricua lived in the Talamanca region along the Pacific. Their dialect belonged to the Chibchan language group, common throughout Central America and the Andes. Little is known regarding what is thought to be the oldest indigenous tribe, the matriarchal Corobicis. Grouped into two small, widely separated settlements, the agriculturally oriented, Aztec-influenced Nahuas have been credited with the introduction of cacao into the region.

Columbus intrudes: During his fourth and final voyage of 1502, Christopher Columbus anchored at the present-day port of Puerto Limón. He bartered away trinkets for the gold disks the Caribs wore as pendants. His brother Bartolomé remained behind to explore, only to flee when his party was attacked. Every attempt in the early 1500s to conquer the isthmus, from the very first one by Diego de Nicuesa, ended in failure with *conquistadores* retreating in the face of hunger, disease, and armed resistance. Unlike the Mayan and Aztec regions, there was no single Indian empire to conquer; each tribe had to be fought anew. The Indians would burn their crops rather than allow the invaders to take them. And the would-be conquerers expended a great deal of their time and energy contending with one another. Between 1511–17, many Indians were seized and shipped off to slavery in Cuba; many others fell victim to smallpox. Anthropologists estimate a pre-Columbian population of 400,000; many of them dropped dead of the newly introduced communicable diseases without even so much as seeing one of the intruders.

the first conquests: The first successful expedition was led by Gil González Dávila who traded with the Peninsula de Nicoya's Chorotegas while his *compadre* Diego de Aguero—at least according to the official version—baptized thousands. This settlement ended when González Dávila was arrested in Panama by Pedrarias Dávila, the Governor of Veragua, for trespassing on his jurisdiction. Likewise, a small settlement by Francisco Fernando de Córdova in 1524 ended under threats from Pedrarias. Appointed by the family of Christopher Columbus who had died in 1506, an expedition in 1534 by Felipe Gutiérrez ended in disaster, with some of its members resorting to cannibalism. In 1540 Hernán Sánchez de Badajoz founded the settlement of Badajoz at the mouth of the Río Sixaola. He was driven out by Rodrigo de Contreras, the new governor of Nicaragua. Contreras, in turn, was routed by the Indians who rebelled at his cruelty. Other conquistadors followed but none enjoyed success.

early colonization: In 1539 Costa Rica was separated from Veragua and was organized as a *gobernacion* in 1542. In 1561 Juan de Cavallón established the first settlement at Garcimuñoz at a point on the Río Ciruelas on the Pacific side. Disheartened at the lack of gold in the area, Cavallón deserted the colony in 1562 and was replaced by Juan Vásquez de Coronado who moved the settlement into the Meseta Central in 1564. From the new town of Cartago, Coronado explored the area, surveying Costa Rica's boundaries. Lost at sea during a return visit to Spain, he was replaced by Perafán de Ribera in 1568. That same year Costa Rica was subsumed in the newly-established kingdom of Guatemala. Ribera fought against the indigenous people of the Talamanca region from 1570–72, a costly campaign which again produced no gold. At the time of his departure in 1573, two small settlements had sprung up: Cartago and Aranuez.

early society: Decimated by introduced diseases, intertribal warfare, and by conquest, the Indians declined in number. Many starved to death after they had been driven from their land. By 1569, their numbers in Nicoya had declined to 3,300. Others, such as many of the Chorotega tribe, intermarried with the Spaniards, producing a *mestizo* population that viewed itself as Spanish, not Indian. Other Indians, such as the Changuenes were captured by the Zambos Mosquitos (descendants of unions between Miskito Indians and shipwrecked African slaves) and sold to Jamaica by them in conspiracy with English pirates. Other than in such areas as isolated Talamanca, the Indians died out. Black slaves were also integrated through intermarriage. Increasingly viewed as a backwater—its lack of gold exposed—few found the colony attractive. The census of 1700 counted 20,000 inhabitants including 2,500 Spaniards. Owing to the area's limited natural resources, *hidalgos* (gentry) and *plebeyos* (commoners) alike were impoverished. The system of *repartimientos* (allotments), under which Indians were forced into labor on estates, was enforced throughout the Americas; in other Central American nations it resulted in sharp class divisions with a subservient Indian and *mestizo* class at the bottom. In the case of Costa Rica, although 20,000 Indians were pressed into servitude, the system was a failure, and the captives either died or were assimilated. In lieu of the plantation-style estates which developed elsewhere in Latin America, small family-run farms emerged. Well into the 18th C, the economy continued to be based on subsistence agriculture and barter transactions. Money had become so scarce that *cacao* beans were designated the official currency in 1709. The Talamanca highlands remained unvanquished and in the early 17th C, the *zambos* (bandits of Indian-Black heritage) along with the Miskito Indians continually raided the Matina Valley in the Meseta Central. In order to halt the raids, a tribute was paid to the Miskito King from 1779 to 1841. Pirates also plagued the colony, resulting in closure of all of the ports and the collapse of exports. The pirate Henry Morgan and his brigands were turned back in 1666 from their attempt to sack Cartago by an outnumbered band of colonial militia—an episode which was viewed as divine intervention by the Virgin of Ujarrás, the saint whose image they had carried into battle. Things began to improve under the administration of Diego de la Haya Fernández (1718–27). Under his tenure, the port of Caldera was reopened, the Matina Valley was fortified against Miskitos, and *cacao* plantations were developed. He oversaw the rebuilding of Cartago on a grander scale after it was destroyed by a volcanic eruption in 1723. Lacking a resident bishop, the Catholic Church here was not as strong as in other nations. However, the church encouraged farmers to settle near parishes and, in this fashion, Heredia (1706) and San José (1736) were founded.

independence: In September 1821, the Captain General of Guatemala proclaimed the independence of the Central American provinces without consulting Costa Rica. After meeting, the municipal councils of the four major towns (Cartago, San José, Heredia, and Alajuela) formed a junta to draft a provisional constitution. In May of 1822, the newly-crowned Emperor of Mexico, Augustin de Iturbide, declared his authority over the Central American provinces. Whereas two of the four main settlements, Cartago and Heredia, favored union with Mexico, San José and Alajuela favored either independence or union with the rest of Central America. Civil war erupted as Mexican supporters from Cartago and Heredia marched on San José only to be defeated at Ochomongo. In March 1823, a provincial congress in Cartago declared independence from Spain and applied for union with Colombia, in an attempt to forestall an attack from Mexico. After Iturbide was overthrown around the same time, however, opinion shifted, and the Costa Rican Congress voted in August 1823 to join the newly formed United Provinces of Central America (commonly referred to as the Central American Federation) which included Guatemala, Honduras, Nicaragua, and El Salvador. The first *Jefe Supremo* of the Free State of Costa Rica served from 1824–33. In 1824, the inhabitants of Guanacaste seceded from Nicaragua and elected to join Costa Rica. The unstable federation collapsed, and Costa Ricans thereafter were wary of attempts to unite Central America, believing themselves to have little in common with their neighbors in the region.

civil war: In the early 1830s, geopolitical conflict erupted over the decision of where to base the capital. Heretofore, each of the four major cities had operated administratively as city states rather than as parts of the same nation. Under the Law of Movement enacted in 1834 under José Rafael de Gallegos, the capital was to be rotated from town to town every four years. This failed to resolve the conflict and, after the new head of state Braulio Carrillo Colina established the capital at San José, the three rival towns formed the League of Cities under Nicolas Ulloa to oppose Carrillo. Crushing the revolt decisively that October, Carrillo went on to largely disregard the constitution. Defeated in his 1838 bid for reelection, he seized dictatorial power. In 1841 he gave squatters title to government-owned agricultural land, abolished the constitution, and declared himself dictator for life. Carrillo was driven out of power by an alliance between one of his generals, Vincente Villasor, and Honduran Central American Federation proponent Morazán. Shortly after their accession to power, these two also fell into disfavor and were executed.

the first president: In 1847 José María Castro Madriz, a 29-year-old editor and publisher, was named the nation's first president by the Congress. His wife, Doña Pacifica, designed the national flag. Declaring Costa Rica an independent republic the next year, he instituted a headstrong program of reforms—including constitutional changes and replacement of the army with a national guard—which resulted in his replacement by more conservative coffee baron Juan Rafael Mora Porras. Mora Porras encouraged the cultivation of coffee for export, an idea in harmony with the liberal laissez faire capitalism espoused in Europe at the time. Politics, as such, during this era consisted of rivalries between families. Suffrage was restricted by property and literacy qualifications to a small minority.

war with William Walker: In 1855 Tennesseean William Walker was deployed by Nicaraguan liberals at the head of a group of European and American mercenaries and given the mission of overthrowing the conservative government. Instead of handing power over to the liberals as had been originally agreed upon contractually, Walker installed himself as dictator and reintroduced slavery. Prodded on by business competitors of Cornelius Vanderbilt, he nationalized Vanderbilt's transport firm which carried gold seekers bound for California across Nicaragua. Vanderbilt retaliated by encouraging Mora Porras to declare war in Feb. 1856. Walker invaded Guanacaste, but in April the Costa Ricans attacked Rivas across the border. Drummer boy Juan Santamaría set fire to the town, driving out Walker's forces and setting himself up as Costa Rica's first and only national hero. Walker was decisively defeated by a coalition of Costa Rica and other Central American forces during the second battle of Rivas in April 1857. This war has been credited with giving the new nation's people their first sense of national unity. A border conflict with Nicaragua came on the heels of the war's finale. Under the Cañas-Juarez treaty of April 1858, Costa Rica's title to Guanacaste was confirmed, and, while Nicaragua's right to the Río San Juan was acknowledged, Costa Rica was granted navigation rights.

the Montealegres: After the war, Mora Porras was replaced by coffee baron José María Montealegre after a military coup. A new constitution—providing for limited suffrage as well as indirect election of the president via the Congress—was promulgated in 1859. Although "elections" continued, the army elite and the Montealegre family wielded the real power. In 1870, their chosen president, Jiménez Zamora, was ousted in the aftermath of a coup led by populist General Tómas Guardia Gutiérrez. His new constitution of 1871 was destined to last until 1949, and Guardia was formally elected in 1872. Although the constitution specified a one-term limit for presidential office holders, Guardia dismissed the new president in 1876 and ruled with an iron fist straight from 1877 until his death in 1882. Although his avowed aim was to break the hold of the coffee barons—by redistributing land and imposing heavy taxes—what he in fact achieved was to replace this elite with another composed of his family and friends. Although Guardia encouraged public education, improved urban sanitation, abolished capital punishment, and provided trade incentives, his foremost achievement was the laying of a railway line from the Caribbean coast to the Meseta Central. The line cost US$8 million and 4,000 lives. All this development came at an additional cost, however, and the nation was saddled with a massive debt which still had repercussions 40 years later.

post-Guardia: Guardia was succeeded in office by his brother-in-law, army commander Fernández Oreamuno. After his death in 1885, power passed to Bernardo Soto Alfaro, who created the nation's first free, compulsory public school system. Soto stepped down in 1889, and ushered in a new era when the first election with an unrestricted press, free debates, and an honest tally was subsequently held. The election of José Joaquín Rodríguez Zeledón marked the first peaceful transition of power from those in power to the opposition. It also brought in members of the "Generation of '89," the young liberals who were to govern the nation and control its political life for all but a brief period over the next half century. Although he came from a long liberal lineage, Rodríguez revealed himself to be yet another despot. Refusing to work together with the Congress, he dismissed it in 1892. That same year saw the formation of the Partido Unión Católica. The nation's first genuine political party, the PUC was organized by German-born bishop Bernard August Thiel. Although the party was organized in reaction to the severe governmental curbs on the church's power (that had begun under Guardia and had continued to grow), it focused on criticizing the nation's economic inequities.

into the 1900s: The century was ushered in by a series of unethical political campaigns. While Rodriguez picked Rafael Yglesias Castro to succeed him, the PUC fronted José Gregorio Trejos Gutiérrez in the 1894 elections. Although Trejos Gutiérrez won a plurality despite governmental fraud, the Congress chose Yglesias, and a revolt in the countryside resulted in the PUC's dissolution. Another in what was fast becoming a long line of authoritarian presidents, Yglesias arranged to have the constitution amended so that he might succeed himself in 1898. Ascensión Esquivel Ibarra, a compromise candidate agreeable to both the government and opposition, was selected in 1902. Esquivel was instrumental in fostering new democratic reforms and advancements in education, and his policies were continued by Cleto González Viquez, elected in 1906 in a five-way race. Although González had received the highest number of votes, his election was secured only after Esquivel had exiled the three candidates with the lowest count! Ricardo Jiménez Oreamuno, who succeeded him in 1910, successfully pushed for a constitutional amendment, ratified in 1913, which established direct presidential election and, although the numbers still remained small, expanded voter franchise. Despite these improvements the politics of *personalismo* still prevailed, and parties remained dormant until election time when they awakened from hibernation to support their "liberal" candidate. By this time Costa Rica's population had tripled (to 360,000) since 1860. A large number of immigrants had arrived from Spain, Germany, and Italy, and a new rural elite, comprising small farmers, were making their presence felt in local government.

the Tinoco dictatorship: Alfredo Gonzales Flores, picked as a compromise candidate by the Congress in 1914, followed Oreamuno. He faced a severe economic crisis brought on largely by falling coffee prices and the closure of the European markets due to the onset of WWI. Gonzales Flores attempted—through higher export levies on coffee and by proposing increased taxation of the upper classes—to prevent capital flight to the US, moves which lost him the elite's support. His cuts in government expenditures and civil service salaries proved unpopular among local politicians. And governmental corruption lost him his popular backing. His government was overthrown in a Jan. 1917 military coup led by his own secretary of war, General Federico Tinoco Granados. Tinoco, too, soon lost his own widespread support. Woodrow Wilson had announced a policy of nonrecognition for governments which had not been democratically elected—a policy which had repercussions on trade with the US. In Aug. 1919, Tinoco handed over command to his vice president Juan Batista Quiros Segura. The American Government, however, was still insistent on new elections. The US positioned the cruiser *USS Denver* off the coast, thus forcing Quiros's resignation. A former vice president under Gonzalez Flores assumed command until Juan Acosta Garcia, who had been Gonzales Flores' foreign minister, was elected in 1920. Meanwhile, in 1916 Costa Rica had filed suit in the Central American Court, protesting the perpetual rights granted the US to build a transisthmian canal through Nicaragua, a canal which would use a portion of the hotly contested Río San Juan. Although the court ruled against Nicaragua and the US in 1918, the defendants ignored the decision, and the discredited court subsequently disbanded. The southern border with Panama had been disputed since the days that nation was part of Colombia. A conflict in 1921 between the two nations was settled only after US intervention.

"democracy" restored: In 1919 Julio Garcia was elected, taking office the following year. For the next three four-year terms, the presidency alternated between "liberal" past presidents Jiménez Oreamuno (Don Ricardo) and Gonzalez Viquez (Don Cleto). Despite the lack of any substantive differences between candidates in the 20s and 30s, campaigns were hotly contested, with frequent charges on both sides of voter manipulation and fraud. Secret ballots and yet wider suffrage was introduced during the 20s. Jiménez Oreamuno, under pressure from discontented laborers, pioneered minimum wage legislation, underwrote the establishment of a government-owned insurance monopoly offering low cost coverage, and purchased untilled acreage from the United Fruit Company—out of which plots were distributed to landless farmers. Over the course of time, the efficacy of the educational system had produced political awareness which gave rise to social dissent. During the 1930s, workers organized themselves, farmers became increasingly vocal, and the educated urban upper middle class complained about deficiencies in health care, housing, and transportation. Discontent focused on the prevailing system of liberal elite rule, concentrated in the hands of only a few families, and on its symbiotic relationship with a bureaucracy selected by patronage. Returning from theological studies in Europe in 1912, Jorge Volio Jiménez published a journal propounding "social Christianity" rooted in recent Catholic thought. Mercurial, often demagogic and enigmatic, Volio was politician, priest, scholar, and soldier—possibly the most original thinker and theorist of his era. Founding the Partido Reformista, he entered the 1923 election on a platform calling for union legalization, taxes on the ruling class, and other broad social reforms. Coming in third, he became second vice president in the Jiménez Oreamuno administration, a position which compromised him in the eyes of his supporters, marking the demise of his party. After Volio was implicated in a coup attempt, President Oreamuno explained that he had suffered a mental breakdown and shipped him off to Europe for an extended treatment. Volio continued to fight with his ecclesiastical superiors and was eventually defrocked.

the left emerges: Organized by 19-year-old student Manuel Mora Valverde in 1929, Bloque Obreros y Campesinos (Workers and Peasants Bloc) fielded candidates in the 1932 election. By the late 1930s, the BOC had gained control over important sectors of the labor movement, including Spanish-speaking banana plantation laborers. The party organized a 1934 strike which shut down the nation's banana production and forced United Fruit to equalize wages paid to Jamaican and Costa Rican workers. León Cortés Castro, the PRN candidate, followed Jiménez Oreamuno to power in 1936. Like Oreamuno, Cortés intervened in order to stabilize prices and to encourage the growth of the banana industry, approving an extension of the Pacific railway. Suspected of being a Nazi sympathizer because of his ties to rich German expatriates, Cortés appointed a native German immigration official to prevent entry by Jews. He cracked down hard on the left, and his political opponents' civil rights were frequently curtailed. In order to challenge Cortés in the 1940 election, Jiménez Oreamuno formed the Alianza Democrática (Democratic Alliance) which included the BOC, but he was forced to resign as its leader after obstructive pressure from Cortés. Cortés handpicked physician Rafael Angel Calderón Guardia to represent him until he could legally run for office again. Facing only token opposition, Calderón won by a landslide.

the Calderón era: Suprising Cortés, Calderón proved to be independent. Relying on patronage and *personalismo* for his support, the new president was the first to stress social and economic reforms as a priority. A staunch Catholic, he sought *rapprochement* with the Catholic church. A paternalistic elitist, he dictated reforms from above, reforms which made others in his social stratum view him as a traitor to his class. In 1941 Cortés broke with Calderón to form the Partido Demócrata. While the PD opposed Calderón's proposed reforms, other critics charged that government inefficiency and corruption, rather than constitutional restrictions, stood in the way of their implementation. Other harsh critics were the Acción Demócrata, an organization formed by Francisco Orlich Bolmarcich and Alberto Marten, and the Centro para el Estudio de Problemas Nacionales (CEPN), which produced critiques and studies. On Dec. 8, 1941, Costa Rica declared war against Japan—largely a symbolic gesture since the nation had no men or other resources to offer. After the United Fruit Company's merchant vessel the *S.S. San Pablo* was torpedoed by a German submarine killing 27 and, consequently, seriously hampering exports, Calderón enacted an alien property act which enabled him to seize the property and assets of wealthy resident German and Italian families. Encouraged by the CEPN, largely unknown landowner José Figueres Ferrer purchased airtime, using it to make a speech highly critical of governmental policy. Figueres was later arrested and sent into exile. A series of 15 constitutional amendments, known collectively as the Social Guarantees, passed in 1943, gave the Congress wider authority, paving the way for the administration's agenda of interventionist legislation. The bills enacted encompassed passage of social security legislation which included health insurance, a law allowing squatters title to land, and a comprehensive labor code—one which guaranteed some types of workers a minimum wage, ensured job security, mandated collective bargaining, and legalized strikes. Calderón, together with the church under the leadership of Archbishop Sanabria, permitted the communists participation in the civil service, police, and government in exchange for their support. The POC changed its name to the Partido Vanguardia Popular and included other leftist organizations, and Sanabria allowed Catholics to join the PVP. At the same time he encouraged Father Benjamin Nunez Vargas to form the Confederacion Costarricense de Trabajo Rerum Novarum (Costa Rican Confederation of Labor Rerum Novarum), a Catholic labor union which would compete with the other, communist-led ones. In order to back Teodoro Picado Michalski, Calderón's hand-picked successor, the PRN and PVP formed the Bloque de la Victoria (Victory Block). Anti-communist conservative Picado accepted the PVP's participation as necessary in order to defeat Cortés. In a record turnout of 137,000 voters, Picado defeated Cortés two-to-one in the Feb. 1944 election and also scored a similar victory in the legislature.

the Picado administration: The Partido Social Democrata, PSD, was formed several months later, merging the Accion Democrata with the CEPN. This left-of-center, anti-communist party's platform advocated systematic progressive reform based on the prewar European social democratic party model. Decrying both present and past corruption and election manipulation, the PSD sought a complete overhaul for the system. Returning from exile in May 1944, Figueres joined the party leadership, but, in spite of its staunch middle class backing it remained a marginal force. After Cortés' sudden death in 1946, Figueres joined the PD. His hopes were dashed, however, when he was defeated in his bid for leadership by conservative businessman Fernando Castro Cervantes. He then went on to form a splinter party with Cortés's son. Reviving the party name Partido Unión Nacional (PUN) and backed by business interests who feared Calderón's return to power, venerated conservative newspaper editor Otilio Ulate Blanco entered the 1948 election as the party's standard bearer. In the meanwhile, the violence that had scarred the 1944 election campaign had continued to escalate. Demonstrations, strikes, and coup attempts plagued the Picado administration, leaving it increasingly dependent on the communist-controlled worker's militia to provide security. Governmental opponents were periodically abducted and questioned without regard for their civil rights, and some were forced into exile. In 1946, after troops fired into a crowd protesting irregularities in off-year congressional elections, killing two and wounding a number, Picado disavowed all responsibility. The Huelga de Brazo Caidos (Strike of the Fallen Arms)—which brought the nation to a virtual standstill for two weeks—was staged by merchants and managers in major cities. The communist militia attempted to break the strike by breaking into shops and distributing merchandise. However, Picado was forced to capitulate, signing an agreement to place controls on the security forces and pledging that the next election would be fair. While in exile, Figueres had plotted to overthrow the Calderón government, forming the Caribbean Legion which was supported by Guatemala and Cuba. At Lucha Sin Fin (Struggle without End), his farmhouse base located S of Cartago, Figueres continued to build his militia. Negotiating in Guatemala with other exile groups in 1947, he signed the Pact of the Caribbean in which he pledged to use Costa Rica as a base for liberating other countries struggling under dictatorships—including Honduras, the Dominican Republic, Venezuela, and Nicaragua—if they helped him to overthrow the Picado/Calderón regime. Supported by both the PRN and the PVP, Calderón still commanded working class backing when he ran again in 1948. He also had the bureaucracy and the government apparatus to support him. Castro Cervantes and the PD opted to support Ulate. The reformist PSD also threw in its support. All denounced the violations of civil liberties and the governmental inefficiency which hallmarked the regime. Despite Picado's pledge, the security forces disrupted meetings and attempted to intimidate voters. With 100,000 votes counted on Feb. 8, preliminary results showed that Ulate had won by a 10,000 vote margin. Both parties claimed that election irregularities had adversely affected balloting. After examination, the election commission upheld the results by two to one. Maintaining that the one dissenting member had invalidated its decision, the Picado administration insisted that the president be selected by the Calderón-controlled current legislature which voted 28 to 18 for annulment—a move which left it open for them to name Calderón as the new president. Ulate was arrested and released the next day, an indication that the government was committed to holding on to power by whatever means necessary. Over the next two weeks Archbishop Sanabria attempted to mediate as Figueres assembled a 600-man volunteer army at La Lucha. The rebels were up against a small army and police force, the PRN-armed *calderonistas*, and the communist-run 3,000-man militia. Shortly after capturing an airfield and blocking the Inter-American highway, Figueres was forced to retreat into the nearby mountains, leaving forces behind to cover the airfield. Capturing Puerto Limón and Cartago, Figueres forced the government's fall. On April 19th, Picado and his lieutenant, Núñez, signed a pact allowing for the government's conditional surrender at the Mexican Embassy in San José. Amnesty was granted to all those fighting on the government side. No one would be responsible for property that had been damaged or lost during the conflict, and the PVP as well as the communist controlled labor union were guaranteed continued legality. Finally, it was agreed that the Social Guarantees would not be repealed. Calderón and Picado were exiled to Nicaragua and 74-year-old-Santos León Herrera, who had been completing his third term as vice president, was appointed caretaker president. Known as the "War of National Liberation," this short-lived but brutal and divisive civil war left bitter aftereffects. More than 2,000 died—mostly on the government side—and many more were wounded. Intervention by Nicaragua, which sent troops in to Guanacaste in order to buttress the government, was insufficient and arrived too late.

the Ulate-Figueres era: Cognizant of the difficult realities facing the nation, Figueres and president-elect Ulate suppressed their differences of opinion for the common good. They both agreed to give power to an interim government for an 18-month period in which a constituent assembly would be elected and prepare a new constitution. On May 8 Figueres become the president of the Junta Fundadora de la Segunda Republica (Founding Junta of the Second Republic) whose members were Martén, Orlich, and Núñez. During the first 18 months the junta passed 834 decree-laws, many of which violated the suspended constitution as well as the cease fire agreements. One of the more notable of these was the law granting suffrage to women. Meanwhile, hundreds of *calderonistas* remained across the border in Nicaragua. The exposure of a counterrevolutionary plot as well as a large weapons cache enabled Figueres to renege on his pact with the former government. The PVP was outlawed, the communist-run unions banned, critics were purged from governmental posts and teaching positions, and over 200 communists were arrested. The Court of Immediate Sanctions, a special tribunal, was set up in order to retroactively punish alleged crimes committed during the previous administration and during the civil war. Operating outside of the regular court system, no appeals were permitted. Astutely, Figueres abolished the army—a force not loyal to him—in Dec. 1948, replacing it with a 1,500-man Guardia Civil. His Caribbean Legion, however, continued to operate independently. At the beginning of that same month Costa Rica had ratified the Inter-American Treaty of Reciprocal Assistance (Rio Treaty), a mutual defense pact between Central American nations in which the US served as guarantor. On Dec. 10, a week after its ratification, 800 well equipped *calderonistas* poured in from Nicaragua. When the envisioned general revolution failed to materialize, the insurgents pulled back. While the OAS harshly criticized Nicaragua for its support of the invasion, it also rebuked Costa Rica for permitting Nicaraguan exiles to train on its territory and advised that the Caribbean Legion be disbanded. In April 1949 the minister of public security, Colonel Edgar Cardona Quirós, attempted a coup which garnered no support. The youthful PSD activists, who were in charge of drawing up proposals for the new constitution, had their radical recommendations largely rejected by the mostly-PUN constituted assembly. The body even omitted the term "Second Republic" from the constitution's final version. The 1949 constitution, Costa Rica's eighth since 1825, established separation of powers and embodied the substance of the Social Guarantees. The function of the Figueres-devised Tribuno Supremo de Eleciones (TSE) was to supervise elections. On Nov. 8, 1949 Ulate and the Legislative Assembly took power. Most of Figueres's changes were left intact by the Ulate government. The high price of coffee and the reopening of the banana plantations brought revenues in, and the external debt left by the junta was reduced by US$30 million during the first two years. The World Bank financed construction of a new airport as well as the purchase of agricultural and industrial equipment. The US aided in financing the building of a dam and power plant on the Rio Reventazón. In late 1951 Figueres formed the Partido Liberación Nacional and announced his candidacy for the July 1953 election. Incorporating the PSD, the broader-based social democratic PLN identified itself with the Figueres-led victory and the as-yet-unfulfilled promise of a Second Republic. Its platform stressed that institutional reform and modernization were prerequisites to substantive social reform. This could be achieved through improved efficiency, applying advanced technology, and long-term planning. Despite the party's pro-American stance, it advocated monitoring and regulation of foreign companies and investment. Although Figueres designed the party as a permanent organization—one which would operate independently of any specific individual, it came to revolve, nevertheless, around "Don Pepe," as Figueres was known to his followers.

Figueres's second term: In the 1954 elections the PUN candidate withdrew, and both the PUN and the PD united behind the candidacy of conservative businessman Fernando Castro Cervantes. Figueres's promises to end poverty and improve the standard of living for all classes contrasted sharply with Castro Cervantes, who put forward no program other than opposition to Figueres. Figueres was elected by a two-to-one margin in July. His controversial administration renegotiated its contract with United Fruit, doubled income taxes imposed on the wealthy, financed agricultural development and food processing projects with revenue generated by the governmental alcohol monopoly, and hiked import duties in order to shelter fledgling industries. Critics charged that these expansive policies increased inflation, indebtedness, and economic instability. In pushing through his legislative agenda, Figueres had faced bitter opposition in the Legislative Assembly from both the PLN and the conservative opposition. No love was lost either between Nicaragua's dictator Somoza Garcia and Figueres. Both men hated each other's guts and actively plotted one another's demise. After captured members of a coup attempt revealed that they were Costa Rican trained, Somoza Garcia challenged Figueres to a duel. Figueres responded by advising him to "grow up." Figueres also sheltered opponents of dictators ruling in the Dominican Republic and Venezuela.

insurgents invade: On Jan. 11, 1955, several hundred *calderonistas*—well armed and equipped—poured across the border from Nicaragua. Moving swiftly, this self-proclaimed "Authentic Anti-Communist Revolutionary Army" captured Quesada, lying about 50 km NW of San José, and took over sections of Guanacaste. One of their aircraft strafed San José. Two days later an OAS fact-finding mission decided that, despite Nicaragua's denials, the forces had come from Nicaragua, and Nicaragua was told to capture the insurgents operating from its territory. Fulfilling the terms of the Rio treaty, the US sold Costa Rica four fighter aircraft for US$1, a move which served to deter any additional air attacks. Somoza Garcia, protesting the shipment, claimed that the US was "putting dangerous toys in the hands of a lunatic." Quesada was retaken on Jan. 21, and the two nations agreed on a demilitarized zone. The OAS-recommended formal treaty of friendship remained unsigned until Dec. 1956, three months after Somoza Garcia's assassination.

Echandi's administration: In the 1958 election Ulate was still ineligible to run again under the constitution so Echandi was again selected as the PUN's candidate and this time won. The PR's strong showing of 11 seats evidenced that Calderón's support base, even after a decade in exile, was still considerable. Lacking a majority in the legislature, free enterprise advocate Echandi was unable to alter Figueres's basic programs and policies. After coffee prices plummeted in 1957, Echandi was forced to borrow money abroad, and the national debt mounted up further.

the 1960s: A close friend of Figueres, Francisco Orlich Bolmarich won the 1962 election. Although the administration expropriated unused United Fruit Company land as well as large individually owned estates for redistribution to landless farmers, support waned as the economy plummeted headlong into a recession. Striking banana plantation workers blamed Orlich for the industry's decline. Irazú's untimely March 1963 eruption, which coincided with US President Kennedy's visit, devastated the vital agricultural region surrounding San José. And the right wing assaulted the cancerous growth in the public sector which, according to some estimates, consumed half of the GNP. Despite their past roles as opponents in the civil war, Ulate and Calderón swallowed their differences and, together with former president Echandi, formed the conservative Unificacion Nacional. For the 1966 presidential election, they threw their support behind anti-PLN candidate Trejos Fernandez, a little-known university professor. Figueres, although now constitutionally eligible once more, deigned not to run, and the PLN selected the party's aggressive left wing leader Daniel Oduber Quiros, who had challenged Orlich for the nomination four years earlier. Trejos's "neo-liberal" candidacy promised an administration attentive to the needs of the private sector. His influential backers propagated fears that another PLN victory would lead to a one party state. Backing given Oduber by the communist Allianza Socialista Popular, an organization which had been determined to be constitutionally ineligible to field its own candidate, did him more harm than good. In the end, Trejos won 222,800 votes to Oduber's 218,000. Introducing a sales and import tax, Trejos worked to slash public sector expenditures. His grant of a strip mining concession to ALCOA aroused ire.

Figueres returns: Representing himself as a candidate of the "democratic left," Figueres handily triumphed over Echandi in the 1970 presidential contest, harvesting 55% of the vote. His second administration concerned itself with improving and extending past PLN-initiated programs rather than breaking new ground. Attempts were made to diversify the economy in order to loosen its dependence on bananas and coffee. Just before his inauguration in April 1970, student and non-student demonstrators stormed the legislature buildings in order to protest approval of ALCOA's strip mining concession. This and other subsequent disturbances were blamed on communist agitation. Figueres was tainted by his association with Robert Vesco. When Vesco—who had invested heavily in the country and applied for citizenship—was indicted in the

US, a Costa Rican judge refused to issue extradition papers, claiming that its extradition treaty with the US failed to cover the charges against him. Allegations uncovered in the US linked Figueres with this white collar criminal, claiming that Vesco had showered him with campaign contributions, personal gifts, and investment capital for one of his businesses.

the mid '70s: In 1974 Oduber broke with the nation's informal each term/different party tradition by securing 42% of the vote in a field of eight candidates. During the campaign, the issue of alleged communist subversion had been so intense that the election tribunal banned the use of the words "Marxist" and "communist" from the campaign. Oduber called for nationalization, higher taxes, land redistribution, and strengthening of the public sector in order to increase employment and raise the standard of living. After the party's proscription had been lifted by a constitutional amendment, Mora Valverde reestablished the PVP. Oduber reopened trade with Cuba and reestablished diplomatic relations, broken under the Orlich administration in 1962. After the tax on banana exports was raised by more than a third in May 1975, Oduber had to threaten the multinational fruit companies with expropriation in order to force them to pay the tax. He encouraged export-oriented agricultural production at the expense of local industries which produced goods for local consumption. In mid-1976, a party crisis appeared when Figueres pressed for a constitutional amendment that would allow the president to succeed himself. To add to the tense atmosphere, electrical workers struck, and a plot to overthrow the government was unveiled. As Oduber's administration reached its finale, Figueres withdrew from party activities, the economy continued to worsen, and the *sandinista* struggle against dictator Anastasio Somoza Debayle in neighboring Nicaragua threatened to suck Costa Rica in. In the 1978 election, Figueres deigned not to campaign for Monge, the PLN's candidate. The greater part of the opposition, composed of right-of-center groups, organized the Unidad Opositora (Unity Opposition) which fielded businessman and former PLN-member Rodrigo Carazo Odio. Taking a firm anti-communist line, Carazo pledged to recall the

Costa Rican ambassador in Moscow. He also promised to expel Robert Vesco. As head of his own party in 1974, Carazo had won only 10% of the vote. But this time he took 49% of the vote in the five-candidate race to Monge's 42%.

the turbulent 1980s: Relations with Nicaragua had deteriorated throughout the end of the 70s, culminating with Costa Rica's breaking relations in November 1978, calling for its expulsion from the OAS. Costa Rica actively supported the *sandinistas* in their struggle, serving as a conduit for supplies and arms—a very profitable business—to the 5,000 Costa Rican-based troops under Eden Pastora Gomez. After Somoza fled in July 1979, Costa Rica recognized Nicaragua's provisional junta. Banana plantation workers struck again in 1979 and in 1980. In March of 1981, three USMC American Embassy guards were wounded when Costa Ricans attacked their vehicles. A San José shootout with terrorists in June left three Civil Guardsmen dead. A public rally in San José, called to protest the government's perceived lack of effectiveness in dealing with violence, turned violent itself when guardsmen, attempting to intervene when the crowd called for Carazo's resignation, were stoned. Relations with Cuba were again severed that May. As Unidad fought within itself and the PLN refused to cooperate, Carazo was forced to govern again and again by presidential decree. By the end of his term, the nation's foreign debt climbed to a staggering US$3 billion, up from US$800 million, and foreign reserves were depleted. Its per capita indebtedness was calculated to be the world's highest, and unemployment rose to 14%. In September 1981, the government officially suspended payments on its external debt and, in November, it halted bond repayments and requested debt payment rescheduling. This move, along with other violations of a pact reached earlier in the year with the IMF, caused the fund to suspend the release of scheduled loan funds and close down its Costa Rican office.

Monge's tenure: Distancing itself from the now battered and beleaguered Carazo, Unidad nominated 33-year-old Rafael Angel Calderón Fournier, son of a former president. In Feb. 1982, the PLN's Monge won 53% of the vote against Calderón Fournier's 33%. The remaining 10% was distributed among the other candidates including former president Echandi Jiménez. The PLN increased its seats to 33 in the Assembly, a comfortable majority. Doctors struck in April 1982 for 42 days after the government refused them a US$40 increase in their base pay. At Del Monte's Banana Development Company, 3,000 workers struck, demanding an increase; their wages averaged 67 cents per hour! Six strikers were wounded after Rural Guards fired at them. Monge had run on a *"volvamos a la tierra"* or a "Return to the Land" slate, and he continued and even increased agricultural subsidies. Monge also announced a "100-Day Plan" which was designed to deal with the weakening *colón,* the enormous public deficit, rising inflation, and a decline in confidence by foreign investors. Under his administration, although the economy's decline was stabilized, with marked reductions in inflation and unemployment, the nation's economic problems remained severe. In 1983, teachers, telephone workers, and petroleum workers struck. In Sept. 1983 thousands marched through the streets of San José in reaffirmation of the nation's neutrality. On Sept. 28, the CIA instigated a confrontation at the Peñas Blancas border crossing, using anti-*sandinista* guerillas belonging to ARDE, Eden Pastora's Democratic Revolutionary Alliance. The foreign debt climbed to US$3.8 billion by 1984, exceeding the US$3.1 billion Gross Domestic Product, and a more than threefold increase since 1981 when the debt stood at US$1.1 billion. Between 1979 and 1984, the GNP per capita declined 13%, the offical unemployment rate increased 69.5%, the *colón* was devalued by 550%, and both imports and exports declined. With intraregional commerce cut off and depressed agricultural export prices, the economy was in trouble. Monge also brought back the army in the camouflaged form of the paramilitary Organizacion Para Emergencias Nacionales (OPEN). In May 1984, 20–30,000 people marched through San José, demanding that Monge uphold the nation's policy of neutrality after the nation received US$4.6 million in military aid that year. In an attempt to counteract this drift to the right, which was necessitated by the nation's dependence upon the US, Monge embarked to Europe on a "Truth Mission" in June and July; although promises of US$375 million in aid agreements were announced, only a trickle of that amount ever came in, and US aid continued to exercise a dominant influence. Also that year a new labor law replaced the nation's trade union movement with a system of worker-employer cooperatives.

the 1986 elections: In a break with two traditions—one in which parties customarily alternate terms and the other of not electing a candidate on his first try—PLN-candidate Oscar Arias Sanchez won over PUSC-candidate Rafael Angel Calderón Fournier. Holder of a doctorate in economics from the University of Essex, Arias came from a wealthy family. The PLN also retained a slim legislative majority with 29 of the 57 seats. After the US Army Corps of Engineers arrived to begin public works projects involving bridge construction on the Pacific highway, President-elect Arias, while supporting the plan, made this controversial statement: "If I were President Reagan I would give the US$100 million (in contra aid) to aid the economies of Costa Rica, El Salvador, and Honduras instead." Just before the election he inaugurated the last of 80,000 homes promised under his National Housing Program.

the 1990 elections: Successful at last after three tries at the presidency, lawyer Rafael Angel Calderón defeated economist and conservative PLN leader Dr. Carlos Manuel Castillo, whose party was plagued by political infighting during the campaign, by a 51.3% to 47.2% margin. As there were few substantive differences between the two candidates—both living in glass houses which the other had the stones to break, the campaign was a ho hum affair with the issue of corruption lying dormant. In the Liberation primary, Castillo triumphed over the younger Rolando Araya after $750,000 in alleged drug money was found wrapped with Araya campaign stickers and after top Araya aide Ricardo Alem was charged with attempting to launder money. (Araya was later cleared of the charges.) The resignation of Liberation deputy Leonel Villalobos was also demanded after he allegedly performed improper favors for naturalized Costa Rican Fernando Melo who was accused of links to drug traffickers. After denying it at first, Castillo was forced to admit that he had received a $2,364 donation from Melo in 1985, thus throwing his credibility and morality into doubt. To top this all off, his close friend and former boss, ex-president Daniel Oduber admitted receiving a one million *colón* contribution from US citizen James Lionel Casey, who is wanted for drug charges in the States. On the other hand, Calderón denied an accusation that he had received cash donations of $500,000 in 1985 from Panama's General Noriega.

Calderón days: With a background that includes a two year stint as head of the Costa Rican Association for the Defense of Democracy and Liberty (an organization closely linked to the US Republican party) and a personal friendship with George Bush whose mastermind consultant Roger Ailes contributed to his campaign, there is no mistaking Calderón's right wing orientation. Despite his father's reputation and his nickname of "Junior," he is definitely no friend of the left. Called by his detractors a *caballo con ropa* (a "horse with clothes"), Calderón swiftly moved to help the poor by raising prices across the board, affecting clothing, housing, fuels, power, water, and telephones. Calderón's administration was marred by an incident in which a drug raid by the Green Beret-trained section of the elite Immediate Action Unit resulted in the accidental death of a 12 year old. Despite the trauma it caused, the unit was not dissolved despite early assurances it would be, and the boy's killer has so far been dealt with more leniently than the average five-and-dime thief. Calderón has also promised to cut the fiscal deficit from 30 million *colones* to 20 million. In addition to promising to cut public sector spending, he also promised to increase employment, jail all pickpockets, provide small farmers with credit, construct thousands of new homes, repair roads, and cut taxes. Promises, promises!

IMPORTANT DATES IN RECENT COSTA RICAN HISTORY

1948:   Nationwide strike, Huelga de Brazos Caidos. Civil War leads to victory for the forces led by José Figueres and the flight of Calderón and Picado to Nicaragua.

1949:	Ulate becomes president. Catholicism is declared the official religion.
1952:	Figueres forms Partido Liberacion Nacional (PLN).
1954:	Election of Figueres.
1955:	*Calderonistas* invade and are dispersed.
1958:	Conservative Mario Echandi Jimínez elected.
1962:	Francisco Orlich Bolmarich elected president.
1963:	Costa Rica joins Central American Common Market.
1966:	José Trejos is elected president.
1970:	José Figueres elected to a second presidential term.
1974:	Daniel Oduber Quiros elected president.
1978:	Unity party candidate Rodrigo Carazo Odio is elected.
1979:	Costa Rica supports Sandinistas.
1982:	PLN's Luis Alberto Monge Alvarez is elected. Debt repayment halted.
1983:	Presence of contras on Costa Rican soil raises problems with Nicaragua. IMF agrees to reschedule external debt.
1984:	La Penca terrorist bombing. Monge reaffirms neutrality but US opposition to this move results in resignation of foreign minister.
1985:	United Brands sells its banana plantations.
1986:	PLN-candidate Oscar Arias Sanchez triumphs over PUSC-candidate Rafael Angel Calderón.
1989:	President Arias receives Nobel Peace Prize.
1990:	PUSC candidate Rafael Angel Calderón elected President.

GOVERNMENT

With the strongest democratic tradition in the Central American region, Costa Rica is one of the most politically stable nations in the hemisphere. The nation has had only two violent interludes in its history: 1917–19 and 1948–49. Of the more than 50 presidents, only six have been considered to be dictators and only three have come from the military. The nation's relatively homogeneous population, its large middle class, traditional respect for the rule of law, geographical isolation, and lack of a large military establishment have all contributed to its political stability.

political structure: Despite having declared itself a sovereign republic in 1848, Costa Rica has gone through a number of changes in its constitutional format. Established as a democratic and unitary republic by the 1949 constitution, the Costa Rican government is divided into executive, judicial, and legislative branches. Although there is a carefully designed system of checks and balances and presidential power is limited by Latin American standards, the president commands the center position of power. His control is limited by the legislature's right to override his veto, the Supreme Court's ability to establish the constitutionality of administrative acts and legislation, and the one-term, four-year limit. There is no official army, and the large police force reverts to the control of the Tribunal Supremo de Eleciones (TSE), which supervises the elections (the so-called *Fiesta Política*) during campaigns. A fourth branch of government are the state's 200 autonomous institutions, including the Pacific Electric Railroad, the Social Security Institute, the Electric Institute, the University of Costa Rica, and all banks including the Central Bank. The executive branch consists of the president, two vice presidents, and the *consejo de gobierno* (Council of Government). A unicameral body elected for a four-year term, the National Assembly has 57 members, distributed proportionately, with one for every 30,000 Costa Ricans. It may override a presidential veto with a two-thirds majority. No rubber stamp, its exclusive powers include the right to declare war and peace, determine the national budget, impeach the president, and—disturbingly—suspend civil rights for up to 30 days.

local government: Ruled by appointed governors, the nation's seven provinces all have capitals of the same name with the exception of Guanacaste whose capital is Liberia. While Alajuela, Heredia, San José, and Cartago lie entirely inland, Guanacaste, Puntarenas, and Limón border the coasts. Provinces are divided into a grand total of 81 *cantones* (counties). These in turn are divided into 344 *distritos* (districts). The

Mouse opposum, Marenco Biological Station (Sergio Miranda)

Street scene, Horquetas

Cattle ranching, Horquetas area

municipalidad (municipal council) of each *canton* controls services ranging from trash collection to road maintenance.

political parties: Largest and most influential of these is the Partido de Liberación Nacional (PLN, National Liberation Party), founded by the nation's famed statesman José "Don Pepe" Figueres. Opposition comes from the currently-ruling, more conservative Unidad Social Cristiana (USC, Social Christian Unity), a loose confederation of four different parties which was known from 1978 to 1983 as the Coalicion Unidad. Other, much smaller and less influential parties include the Partido del Progreso (Progressive Party), the religious and conservative Partido Alianza Nacional Cristiana, the Trotskyite Partido Revolucionario de los Trabajores en Lucha (Revolutionary Party of Workers in Struggle) and the Pueblo Unido, a coalition of two left-wing parties. In recent elections, their combined share of the vote has dropped from 8% to around 1–2%. Some voters, disheartened and disillusioned with the two major parties, turn in blank ballots. In the 1990 polls one witty soul plastered pictures of cattle (including one wearing a suit and tie) and of two pigs (one of them feeding) on his ballot, scrawling the word "no" prominently in three places.

elections: Costa Rica has universal suffrage for all citizens over the age of 18, and voting is compulsory for all citizens under 70. Turnout has been about 80% in the past few elections. Voting is by secret ballot with the voter indicating his choice by placing a thumbprint in a box under the party's name, full color flag, and the candidate's photo. There is also a separate ballot for the congressional and municipal races. Here one votes for the party with its full slate of candidates rather than picking each individual candidate. After voting, each citizen has his or her right index finger dipped in a jar of purple indelible ink. Citizens are automatically registered to vote on their 18th birthdays if they receive a *cedula de identidad,* a numbered identity card complete with name, address, fingerprints, and photo. The autonomous Tribunal Supremo de Elecciones (Supreme Electoral Tribunal) supervises the electoral process. Composed of three magistrates and three alternates, all selected by the Supreme Court and serving staggered six-year terms, the TSE commands complete control, even having the right to ban an already established party. Even though additional advertising is affordable only by the two major parties, all registered parties are granted equal TV and radio airtime. Although the government also contributes funds for campaign expenses, .5% of the national budget is distributed to parties in proportion to the votes they received in the previous elections. (The catch is that a party must have received a minimum of 5% to qualify). National assemblies (party conventions) choose candidates. Every four years elections are held on the first Sunday in February. The weeks previous to the election are marked by *plazas publicas* (demonstrations featuring sound systems, speakers, and bands), car honking, and flag waving. If the president and two vice presidents fail to receive 40% of the vote, a special runoff election pits the two top contenders against each other. In the unlikely event that the top two contenders receive the exact same percentage, the oldest will be selected.

ECONOMY

In order to understand Costa Rica's economy one must take into account a number of factors. First of all, the nation's small size and relatively small population have hampered industrial development. The incessant regional instability, along with socio-cultural and political differences, have served as obstacles to development of a truly unified regional economic block. Secondly, the nation has always been a plantation economy with agricultural exports commanding chief importance. Finally, the same lack of industrial development that has hampered the economy in other ways has also made it necessary to import a large number of items from the "developed" world (the US in particular), thus running up a substantial deficit in the process. Another factor to consider is the government's role as employer: about 20% of the population works directly or indirectly for the public sector.

recent economic history: Between 1960 and the late 70s the Gross Domestic Product grew 6% in real terms annually, with low inflation except for the period surrounding the oil crisis. Per capita income has risen from US$838 (1960) to US$1,630 (1979)—a level well above that of any other Central American nation. The economy hit its peak in 1976–77, slowing down thereafter as agricultural expansion peaked and new markets shrank. The 1980s were turbulent times. President Carazo (1978–82) floated the *colón* in Sept. 1980, and it dropped from 8.54 to the US$ in Nov. 1981 to 52 during May of 1982. The national debt reached US$1.3 billion in Dec. 1982, nearly 85% of the GNP. The inflation rate hit 100% that year. After Monge took over, the situation improved as he achieved two reschedulings of the nation's $4 billion foreign debt. By early 1983, average industrial wages had dropped to a point where they were, at less than 20 cents per hour, on a par with Haiti. During 1983 aid rose to $350 million, and the trade balance had improved to minus $30 million by the end of the year. The 1988 inflation rate hit 25.3%. Although the administration had agreed with the IMF directive to limit the 1989 deficit to not more than 7 billion *colones* (about $81 million), it has been estimated at 14 billion *colones*, an all-time high. Inflation topped 20% in 1990. In May 1990, Costa Rica repurchased two thirds ($1.2 billion) of its outstanding $1.8 billion foreign debt from international banks for the bargain price of $253 million, a deal which was the final achievement of the Arias administration. Under Calderón, the current president, the currency has continued to lose its value. Although devaluation adds to the wealth in local currency of the wealthy agroexporters, it hurts the poor who must cope with the resulting inflation, and the gap between rich and poor widens still further. It also makes domestic assets cheaper, expediting their passage into foreign control. According to official estimates some 40,000 Costa Rican families live in extreme poverty with each household averaging at least seven members. In Los Cuadros, an urban slum (*tugurio*) located a few miles from San José, households have an income of only 10–15,000 *colones* per month. Single mothers, who constitute 25% of the population here, have incomes of only 3–5,000 *colones* a month! Countrywide, the average income is around $175 per month, but the cost for a basic basket of 69 staple items is around $165.

US aid: One cannot discuss the nation's economy without considering the enormous influence of the US government. Foreign assistance in the years 1981–84 totalled US$3 billion, without which the economy would have collapsed. The economy's small size (with a 1985 GDP of just over $4 billion) meant that these donations had great impact. Much of the money was kept out of government hands as the Agency for International Development (AID) established parallel institutions resembling a "parallel state." In 1984 Costa Rica received US$181 million from US AID, making it the highest per capita recipient (after Israel) of such contributions. The next year the total rose to $231.2 million including $11.2 million in military aid. The figure dropped off during the Arias years, after he refused to make the nation a center for contra resistance, and, today, assistance is on the wane. The Bush administration proposed reducing aid to Costa Rica from $90.4 million in 1990 to $65 million in 1991. All of this money does not come without some advantage to the US: in 1989, 43% of the nation's imports came from the US.

foreign investment: One recent element in the economic mix is Japanese investment. Businessmen, who have invested $52 million in the country, are expected to bring in another $100 million for the development of a large tourism complex on Nicoya's Playa Carrillo. To date, they have invested in luxury hotels and other tourist projects, and have purchased a 45% share in LACSA.

Solidarismo: Any discussion of the economic situation would be incomplete without mention of *Solidarismo*. Created in 1948 by Alberto Marten as an alternative to the Communist-run labor unions, the over 1,300 *Solidarismo* associations operating nationwide are savings associations which work hand in hand with management. The workers invest a fixed percentage of their wage (generally 5%) into a savings fund, an amount which the company then matches with money from a severance pay fund. (Companies are legally obliged to deposit 8.33% of their payroll in a fund which covers payoffs for dismissals). While some find the system works well for them, there have been complaints of abuses from members as well as from unions, who claim the *Solidarismo* philosophy is designed to destroy their collective bargaining groups. It is also alleged that many *Solidarismo* groups are run by patsies for management who do not have the best interests of workers in mind.

light industry: The nation's manufacturing industry dates from the early 20th C when factories to produce such consumables as textiles, cigarettes, beer and other items were established. During the second half of the 20th C, the government adopted the policy of *desarrolo hacia adentro* (internally oriented development). However, its impact has proved disappointing, and the nation is still heavily dependent upon exports. Since WWII, the government has nationalized many industries. At first this was confined to banking, power companies, and telecommunications. In the 1970s, it was expanded to encompass agriculture and industry. The government set up corporations to manage projects which were either too expensive for or not of interest to private firms. Along with the enactment of the 1959 Industrial Development Law, establishment of the CACM (Central American Common Market) in 1960 accelerated expansion of manufacturing. The CACM established intra-regional free trade along with protective barriers against outside competition. The nation's open attitude toward foreign investment, combined with its relatively high educational level, has spurred on the economy. The wide variety of goods produced today include bricks, cement, fertilizers, paints, plastics, solar energy collectors, petroleum products, textiles, cosmetics, adhesives, tubes, tires, yachts, and motor vehicle spare parts. Most of the manufacturing is concentrated in the Meseta Central. Unfortunately, the nation's relatively small population, the vast majority of whom live at or near the subsistence level, limits the market for locally produced goods, and the wages are horribly low: a textile worker might make only 3,500 *colones* for a 48-hour work week.

tourism: This "industry" has grown dramatically with over 400,600 foreign tourists spending US$164 million in 1988; of these 123,600 came from the US and Canada. Now in third place, after bananas and coffee, tourism has become a major economic priority, and a large number of new hotels are under construction. Unfortunately, many of the hotels (especially on the Nicoya Peninsula) are being constructed with only short-term, pecuniary gain in mind, without taking into account what effect such development will have on the local ecosystem and all of its inhabitants. Some believe that it is unwise for any local economy to place too much emphasis on tourism. Instability in the region, a major earthquake, civil disturbances, hyperinflation, even the whims of tourists—any or all of these could depress tourism, sending the economy into a tailspin.

other sectors: Much of the mining is of nonmetals—sand, limestone, and clay. Small amounts of gold, silver, and dolomite are also mined. Various projects have been instituted by Citizens Energy Corporation, a nonprofit organization founded by Rep. Joseph Kennedy III. Much of the potential for hydro-electric power remains untapped. In 1986 the DEA estimated that 20% of the cocaine arriving in the US was funneled through Costa Rica. The largest seizure in history occurred in Nov. 1989 when 568 kg were confiscated at Limón airport along with $13,500 in cash and the plane belonging to the two Colombian pilots. The fact that no arrests were made of Costa Ricans hinted to many of high level governmental links with drug trafficking.

AGRICULTURE

The economy has always centered around agriculture and animal husbandry—exporting coffee and bananas and, more recently, livestock. Despite a surge in growth, the manufacturing industry's structural emphasis on imports has limited its overall contribution. As there are no mineral deposits of note, the most valuable natural resources are the nation's superior pastures and nutrient-rich fields. As elsewhere in Central America, the land distribution here is inegalitarian, with a small minority (11,500) of the larger farms monopolizing the largest portion (some five million acres) of the farmland. Less than 1% of the nation's farms are larger than 1,200 acres but these extend over 27% of the country, and estates with more than 500 acres account for only 3% but occupy more than half of the land area. According to the 1983 census, 71% of the "agricultural" population are landless agricultural laborers. Owing to the topography and the small size of the average farm, mechanization has had little effect on agriculture. If the land were used in an ecologically optimal fashion, it has been estimated that agriculture could supply employment for nearly half of the nation's labor force, which would relieve the pressure on urban areas. In the history of agricultural development, government support and regulation has been crucial: The Consejo de Nacional Producción (CNP) buys basic grains from farmers at subsidized price levels and distributes them through its *expendios*. A problem for small farmers has been that loans have been available mainly for export-oriented rather than local production. Traditional export crops include banana, sugarcane, coffee, and cacao.

environmental problems: Sadly, the Hispanic-American farmers learned little about agricultural methods and techniques from the Indians. Whereas the indigenous peoples lived in harmony with the environment—using the forests as a resource, growing different types of vegetables in order to stave off soil depletion—the new arrivals have radically transformed the natural environment, to the point where deforestation, soil erosion, and changes in river ecology have reached crisis proportion. These ecological colonialists attempted to institute temperate land use patterns—such as monoculture and the transformation of rainforests into pasture—that have wreaked havoc on the environment. Forests on steep slopes and in areas of heavy precipitation, which protected the soil from erosion and regulated water supply to the drainage system, were indiscriminately wiped out, setting off a chain reaction. Today ecologists estimate that 30% of the nation faces serious water and wind erosion. Pesticide use, along with its effects, constitutes another major problem. Export-oriented crops, such as cotton, fruit, vegetables, and cut flowers—temperate products produced in the tropics—must be deluged with pesticides. Pesticide use can also lead to tragic results. One recent example was DBCP, a pesticide used in Standard Fruit's Río Frio banana plantations to control nematodes. After the chemical was found to cause sterility in humans, its use was suspended in 1977 in the US. In Costa Rica, however, it was banned only in Aug. 1988. In addition to abuse of legal pesticides, unregistered pesticides have also been found in use. Pesticide bombardment of the mining fly, which plagues the potato fields, has become so heavy that the fly has developed a resistance. Costa Rica spends an estimated $40 million on imported pesticides.

nontraditional agriculture: Termed the *cambio,* nontraditional agriculture is growing in importance. Since the early 1980s the government has stressed the export-oriented production of crops such as coconuts, ornamental plants, flowers, pineapples, macadamia nuts, and melons. Income from nontraditionals soared from $336 million in 1984 to $729 million in 1989. In the near future, the greatly increased acreage planted in macadamias will make Costa Rica the third largest producer of these nuts. However, because of the capital requirements and the high interest rates, it is difficult for the small farmer to switch to crops like strawberries, miniature vegetables, mangoes, and flowers. Support for nontraditional farmers has been misdirected because it has been supplied in the form of CATS or tax certificate bonds valued at up to 15% of the value of the crops. These investments can be claimed as discounts on taxes or they can be sold to investors for immediate cash. Unfortunately, the small farmer often sells to an exporter who then cashes in on the small farmer's benefits.

coffee: Coffee production began in 1779 in the Meseta Central, an area which has near-perfect soil and climate conditions. A native of Ethiopia, the introduced Arabica blend had been first cultivated in Saudi Arabia. Coffee growing soon surpassed cacao, tobacco, and sugar in importance. By 1829 it had become *the* major source of foreign revenue. As a nonperishable commodity in an age of slow and costly transport, coffee proved an ideal product, and it has remained the nation's major export ever since. Exports to neighboring Panama began in the late 1820s. After a load was sent directly to Britain in 1843, the British began investing heavily in the industry, becoming the principal purchaser of Costa Rican coffee until after WWII. The largest growing areas are the San José, Alajuela, Heredia, Puntarenas, and Cartago provinces. Costa Rican coffee is high both in quality and caffeine content; it is often blended with inferior varieties. Local coffee, set at a much lower government-controlled local price, is tinted in order to prevent diversion to the export market. Labor-intensive, coffee production depends upon cheap, seasonal labor: workers receive a mere 80 *colones* per basket picked, and many workers are refugees. A major blight struck in 1983. As with any plantation crop, one of the major drawbacks is that income is subject to major price fluctuations. When world coffee prices plunged 40% after the collapse of the world quota cartel system, Costa Rica joined Honduras, Guatemala, Nicaragua, and El Salvador in June of 1989 in a coffee retention plan. This would entail selling their coffee in installments in order to ensure price stability.

bananas: Thought to be a native of tropical Asia, the banana (*plátano, banano*) was introduced into the Caribbean and subsequently to Central America sometime after the Spanish invasion. The fruit became well known in the US only after the mid-1860s, and the production of the popular Gros Michael variety was begun by American Minor Cooper Keith. He shipped his first fruit, 360 stems, to New Orleans in 1870. Taking over the nation's debt to cutthroat British bankers in 1883, Keith was offered in exchange control of the completed railway and 800,000 acres or 7% of the national territory. Although much of this land was returned, the remainder became the basis for the company's Costa Rican empire and Keith's influence seeped into every sector of the economy. A century later, exports surpassed 50 million 40-pound boxes. In the 1890s, financial difficulties drove Keith to merge with the United Fruit Company, a firm which monopolized the nation's banana exports until the late 1950s. The Standard Fruit Company began production in 1956 with exports beginning in 1959. A third major transnational, the Del Monte subsidiary BANDECO, the Banana Development Corporation, began operating plantations. United Brands subsidiary Compañía Bananera closed down operations in 1985 following rising costs and a 72-day strike in 1984 which cost the company US$12 million in lost production. In addition to domination of exports by transnationals, another problem with banana cultivation has been the crop's susceptibility to disease, namely Panama disease and Sigatoka (leaf spot) disease. Epidemic diseases in the first quarter of the century led to the temporary abandonment of the Caribbean coastal area and to the establishment of plantations on the Pacific side. With the formation of the Asociación de Bananeros S.A. (ASBANA), a government-subsidized private association, the Atlantic Coast banana plantations took off once more, producing an estimated 75 million boxes of bananas and generating $250 million for the local economy. But this development has not come without a stiff price. Much of the new acreage came through destruction of thousands of acres of virgin jungle near Guapiles. In 1990, Limón's bishop Alfonso Coto denounced the conditions under which workers labor. He contended that they are treated unfairly, the wealth is concentrated in too few hands, the industry aggravates deforestation and contamination of rivers, and that the labor organizations (*Solidaristas,* which have replaced the unions) provide neither job security nor adequate working conditions. Today, most bananas are shipped to the US and Europe.

sugarcane: Caña (*Saccharum officianarum*) probably originated in New Guinea; it has become a major crop only since the late 1950s. While it is grown all over the country, the largest areas for sugarcane growing and processing are concentrated in the Meseta Central, in Guanacaste province, in northern Puntarenas province, and in northern Alajuela province. An estimated 113,700 acres are under cultivation. Except in labor-scarce Guanacaste, almost all the cane is cut by hand, and the land is burnt before harvesting (Jan. to May) in order to expedite cutting. Large sugar mills (*ingenios*) are prevalent although the oxen-powered mills (*trapiches*) can still be found. During the pre-Castro 1950s, little cane was grown, and sugar was imported until the middle of the decade. Stimulated by the Cuban embargo, exports to the US climbed to 60,000 tons by the mid-1960s. In 1989, 45,300 tons were produced.

cacao: Thought to have originated in the Amazon basin on the E equatorial slopes of the Andes, *Theobroma cacao,* the "food of the gods," has been cultivated for upwards of 2,000 years. After the Spanish conquest, cacao (known as chocolate or cocoa in its refined form) became the most important crop, and it was used as currency until the 19th C. when it was replaced by coffee. It only re-emerged as an export crop in 1944. Today, cacao is the only export crop grown under adverse conditions. The vast majority of the crop is produced in the Caribbean coastal lowlands, an area which is really too wet to grow cacao properly. While the NE lowlands are superior, cultivation in the region is hindered by the lack of coastal transport; most of the current crop grown there goes to Nicaragua. Owing to the lack of controlled fermentation, quality of the processed cacao is low. Devastated by the fungus *monilia* since 1979 and plagued by plummeting prices on the world markets, cacao seems to be on its way out. The Ministry of Agriculture has even recommended that farmers substitute other crops.

palm oil: Native to W Africa, the African oil palm (*palma de aceite*) was transported to this hemisphere along with the slave trade. The primary oil in use during the Industrial Revolution, it helped to cement the colonial linkage between Europe and Africa. In Costa Rica it was introduced in the 1940s to fill the domestic need for cooking oil. After the pullout by United Brands in the 1980s, it replaced bananas on the W coast. It is cultivated by the Chiquita-owned, government-controlled transnational monopoly, Cia. Palma Tica (formerly Compañía Bananera) whose subsidiary (Grupo Numar) in San José processes the unrefined oil into cooking fat. It also blends it with imported soybean oil to make cooking oil and margarine. Because of the high volume of saturated fats in the palmitic acid contained in the oil, palm oil, along with palm kernel and coconut oil (the other "tropical" oils), has become the center of a worldwide controversy. The oil and its food products are of major economic importance. Costa Rica exports 12,000 metric tons of it annually, with a market value of over $4.6 million.

other crops: Maize, beans, potatoes, plantains, rice, onions, and sorghum are the main crops cultivated for domestic consumption. The most important cereal grain in Costa Rica, corn is used as a staple food (in forms ranging from *tamales* to *tortillas*), a raw material for industrial products, and as animal feed. Most of the corn is grown on small to medium-sized farms and is usually planted using a digging stick, with two or three seeds inserted in each hole. Approximately 90% of the rice crop (*Oryza sativa*) is grown without irrigation. Unlike maize, it is grown by large-scale growers using modern methods. Although Guanacaste has been the traditional stronghold for rice cultivation, irregular rainfall has spurred the development of new areas near Puntarenas. Less important crops include cassava, tobacco, and cotton. Quantities of maize, beans, and sorghum must still be imported.

animal husbandry: First brought here in the 1500s, cattle are the most important component of the livestock industry. Until after the end of WWII, beef, the favorite meat of Costa Ricans, still had to be imported. Export of live cattle (*ganado*) to the US began in 1954, but exports switched to beef so that hides and offal could be used locally, and it continues to be the major export after bananas and coffee. Local consumption, however, has actually declined as escalating prices have made beef more and more of an unaffordable luxury. Graded low because the cattle is grass-fed and therefore lean, most of the exported beef is made into pet food, TV dinners, and fast food hamburgers. Although cattle ranching has been hailed because of its ability to magnetically attract greenbacks, it has had devastating ecological consequences, wiping out forests and resulting in severe erosion. The massive deforestation occurring between the 1960s and early '80s was largely the result of a boom in cattle ranching. While beef exports tripled between 1960 and 1978, the percentage of pasture vs. agricultural land grew to more than 50%, and an estimated 80% of trees felled were either burned or left to rot on the ground. In a pattern that has become alarmingly typical, small farmers cut down the primary forest, farm the land for a few years until it is depleted, resell the land to a rancher, and then move on to the next virgin tract. Although cattle ranches consume vast areas of land, they provide little employment. At their height, beef exports never surpassed 8.6% of total exports. During the 1980s, the price of beef began to drop, and a 1988 boycott led by the San Francisco-based Rainforest Action Network led Burger King to stop purchasing Costa Rican beef. Along with the Alajuela province's Llandura de San Carlos region, the largest cattle raising areas are Guanacaste and northern Puntarenas provinces. Only a few farms raise pigs commercially. Horses far outnumber mules, sheep, and goats. Although all three birds were introduced by the Spaniards, chickens win out numerically over ducks and geese. There are also turkeys and even quail, which produce eggs for export.

forestry: Much of the forest has been sold without directly benefiting the economy. Although the Arias administration claimed to have cut the deforestation rate to 75,000 acres annually while increasing reforestation tenfold, some experts believe the deforestation figure to be much higher. Although it is now a felony to illegally cut or transport wood, violators are consistently fined rather than jailed. Much contraband wood is transported at times when forestry officials are off work. Although the lumber industry accounted for less than 4% of the nation's agricultural earnings in 1985, thousands are employed in the process of milling and transporting logs. As wood grows scarcer, the price of timber has risen and the number of mills has dropped from 220 in 1984 to around 150 in 1990. Many of the bankrupt mills made inefficient use of wood and were wasteful. At the current rate of deforestation, the nation's productive forests will be depleted sometime this decade. This might cost the government up to $150 million a year to

import wood sufficient for its needs. Even though annual reforestation is planned to equal the area cut, there is still a 15–20
year gap between the time of forest exhaustion and the time
when the reforested trees are ready for harvest. Although exports of logs along with wood that has been made into timber
is prohibited, the nation exports around $22 million worth of
wood products annually.

fishing: The fishing industry accounts for only a small part of
agricultural production. While lobsters are caught in the Caribbean, tuna, herring, sardines, and shrimp are caught in the
Pacific waters.

THE PEOPLE
(Los Costarricenses)

As is true all over Latin America, one cannot discuss the culture without mentioning Spain and its influence. Although
hardly more than a few thousand Spaniards immigrated between 1502 and 1821, their impact upon the society was tremendous. Costa Ricans call themselves "Ticos" after the
peculiar diminutives they add to their speech. Throughout
Latin America, diminutives are commonly added to speech, for
example *momento* becomes *momentito,* "in a little while." But
Costa Ricans change this into *momentico,* using their own peculiar diminutive. Despite the official version of a Euro-
American "white" Costa Rica, there has been a great deal of
racial mixing over the centuries. Still, Costa Rica is unques-
tionably the most homogeneous—both linguistically and
ethnically—of all Central American nations. Although there is
a definite infusion of African and Native American blood, Ticos share the same language and consider themselves to be

Caucasians. Because Ticos have traditionally viewed themselves as egalitarian yeoman farmers, they sometimes refer to
their society as classless despite glaring differences in income
status, power, and distribution. In fact, the independent
farmer is a dying breed, but other social classes remain strong.
In addition to the Spanish stock, French, British, Germans,
and Italians have arrived over the centuries and been ab-
sorbed into the mainstream.

population: At the time of Independence, there were approximately 65,000 Costa Ricans. Their numbers grew to 100,000
by 1850, 250,000 by the early 1900s, nearly 500,000 by 1927,
2,655,000 in 1985, and nearly 3,000,000 in 1990. An average
of 13.8 deaths occur for every 1,000 births. With a current
annual growth rate of 2.6%, the population is projected to be
3.4–3.7 million by the end of the century and 4.9 million by
2025; 20% of households are headed by single mothers. Of the
80,000 births recorded annually, teenage pregnancies account
for over 14,000, and more than half of all births are out of
wedlock. Over half of all Costa Ricans live in the Valle Central
which comprises portions of four provinces: San José, Alajuela,
Heredia, and Cartago, with the largest portion living in the
San José metropolitan area. Although this area encompasses
only 5% of the land surface, the population has actually been
even more concentrated percentagewise in the past with many
other areas becoming significantly populated only in the 20th
century. Most emigrants go to the US, and that nation receives
a higher percentage of immigrants, relative to Costa Rica's
total population, than from any other Latin American nation.

class structure: In the earliest times, there was a sharp divi-
sion between the minority *hidalgos* (gentry) and the *plebeyos*
(commoners). The former had servants and owned all of the
slaves. Although these differences had largely dissolved by the
beginning of the 1800s, a small elite still dominated the nation. In fact, 21 out of the 28 who signed the act declaring the
nation's independence were closely related. These *cafetaleros*
(coffee barons) came to control the best coffee growing lands
along with the *beneficios* (coffee processing plants). Their political power reached its apex between 1821 and 1915. Now

known as *la sociedad* (the society), the descendents of the coffee barons, no longer as economically and politically dominant
as in the past, still reside in San José. This elite has been
joined by other immigrants who made their fortunes in the
20th C, and these days wealth is more likely to impress than
family status. Having expanded substantially during the 20th
C, the upper and lower middle classes also reside in the capital. The middle class believes manual labor to be degrading
and has a strong belief in the power of education; conspicuous
consumption is their badge of success, even though it may be
financed by steep debts. Below these classes, the members of
the working class, traditionally referred to as *clase obrero* or *el
pueblo,* are the "marginals"—many of whom are employed in
illegal occupations. One social class which has become virtually extinct is the *gamonal,* well-off peasants with a traditional, non-cosmopolitan Tico lifestyle. Usually the wealthiest
member of his community, the *gamonal* was highly respected
by the villagers and, because they would follow his advice, he
was often courted by sharp politicians. If you ask an affluent
Tico about poverty in his country, you'll hear about the illiter-
ate, barefoot peasant "who may look as if he has nothing but
is very rich." He's referring, of course, to the *gamonal.*

male and female relationships: Despite the idealized official version of family life that originates with the Catholic
Church, "free unions" are extremely common and some 40–
50% of all births are illegitimate. In some 20% of these the
father is listed as "unknown." Today, to be a *hijo naturale* (illegitimate) is not necessarily shameful. In the upper classes,
because patrimony and purity of blood lineage are viewed as
being of paramount importance, chastity is vital for women
although men are free to screw around. The twin pillars of
male-female relations are *machismo* and *marianismo.* While
the myth of *machismo* rests on innate belief in the superiority
of men in all fields of endeavor, whether it be in work, in politics, or in the arts and sciences, *marianismo,* which holds
women to be morally and spiritually superior, allows women to
feel virtuous through their suffering at the hands of men. The
supreme compliment paid to a wife and mother is to call her

abnegada, self sacrificing. Traditionally, marriage for women is a cross to bear which gains her brownie points both with society and with God. In a society in which men hold the privileges and dominate, female nomenclature is defined in terms of their relationship with men. Unmarried women are called *señoritas* or *muchachas buenas* (a "good girl," therefore a virgin); single, unmarried females are *mujeres* (women); loose women are *zorras*; prostitutes are *putas*; and *señoras,* married or not, are housewives. Women in consensual unions are legally referred to as *compañeras,* and they have all the legal rights of wives except that they may be forced to testify against their husbands in criminal cases. Common among the poor are so-called "Queen Bee" families in which a grandmother runs the house and looks after the children while the daughters go out and work and bring home the bacon. While many middle and upper class young women tend to have an idealized view of marriage, with some even believing their match to be predestined, their poorer cousins tend to be more pragmatic, viewing a relationship with a man as a way to escape their parents' clutches. While lower class housewives still find themselves housebound, these days things are changing for upper class women. But many of these women still view themselves as extensions of their husbands' occupations; as is the case with their lower class comrades, many also have little interest in political or cultural affairs and are preoccupied almost totally with their children.

names: Descent is traced through both male and female lines. Children receive both a paternal or first surname and a maternal or second surname, which is frequently abbreviated. If your father is "unknown," you have only your mother's surname.

MINORITY GROUPS

As black slaves were few in number and the Indians were mostly assimilated or dispersed, Costa Rica retains few minority groups. Blacks, Indians, and Chinese constitute only 3–5%

of the population. But few though they are, these groups are of great importance for they continue to influence the nation's future just as they have affected its past. All still suffer the sting of prejudice: national passports still specify skin color, and many Ticos still mistakenly believe white to be superior, resulting in condescending attitudes not only towards national minorities but towards citizens of neighboring countries.

mestizos: Costa Ricans have often referred to a *mestizo* class. Said to compose 15% of the population in the 1950s, they had shrunk to 7% by the 1970s. Since it seems unlikely they were captured by visiting alien anthropologists for transport to a research lab on a distant planet, there is only one possible explanation for the shrinkage: "*mestizos*" had been classified as such not on racial but on cultural grounds. As they acculturated they were accepted, and no longer considered to be separate. Most *mestizos*, descendants of unions between Spanish and Chorotega Indians, today live in Guanacaste Province and are also known as Guanacasteans. They retain some Indian customs, and they have a distinct dialect.

Jamaicans: Although the first African Americans came to Costa Rica as early as 1825 to farm and hunt turtles, most are the descendants of Jamaicans who were brought in to help build the railroad. After its construction, they stayed on—confined to the area around Limón from which they were forbidden to relocate, a restriction that remained in force until 1982. Working as railway men, longshoremen, and as banana plantation workers, the newcomers had no desire to assimilate nor did they have much in common with the Hispanic Americans. Although they still retain their Jamaican patois and their Anglican religious affiliation, the younger generation can speak fluent Spanish. During the 30s, depression, banana disease and falling demand put the Caribbean coast plantations out of business. And United Fruit's 1934 contract with the government for the Pacific coast plantations prohibited "colored people . . . from being employed in the zone." Many emigrated to the Canal Zone or the US, and the majority of the remainder became full-time farmers. A 1948 decree, sponsored by consummate patriarchal politician Figueres, awarded them citizenship. Discrimination and prejudice against them, however, remain strong and have prevented their full assimilation. Today, there are about 30,000 Costa Ricans of Jamaican descent who are noted not only for their domination of basketball and soccer teams but also, increasingly, for their social and political contributions to the society. Many of them have left farming to enter the professions.

indigenous peoples: Of the estimated 5,000–20,000 Indians in Costa Rica, 65–75% live in Talamanca, the mountainous area to the nation's S where they were either brought or ran for shelter. Although actually quite similar, the Bribri and the Cabecare who live in this area view themselves as culturally distinct. Widely scattered on both the Caribbean and Pacific sides of the range, the Indians settled on the Pacific slope tend to be more acculturated. The Chorotegas of Guanacaste have been almost totally assimilated as have the Huetares who reside on the Pacific slope of the Meseta Central and the Malekus who live in the San Carlos region near the Nicaraguan border. Living in three villages in the SW, the 1,500–2,000 Boruca are the only other remaining tribe of note. Although they are almost totally assimilated, they retain community ownership of the land and some still practice traditional weaving. A 1939 governmental declaration granted the Indians certain lands, and the Council for the Protection of the Native Races was established in 1945. But Indians have lost much of their land through deception or violence. During the 1960s, a congressional investigation revealed that most of them live in extreme poverty and many have succumbed to demon alcohol. In 1976 President Oduber declared a state of emergency within the Indian areas and established five zones in which non-Indians were prohibited from renting or buying land. Today, although these laws remain on the books, they are unenforced, and the state of the nation's indigenous peoples remains unchanged. Most have made the transition from tribal to peasant culture, and only an estimated 5–6,000 still predominantly preserve their culture, including their language. Hunting has been replaced by husbandry and the Cabaceres, for example, raise pigs for sale. Given the increase in interracial marriages along with the overall situation, the indigenous cultures appear destined for gradual but inevitable extinction through acculturation and assimilation. In 1990 Guayami tribespeople came to San José to protest their inability to secure *cedulas* (identification cards). Many of them emigrated from Panama 50 years ago. The process is now underway to pass a law granting them cards. Without a *cedula* you cannot vote, borrow money, or use the benefits of the government health system.

the Chinese: Once a separate, socially segregated community, the nation's Chinese (*Chinos*) are becoming more and more acculturated. While the oldsters still speak Chinese and believe in the old ways, the Spanish-speaking young are intermarrying and converting to Roman Catholicism. Traditionally, Chinese either stayed out of politics or supported the most conservative candidate. As is true elsewhere in the world, the small, closely knit Chinese communities exercise considerable economic control relative to their numbers, and rise to resentment on occasion. The Chinese emigrated to Costa Rica from 1873 to work as railway navvies and farm laborers. They were harshly exploited. Never confined to the Caribbean lowlands, they spread and established shops, inns, and restaurants.

other groups: Sephardic Jews have been living in Costa Rica since the beginning of colonization and have been fully assimilated. Before and after WWII, a small number of Polish Jews arrived. Because they earned their living by selling door to door, they were dubbed *polequeando.* There are also many Panamanians, Nicaraguans, Honduran, and Chilean refugees. Although they are the butt of considerable resentment and prejudice, the estimated 200,000 Nicaraguan refugees provide badly needed cheap labor, especially in the coffee fields. Because the vast majority lack legal status, they are readily exploited—performing low-paying, low-prestige, and backbreaking work shunned by Ticos. Resident Americans include multinational corporate employees and pensioners. There's also a small but valiant band of Quakers who have set up a cheese factory in the vicinity of Monteverde in Puntarenas Province, and a colony of Italians in the town of San Vito in the S part of the same province.

RELIGION

As in every other Latin American nation, the Roman Catholic Church reigns supreme here. Although 95% of *Costarricenses* claim to be practicing Roman Catholics, and most of these attend church, the strength of religious belief and practice varies with each individual. With the ratio of one priest for every 4,000 Costa Ricans, the nation has the most clergy per capita of any Central American nation and is touted as the most staunchly Catholic nation in the isthmus. Surprisingly, the government has frequently been anticlerical. This attitude, combined with 19th C liberal values, culminated in the Liberal Laws which permitted divorce, ended religious instruction in public schools, secularized cemetaries, and drove a firm wedge between Church and State. These were repeated during the 1940s by President Rafael Angel Calderón Garcia, a staunch Catholic, who re-introduced religion to the public schools. Today, Catholicism remains the state religion, and the only church marriages that have civil validity are those performed by Roman Catholic priests. Although the official Church teaching is that God is all powerful and the saint is only an intercessor on behalf of the petitioner, in actual practice Ticos act as if the saints are all-powerful and have the ability to directly grant their requests. Undoubtedly a reaction to the popularity of evangelical Protestantism, a new movement has emerged in recent years. Known as Catholic Pentacostalism or Spiritual Renovation, this intensified Catholicism involves speaking in tongues, uttering prophesies, and other such activities. Although the Church leadership initially looked askance at such activities, it is now an accepted form. Another innovation is the *Cursillos de Cristianidad,* three-day intensive study courses which have attracted tens of thousands of participants over the past 25 years.

Protestantism: When the Central American Mission arrived in 1981, they encountered vehement hostility: they were stoned and beaten, and the Catholic Church attacked them. The missionaries responded to these attacks by calling the church "utterly debased and idolatrous." Although the government refused to expel them, in 1901 it forbade them to preach in public, advertise their meetings, or establish schools. Despite this, the Protestants persevered, and other sects arrived. When Billy Graham arrived in 1958, the Catholic Church was able not only to suppress any announcement of his arrival but was able to blackout any radio, magazine, or newspaper coverage of his visit, which included a service that was attended by 8,000. Similarly, the Church was able to block a 1961 parade of various sects commemorating the 70th anniversary of the arrival of the Protestant Mission. Today, it is common to see the declaration "Somos Catolicos" posted by the door; this is not an affirmation of religious faith as much as an attempt to deter annoying door-to-door religious peddlers. Over the decades, however, the prejudice has abated. Ironically, as Catholic-Protestant relations have improved, the sects have grown apart from each other. Today, there are an estimated 40,000 Protestants. With Costa Rica the headquarters for the Latin American missionary movement, there are a large number of bible colleges, and publishing houses. Evangelical Protestant sects include Methodists, Baptists, and Pentecostals. They comprise an increasingly large percentage of the population. Most of the Anglicans are Jamaican emigrants and their descendants. Small sects include Jews and some Indian religions.

FESTIVALS AND EVENTS

Jan 1	New Year's Day
March	Festival in Puntarenas
March 19	St. Joseph's Day
April	Easter (three days or more)

April 11	Anniversary of the Battle of Rivas
May 1	Labor Day
June 29	Day of St. Peter and St. Paul
July 25	Anniversary of the Annexation of Guanacaste Province
Aug. 2	Virgin of Los Angeles
Aug. 15	Mother's Day
Sept. 15	Independence Day
Oct. 12	El Día de la Raza (Columbus Day)
Dec. 8	Conception of the Virgin
Dec. 25	Christmas Day

note: On each of the 17 official holidays (*feriados*) most government and professional offices, some banks, and many stores are closed. During Easter and Christmas weeks, the entire country shuts down almost completely.

January

Fiesta Patronales de Alajuelita: Held in honor of the Black Christ of Esquipulas, this festival features a colorful oxcart parade, a pilgrimage to the large iron cross overlooking the town, and plentiful consumption of *chinchivi,* a homemade corn beer.

Fiestas de Santa Cruz: Also held in honor of the Black Christ of Esquipulas, this celebration, held in Guanacaste's cultural capital, includes folk dancing, bullfights, and marimba music.

Copa del Café: This week-long tennis tournament draws an international collection of talented players, all less than 18 years of age.

February

San Isidro de General: This town's *fiestas civicas* are held from the end of Jan. to the beginning of Feb. Activities include a cattle show, agricultural and industrial fair, bullfights, and an orchid exhibition.

Fiesta de los Diablos: The sole remaining Indian festival, this takes place in the village of Rey Curre in SW Talamancas. In an allegorical recreation of the struggle between the *Diablitos* (the local Boruca Indians) and a bull (representing the Spaniards), masked *Diablitos* pursue the bull, which is made of burlap topped with a carved wooden head. Local crafts, corn liquor (*chicha*), and *tamales* are for sale.

March

Carrera de la Paz: In this footrace, around a thousand people run from San José's National Gymnasium to the campus of the University for Peace in Villa Colón.

National Orchid Show: Featuring 500-plus species, this weekend-long festival takes place in the Colegio de Medicos y Cirujanos headquarters in Sabana Sur.

National Oxcart Day: Taking place on the second Sunday in March, this celebrates the *boyero* (oxcart driver) and the *carreta* (the wooden-wheeled painted cart); the locus for the celebration is in San Antonio de Escazú near San José.

Farmer's Day: Held March 15, Farmer's Day is a nationwide celebration headquartered in Tierra Blanca near Poás (whose farmers celebrate deliverance from a plague of locusts in 1877). The day is devoted to the farmers' patron saint, San Isidro, a humble 12th C Spanish farmer.

Ujarras pilgrimage: Held mid-month, this Orosi Valley procession from Paraíso to the ruined church in Ujarras, commemorates the rescue of Ujarras from floods by the Virgin. Her graven image returns along with the crowd for the occasion.

Bonanza Cattle Show: The nation's cattlemen assemble at the Bonanza Fairgrounds on the airport highway for this event. Featured are prize bulls, bullfights, rodeos, horseraces, and mechanical bulls.

San José Day: On this day (Mar. 19), local families traditionally visit Volcán Poás for a hike and picnic.

Crafts Fair: Taking place on the Plaza de la Cultura, 150–200 local artisans exhibit their wares.

April

Día de Juan Santamaría: Held in Alajeula, this day's events—a parade with marching bands and majorettes—commemorate Juan Santamaría, Costa Rica's only national hero and the town's pride and joy.

Earth Day: In San José's Plaza de la Democracía, an annual three-day Festival of Indian handicrafts is followed by the celebration of Earth Day.

Semana Santa: Much of the country shuts down during Easter Holy Week from Wed. noon through Sun. Its highlight is a series of processions, the most famous of which are held in Cartago, Santo Domingo de Heredia, San Antonio de Escazú, San José, San Isidro de Heredia, and in San Joaquín de Flores—where all the procession's characters are people instead of sculpted images. Held only in Santo Domingo and Cartago, the Procession of Silence takes place at 11 PM. The Encuentro procession takes place at mid-morning on Good Friday. The Procession of the Holy Burial (in which Christ is slowly marched to the cross accompanied by a grieving Mary, the Apostles, and a band of mourners clad in black) occurs later between 4 and 5. Holy Saturday ("Judas Day"), is marked by firecrackers and in some villages an effigy of Judas is hanged to the accompaniment of speeches and petitions. Featuring shepherds and pint-sized angels, the triumphant Procession of the Resurrection takes place mid-morning on Sunday. If you have a car, you can catch the beginning of a procession in one town and then move on to another town and catch its finale. Procession schedules are available at each Casa Cural.

May

May Day: On the first, workers march and the president gives the annual "State of the Nation Address." The Limón area celebrates with cricket matches, picnics, quadrille dances, and domino matches.

University Week: Taking place around the beginning of the month, University of Costa Rica students crown a queen, and participate in sports events and a parade. Many local bands also perform on campus.

Día del Boyero: May 15 is traditionally the start of the rainy season, and San Isidro Labrador is honored on this day, the "Day of the Oxcart Driver." Locuses for celebration are in all of the San Isidros and in San Antonio de Escazú near San José. Activities include parades featuring bright colored oxcarts, the blessing of animals (extending right down to puss and Fido) and crops by the local priest. The oxen, in turn show their religious piety by carrying paper money on their horns to the church.

Carrera de San Juan: Taking place on San Juan Day, May 17, around 1,500 run the 14 miles from El Alto de Ochomongo (near Cartago) to San Juan de Tibás, N of San José.

July

Mango Festival: The highlight of Alajuela's year, this celebration offers nine days of parades, music, outdoor food markets, and arts and crafts fairs.

Puntarenas Carnival: Beginning on the Sat. nearest July 16 in this port town, the Fiesta of the Virgin of the Sea is celebrated with a regatta featuring beautifully decorated fishing boats and yachts. The carnival which follows has parades, concerts, dances, sports events, fireworks, and the crowning of the queen. Similar events take place in Nicoya's Playas del Coco.

Annexation of Guanacaste: Held every July 25, the Anniversary of the Annexation of Guanacaste Province commemorates the province's secession from Nicaragua. Fiestas in Liberia and in Santa Cruz feature folk dancing, marimba bands, horse parades, bullfights, rodeos, cattle shows, and local culinary specialties.

The Virgin of Los Angeles: This festival is Cartago's largest. Every August 1, thousands assemble around Av. Central near Plaza de la Cultura and march towards Cartago. In contrast with the awe that one might expect during such a momentous religious event, the atmosphere is lively, and the devotees evidence an intimate, convivial relationship with the *Virgen. Fiestas patronales* continue the celebrations on through the month.

Día de San Ramón: In this colorful tradition, nearly 30 saints from a neighboring town are taken on Aug. 31 for a visit to San Ramón, who resides in the town named after him. His image is taken for a spin around town with the others. The celebration continues as the saint's guests take up residence in the church for over a week.

Semana   Afro-Costarricense: Celebrating   International Black People's Day and taking place in San José, this cultural week's highlights are lectures, panel discussions, and displays.

September

Día del Independencia: Held on Sept. 15, the nation's Independence Day (which is also that of all of Central America) has country-wide parades featuring uniformed schoolkids, majorettes, bands, and the like. At 6 PM the Freedom Torch, relayed by a chain of student runners stretching all the way from Guatemala, arrives in San José, and Ticos join in singing the national anthem. That evening schoolchildren march in *farole* (lantern) parades, carrying handmade lanterns along the route.

October

Limón Carnival: Centering around Columbus Day (Oct. 12), this port city's annual festival is the nation's most famous. Incorporating the Caribbean Coast's African-American traditions, it's a miniature of those found in Río or Trinidad. There are floats and dance groups.

Fiesta de Maíz: Honoring corn, this festival is held in Upala in the uppermost portion of Alajuela Province. Corn Queen contestants don costumes made entirely of corn husks, grains, and silk.

Costa Rica Yacht Club Regatta: Held annually in October–November, this international regatta is open to saiboats 20 ft. and over.

November

All Souls Day: Observed nationwide on Nov. 2, on this day special church ceremonies are held and families visit cemeteries to pay homage to the deceased.

International Dog Show: Sponsored by the Asociación Canófila Costarricense, this San José show features a splendid assortment of dogs.

Coffee Picking Tournament: Held during coffee picking season in the Meseta Central (Nov.–Dec.), *campesinos* compete to pick berries with speed. This televised event includes typical songs, legends, and poems.

International Theater Festival: Held in San José, a variety of theater groups perform plays, puppet shows, and street theater.

December

Fiesta de los Negritos: Featuring wildly costumed dancers in blackface, this festival is held on Dec. 8 in the village of Boruca. Held in honor of its patron saint, the Virgin of the Immaculate Conception, participants dance to flute and drum accompaniment, in time to the movements of the *sarocla*, a frame with a horse's head.

Día de la Pólvora: Honoring the Virgin of the Immaculate Conception on Dec. 8, this nationwide festival includes fireworks, the best of which take place in Jesús María de San Mateo (Alajuela Province) and in La Rivera de Belén (Heredia).

Fiesta de la Yeguita: Held in Nicoya in Guanacaste on Dec. 12. Solemn-faced villagers carry the image of the Virgin of Guadalupe through the streets. To the accompaniment of flute and drums, two dancers, one of whom carries a doll, pass through *La Yeguita*, "the little mare," a hoop with a horse's face. Other festivities include bullfights, fireworks, band concerts, and traditional foods made from corn.

Vuelta Ciclista: An international cycling tournament which starts in mid-Dec. and lasts until the New Year. Contestants cycle across the country.

Christmas celebrations: Beginning Dec. 15, in a traditional practice known as *los posadas,* children go from house to house asking for a place to stay—just as Mary and Joseph supposedly did in Bethlehem thousands of years ago. Accompanied by musicians and carolers, they are given refreshments at each house and are treated to songs in exchange. Confetti battles take place along Av. Central on Christmas eve. *Creches* of the nativity scene are very popular and a competition is held in San José. Before they are taken down on Candelaria in Feb., families gather to pray, sing, drink corn liquor, and eat traditional sweets.

year's end fiestas: Most events take place in and around San José. These begin during the last week of Dec. and extend through the beginning of January. Bullfights are held at the Zapote ring daily; the *topé,* a procession of horses, departs from Paseo Colón, proceeds along Av. Central and ends at Plaza Viquez. Finally, a dance in Parque Central welcomes the New Year. While the Christmas season is a time of partying and all the bars stay open, people turn solemn during New Year's Eve. Some Ticos believe that if God sees them in church on the first day of the year, he'll make allowances if they are absent during the remainder.

FOOD

No one would ever accuse Costa Rica of having one of the world's great cuisines, and this is not a destination to select because of its food. All too frequently overcooked and greasy fried foods dominate. It is a simple and unvarying fare, the product of a nation of farmers struggling to eke out a living on small plots. Despite the legend of spicy Latin food, Tico chefs appear unfamiliar with the use of spices. During your stay, however, you may find that Tico cuisine has its own charms and, back at home, you may find yourself pining away for a breakfast of *gallo pinto*.

typical fare: *Campesino* food has historical roots. The maize and beans grown by the Indians have become staples which, along with rice, are the principal source of protein in the average Tico's diet. The standard diet consists of *tortillas* (thin corn pancakes), rice, beans, salad, and bread. *Agua dulce* (water sweetened with raw sugarcane) is the national beverage. In a typical restaurant, there's one surefire bet: the *casado*. A plate of rice served with salad, beans, and meat, chicken, or fish, this dish—as ubiquitous as the hamburger in the US—will probably be your staple meal. *Arroz con pollo,* one of the most popular local dishes, is chicken with rice and vegetables.

other dishes: Traditional dishes include *olla de carne* (a beef stew including local vegetables like *yuca, ñanpi, chayote,* potato and plantain, among others), *mondongo en salsa* (ox in tomato sauce), and *chilasquiles* (meat stuffed tortillas). A *sopa negra* is made with black beans and sometimes includes a poached egg. Other soups include *pozol* (corn soup) and *guiso de maiz,* fresh corn stew.

desayuno: "Breakfast" appears on the menu throughout the day. *Gallo pinto,* rice and beans fried together, is the staple breakfast food which varies little from place to place except in price. It comes *con* (with) *huevos* (eggs), *jamon* (ham), etc.

seafood: *Ceviche* is a chilled fish cocktail made using *corvina* (sea bass) pickled in lemon juice and mixed with cilantro and onion. It's a meal in itself. *Pescado ahumado* is smoked marlin, a fish which resembles salmon. *Camarones,* usually very small shrimp, are served with fried rice. *Langostinos* (prawns) and *langosto* (lobster) are available but expensive. Fish dishes served *en escabeche* have been pickled Spanish-style. Canned locally, Costa Rican tuna may or may not be tainted with dolphin blood.

Jamaican cuisine: Largely confined to the Caribbean coast, not much has survived the voyage across. The most common dish you'll find is rice and beans cooked with coconut milk and spices, a version infinitely more appetizing than the Tico rice and beans. *Patacones* are mashed and fried plantains which are served like french fries, and *patí* are snacks made of *empañadas* filled with fruit or spicy meat. Two other specialties to watch out for are *johnny cakes* (originally "journey") and *pan bon* (from the English word bun), a sweet and dark bread with designs etched in the batter on top. In some sodas, you'll also find *agua de sapo.* This "toad water" is iced lemon and raw brown sugar. If you're fortunate you may be able to find delicacies such as fritters, fry-bread, roasted breadfruit, ackee, and herbal teas.

Chinese food: You know you're really in a small town when there is no Chinese restaurant. The quality varies from gourmet to grease galore. You may want to ask them to leave out the ajinomoto (monosodium glutamate, MSG), a Japanese flavoring derived from soy sauce that, along with cornstarch, ruins the quality and flavor of traditional Chinese cuisine. Curiously, Chinese food is generally accompanied by twin slices of styrofoam-like bread. Some of the most common Chinese dishes have become an integral part of Costa Rican food. One example is *arroz con camarones* (fried rice with shrimp) which may be accompanied by greasy *papas francesas* (french fries).

on the quick: Fast food franchises, which replicate the US originals and their prices (although the fast food workers are paid a mere pittance comparatively), include McDonald's, Pizza Hut, Burger King, and Colonel Sanders'. Terms you should be familiar with when ordering pizza include *hongo* (mushroom), *aceituna* (olives), and *cebolla* (onion).

snacks: *Tamales* are ground corn and pork wrapped in plantain leaves; they are traditionally served at Christmas. A *tortilla de queso* has cheese mixed in the dough. The term *tortilla* can refer either to an omelette or a small thin tortilla. *Pupusas* are two tortillas fried with cheese inside. *Gallos* are tortillas filled with cheese, beans, meat, etc. *Tortas* are sandwiches which contain meat and vegetables, and *arreglados* are a type of bread filled with meat and vegetables. Invented in Nicaragua, *vigorones* are a combination of cabbage, cassava, tomato, and onion topped with pork rinds. *Empañadas* are corn turnovers filled with cheese, beans, or meat and potatoes, and *enyucados* are *empañadas* made with yucca. *Masamorra* is corn pudding, *pan de maíz* is a thick and sweet cornbread, while *chorreados* are corn pancakes which are often sold by street vendors in San José. While *elote asado* is roasted corn on the cob, *elote cocinado* is the boiled variety. *Plántanos* (plantains) are large banana-like fruit which must be fried or baked. They are often sliced and fried like potato chips. *Huevos de tortuga* are sea turtle eggs which are thought to have aphrodisiacal properties and can be found in bars. As with the sea turtle meat served in restaurants, this food is often illicit and you should not support it.

desserts and toppings: The best ice cream is served at the Pops chain and at Monpik. The former, owned by a consortium, including the right wing publisher of *La Nación*, meticulously weighs each cone dispensed on a scale. *Capuchino* is a cone dipped in chocolate. *Cajeta* is a traditional fudge-like treat; made with coconut, *tapa dulce*, and orange peel, *cajeta de coco*, are delicious. *Tres leches* is a cake with filling and frosting. *Flan* is a sweet custard. *Pañuelos* (lit. handkerchiefs) are a type of pastry. *Melcochas* are candies made from raw sugar. A *torta chileno* is a multi-layered cake filled with *dulce de leche*, and a pound cake is called *queque seco*. *Tamal asado* is sweet cornbread cake. *Tapitas* and *milanes* are foil-wrapped chocolates. Popcorn is known as *palomitas de maíz* or "little corn doves." *Tapa dulce* is strong-tasting unrefined sugar which is

On the way to Limón

Coastline at Cahuita village

sold in brown hunks. *Dulce de leche* is a thick syrup made with milk and sugar. *Natilla,* cream left out overnight, is a popular topping on many dishes. A common dessert, fruit salads often come with jello and whipped cream.

fruits: Papaya is available much of the year. The two varieties are the rounder, yellow-orange *amarilla* and the elongated red-orange *cacho.* Watermelon (*sandia*) are also plentiful in season. Don't mistake them for the *chiverre,* a gourd which is candied during Easter. Originally introduced from Asia, citrus fruits include *toronja,* four types of lemons (*lemones*), mandarins (*mandarina*), and oranges (*naranja*). Mangoes come in several different varieties and are excellent. *Guayabas* (guavas) have a pink, very seedy pulp commonly used in jam or paste. *Cas* is a similar but smaller and rounder sour-tasting, green or yellow fruit, which is used in drinks and ices. Resembling an extraterrestrial beverage, *chan* is a relative of mint and contains furry purple seeds which taste like gelatin as they go down. Another fruit that is commonly served only in beverage form, *maracúya* is an acid sweet fruit which makes an exotic fruit drink. Introduced from Brazil, its taste but not appearance resembles passion fruit. Resembling a cross between a prune and a fig when dried, *marañón* is the fruit of the cashew nut. Brown and similar to avocadoes but with bright orange sweet pulp, *zapotes* are another exotic fruit. An unusual delicacy is *palmito,* the tender and delicious heart of the *pejibaye* palm, which may be boiled or eaten raw. The fruit of the *pejibaye* palm, is treated as a delicacy; it was once a major source of protein for the Indians. Fibrous in taste and texture, these bright orange fruits are usually boiled in salted water, peeled, halved, and eaten. Other fruits include *granadillas* (passion fruit), *mamones* (lychees), *mamón china* (rambutan), *carambola* (starfruit), *aguacate* (avocado), *melocoton* (peach), and *nispero.*

taxes and tips: One thing very confusing for foreign visitors is the system of taxes and tipping. At the better quality restaurants a 10% service charge is levied on all meals above 10 *colones,* and a 10% sales tax is added on top of this. At the cheaper restaurants, the 10% tax is incorporated in the cost of

Loading bananas, Bribri

the meal. The least expensive places, such as *sodas,* incorporate taxes and service in their prices. Costa Ricans almost never leave an additional tip; you can do as you like.

fruit drinks: *Refrescos* are tropical fruit shakes made with milk or water. These drinks are made from *tamarindo* (the seed pod of the tamarind tree), *mora* (blackberries), *cas,* and other fruits. One of the most popular items is *pipas,* green or gold drinking coconuts. These are young coconuts which the vendor opens with a machete. He hacks off a piece from the edge which, after you're finished eating, serves to scoop out the soft white jelly inside. If you want more water than jelly or lots of jelly, just tell the vendor, and he'll hand pick for you.

alcohol: Drinking is a very popular activity, and establishments selling liquor outnumber schools almost three to one. Excellent, locally brewed beers are available in 350 ml bottles in supermarkets, restaurants, *cantinas,* and bars. The brands are the ultra-popular Imperial, the locally brewed Heineken, Bavaria, and (the author's favorite) Pilsen; another brew, Tropical, is a type of ale. *Cerveza cruda* (draft beer) is also available in some local bars. Local bars sell beers for around 50–70 cents, and you are expected to drink it there unless you ask for a cup. Stores sell beer in two varieties of bottles, nonreturnable and returnable, which are so identified in raised letters on the glass. While in the supermarkets you have to get a receipt written out if you wish to be able to return them. Shopowners generally just rely upon appearance—i.e., if it has a price tag it's not ours! Costa Rica also produces a few inexpensive varieties of rum as well as sugarcane-distilled *guaro,* a firewater which is the hands-down popular favorite among *campesinos.* Often drinks are accompanied by *bocas,* small dishes of fried fish, *ceviche,* or other snacks. Sometimes you have to pay extra for these; other times they are included in the price.

café: Aside from alcohol, the most popular drink in Costa Rica must be coffee—the nation's only other legal drug. It is served either as *café negro* or *café con leche* (coffee with milk) and is customarily combined with generous quantities of sugar. The traditional fashion of serving coffee is to deliver one small pitcher of coffee along with another of heated milk which one mixes together according to taste. Sadly, this custom has largely fallen by the wayside. Coffee can be had *en taza* or, somehow more delicious, *en vaso* (in a glass). It comes in two sizes: *pequeño* (small) and *grande* (large). Despite claims to the contrary, the coffee generally served in Costa Rica is not all that delicious unless one compares it with watered down truckstop brew found in the States. Most of the ordinary *sodas* sell coffee made from pre-ground powder which has been either made in a large metal percolator and left to sit, or filtered through a *chorreador,* a cloth filter mounted on a wooden stand. A cup sells for between 20 and 40 cents.

soft drinks: Colored sugar water is very much in vogue here, and imbibers will find a choice selection practically everywhere. Brands include Coke, Canada Dry Ginger Ale, and Squirt. While there is no mineral water, you can ask for *soda blanca.* Although soft drinks come in 500 ml plastic disposables, you might wish both to set an example for the locals and send a message to the multinationals by sticking to glass. Milk costs about 40 cents per liter, and long life milk is also available at a higher price. Both are 2%.

tobacco: Nicotine junkies can choose their poison from well over half a dozen local brands. Males smoke like chimneys as do many *joven, señoras, y señoritas,* or at least those who can afford it. If you wish to cut down or quit, Costa Rica is an excellent place: single cigarettes are priced at about five cents each.

dining out: Most of the nation's finest restaurants—ranging from Swiss to Chinese to Italian—are found in the San José area. While shrimp and lobster are available, they are not cheap. Usual hours for gourmet dining are 11:30–2:30 for lunch, and for dinner from 6 or 6:30 to 10 or 10:30. While some restaurants are open only for dinner, the ones open for lunch usually feature an *almuerzo ejecutivo,* a specially priced "executive" lunch. To find gourmet restaurants check the pages of this guide, the yellow pages, *Guide* magazine, the "On the

Town" column in the *Tico Times*. Out in the country, high quality restaurants are fewer and are usually connected to a hotel.

budget dining: You'll find no lack of places to eat. There are a small number of local restaurants in every town. Alcohol-free *sodas,* which serve everything from *casados* to hamburgers to sandwiches, are your best bet. In a typical soda, the menu (which usually includes a *plato del día,* special of the day) is written on a blackboard or painted on a wall. A glass cabinet on the counter contains baked goods and other snacks. Expect to spend $1–$5 per meal. Restaurants offering counter service are generally less expensive. It's always best to ask the price of food before consuming. Although Ticos are not price gougers like the Mexicans, there *are* unscrupulous people who don't hesitate to jack up the price artificially. In addition, there are the ubiquitous fast-food joints and a proliferation of pizzerias.

tips for vegetarians: This is most definitely a carnivorous society so the more you are able to bend or compromise your principles, the easier time you'll have. If you're a vegan (non-dairy product user), unless you're cooking all of your own food, you will find it even more difficult, but the quantity and variety of fruits readily available may be your salvation. Locally grown fruits such as papaya and mangoes, tend to be much more reasonable when purchased from vendors; prices go down at the end of the day. Fruit salads are often drowning in gelatin (an animal product) and ice cream. Ask to have it *sin helados* and *sin gelatina.* If you do eat fish, you should be aware that locals eat it fried and that it may have been fried in lard or in the same oil as chicken or pork. At the very least, it will have been fried in *manteca,* a type of shortening made from hydrogenated palm oil. Be aware that the word *carne* refers only to beef; a dish may still have pork, chicken, or fish in it. Cheese sandwiches will serve you well in a pinch. If you eat a lot of nuts, plan on bringing your own because those available locally are expensive. The same goes for dried fruits such as raisins. Finally, bear in mind that—outside of tourist restaurants—fish may be in short supply at times. **note**: Places serving vegetarian food are frequently listed in the text.

SPORTS AND RECREATION

WATER SPORTS

beaches and swimming: Aside from the innumerable beaches and rivers, most major hotels and "apartotels" have their own pools; Olympic-size ones are found at the Cariari Country Club and in Parque de Sabana where swim meets are held on occasion. Located S of the international airport, the pools fed by Ojo de Agua springs are cold and fresh. Ironically sponsored by unhealthy McDonald's, the International Swimming Tournament is held at the outdoor club in the E part of San José every July or August.

scuba and snorkeling: Although the former is still an emerging sport here, Costa Rica is an exceedingly fine place to do either. The Caribbean coast's sole coral reef is at Cahuita, S of Limón. One excellent area located in Guanacaste is Playas Hermosa and the nearby Islas Murchélagos is one of the best locations. Another area is just off Bahía Herradura and a visit would have to be arranged by special charter from Quepos or Puntarenas. This is El Jardín, famous for its sea fan and soft coral formations. Just offshore from Limón, the waters surrounding Isla Uvita have a wide variety of fish, sea fans, and coral as well as the wreck of the *Fenix*, a cargo ship. This is recommended for experienced divers only. Other sites include the Isla de Caño off Osa Peninsula in the NW and the distant Isla de Cocos.

surfing: The Pacific coast is famous for its waves. The season in Guanacaste runs from late Nov. to early April. Surfing spots are numerous but hard to reach. To get to Potrero Grande in Parque Nacional Santa Rosa, which features a fast and hollow right point break, rent a boat at Playas de Coco. On the N side of the same park, Playa Naranjo has one of the country's best breaks. Points at Playa Tamarindo are found at Pico Pequeño, El Estero, and at Henry's Point in front of the Third World Bar. Featuring a R and L point break that curls in front of a small river mouth, Langosta is located a km to the S. Avellanas (which has the beach break "Guanacasteco") lies 10 km (6 mi.) S, and Playa Grande is a 20 min. walk (or a shorter drive) to the N. Farther S along the coast are Playa Negra and Nosara. Coyote Manzanillo, and Mal País can be reached by 4 WD during the dry season, but there are no hotels. To the S from Puntarenas are Boca Barranca, Puerto Caldera, Playa Tivites (and Valor, a rocky point), and Playa Escondito—for which you should rent a boat at Jacó. Near famous Playa Jacó are Roca Loca 1.5 km S, Playa Hermosa (best in front of the almond tree), and other points to the S like Esterillos Este, Esterillo Oeste, Bejuco, and Boca Damas. There's good surfing (but polluted water) in the town of Quepos and, to a lesser extent, up at Manuel Antonio. Set 11 km to the R of Ronacador off the road to Dominical, Playa El Rey features R and L waves. Father S are Playa Dominical and (accessible only by boat) Drake's Bay, and Boca del Río Sierpe in Peninsula de Osa. Reachable either by road or by rented boat from Golfito, the L point at Pavones is considered to be one of the world's finest. The southernmost Pacific surfing spot is Punta Burica which can only be reached by boat; there's no accommodation. On the Caribbean side, located to the N of Limón are Playas Bonita and Portete; conditions at the former are dangerous. To the S, a long beach break termed Westfalia extends S from Limón to Punta Cahuita. Other places are Cahuita's Black Beach, "Salsa" at Puerto Viejo, Manzanillo to its S, and beaches near Herradura. To buy or sell your surfboard, try the Mango Surf Shop, 75 feet W of the Banco Popular in San Pedro, or the Tsunami in Los Yoses. Other rental shops are in Limón, Cahuita, Puntarenas, Jacó, and Manuel Antonio.

wind surfing: Conditions for wind surfing are said to be among the best in the world. Chilly Lake Arenal features 35-knot gusts every afternoon. Other spots include Puerto Soley (a half-hour from Cuajinquil), Playas del Coco, Playa Tamarindo, polluted Playa Puntarenas and the nearby Boca Barranca, as well as other spots.

white water rafting: Some of the world's best is found here and it's at its best during the rainy season when the rivers fill up. Beginners will want to try the Reventazón. (See description in "Meseta Central" section). It also has Class V on its lower end. Endangered by a proposed hydroelectric project, the Pacuare flows from the Talmancas to the Caribbean; it is ideal for two- or three-day trips through the tropical jungles. Larger, wider, and more powerful than the Pacuare, the Chirripó is less difficult to navigate. For a relaxing trip, Guanacaste's gentle Corobicí is ideal.

kayaking: Interest in kayaking has grown dramatically in recent years. Featuring Class IV and V rapids, the Reventazón has become world renowned as a winter kayaking training ground. Flowing N from Volcán Poás through the province of Heredia, the Sarapiquí has moderate rapids. Other destinations include the Pacurare, General, and the Corobicí. An alternative to going out on the river is sea kayaking.

angling and deep-sea fishing: Some of the planet's best sport fishing is here. You can expect sailfish, snapper, roosterfish, wahoo, crevalle, snook, tarpon, marlin, wahoo and yellowtail. Freshwater finds include introduced rainbow trout and indigenous guapote and bobo. For the competitively-minded, fishing lodges hold tournaments. A fishing license (US$10) can be obtained through your lodge or from the Ministerio de Agricultura, C. 1, Av. 1, San José, tel. 23–0829. You will need your passport, tourist card and two passport-sized photos. **ar-**

eas and seasons: Lake Arenal's guapote season stretches from Jan. 1 through Sept. 30. Chacon Farm at San Geraldo is one of the locations stocked for trout. Although they peak in size from August through mid-Oct., snook may be caught—near river mouths and along beaches—all year round. Although they may be caught in other months, tarpons are found off the Caribbean coast from Jan. through mid-May. Sailfish and dorado (dolphinfish) are best caught in July through Sept., roosterfish in May and June, yellowfin tuna in July and Aug., and wahoo from June through Sept.

sea excursions: Many boat trips are available. The best known is the cruise to Tortuga Island (See the "offshore islands" section under "Puntarenas to Panama.")

COMPETITIVE SPORTS

basketball: One of the national avocations. Hoops may be had at many a village court, and national games are played at San José's La Sabana.

bowling: There are a number of alleys in San José. Considered to be the most prestigious bowling contest in Latin America, the Tournament of Nations is held on Columbus Day each Oct. 12.

cycling: Despite the dangers of diesel exhaust, cycling is a rewarding experience. The major annual event is the Vuelta a Costa Rica, a 12-day marathon held in Dec. The Recreational Cycling Association offers family excursions on Sundays. For mountain biking excursions contact Costa Rica Mountain Biking (tel. 22–4380) at Apdo. 3979, 1000 San José, Costa Rica.

golf: Set some km W of San José enroute to Alajuela, Cariari Country Club features the nation's sole 18-hole golf course, which has an annual international tournament. Other 9-hole courses are at Los Reyes Country Club near Alajuela, El Castillo Country Club above Heredia, Escazú's Costa Rican Country Club, and Tango Mar near Playa Tambor on the S coast of Nicoya Peninsula.

running: The best place to jog in San José is in the park. Attracting competitors worldwide, there's also a Hash House Harriers Club (tel. 28-0769) who run on Mondays and drink beers afterwards.

squash: Courts include Monte Real in Sabana Sur, and Top Squash (right behind McDonalds in the Sabana area).

tennis: In addition to those found at hotels, public hard and grass courts are maintained at Sabana Park and the nearby Costa Rica Tennis Club, the Costa Rica Country Club, and the Los Reyes Country Club. The Cariari Country Club features the annual World Friendship Tournament in Mar. and April and a tournament for the younger set, the Copa del Café, every Jan.

OTHERS

horseback riding: Costa Rica is noted for its Paso Fino and Andalusian breeds; horses are a national pastime. Instruction is available at the Porton del Tajo (tel. 39-2248) in Cariari Country Club and the Hipico La Caraña (tel. 28-6106, 28-6754), located about 20 km W of San José in Rio Oro de Santa Ana, where international competitions are held annually. Santa Ana's Club Paso Fino (tel. 49-1466) specializes in these purebreeds. It gives lessons and offers accommodation and meals. Horse lovers won't want to miss the Horse Parade, held in San José during Christmas week. Riding is available in places as diverse as Manuel Antonio, Rincón de la Vieja, Cahuita, and Puerto Viejo de Talamanca.

bullfights and rodeos. Cattle capital of Costa Rica, Guanacaste Province features rodeos and bullfights from Nov. to April in the towns of Santa Cruz, Nicoya, and Liberia. The Cariari Country Club also features rodeos, and rodeos and bullfights are held in San José during the Christmas holiday season.

PRACTICALITIES

when to come: When you should come depends upon your motives for coming. The best time is definitely off-season when rates for hotels plummet and there are few visitors to be found in the more popular spots. While it does rain quite a bit during this time, white water rafting improves, the Guanacaste region greens over, and showers (largely confined to afternoon) cool things down. The rain is heaviest in the region surrounding San José. In other regions, such as the Caribbean Coast and around Golfito, there is no clearly defined rainy season; it simply rains much of the time. If you check an issue of the *Tico Times* after arrival, you can window shop rainfall levels and decide which locations to visit. If camping and hiking are important items on your itinerary, it would definitely be preferable to arrive during the dry season. And, if you go to the more inaccessible or untouristed towns, parks, and reserves, crowds shouldn't be a problem no matter what the season.

planning expenses: Expect to spend from $10 pp, pd at a minimum for food and accommodation. Generally, you'll find yourself spending at least $20 total and, depending upon your needs, probably more. The best way to cut down on expenses is to stay in one (relatively inexpensive) location for a time.

ARRIVAL

by air: The best way to get a deal on airfares here is by shopping around. A good travel agent should call around for you to find the lowest fare; if he or she doesn't, find another agent, or try doing it yourself. If there are no representatives offices in your area, check the phone book—most airlines have toll-free numbers. In these days of airline deregulation, fares change quickly so it's best to check the prices well before departure—and then again before you buy the ticket. The more flexible you can be about when you wish to depart and return, the easier it will be to find a bargain. Whether dealing with a travel agent or directly with the airlines, make sure that you let them know clearly what it is you want. Don't forget to check both the direct fare and the separate fare to the gateway city and then on to San José; there can be a price differential. Although you should reserve several months in advance, you should also recheck fares before paying for your ticket. Allow a minimum of two hours connecting time when scheduling. The most prominent carrier serving Costa Rica from the US is now American Airlines, tel. (800) 433–7300. Flying daily from Dallas and out of its Miami hub, it is one of the most convenient airlines to take; connecting flights are available to and from virtually every major city. If you need to change your reservation while in San José, the American Airlines office (tel. 55–1607, 55–1911) is located in the Centro Cars Building, a mammoth reflective-glass structure that houses a VW dealership, at the end of Paseo Colón across from Sabana Este and next to Yaohan. TAN-SAHSA flies from Houston, New Orleans, and Miami with stopovers. Mexicana flies from LA. LACSA, the national airline of Costa Rica, flies nonstop from Miami, from NY (via Guatemala and San Pedro Sula), from New Orleans (via Cancun and San Pedro Sula), LA, and from San Juan, Puerto Rico. Pan American flies nonstop from Miami; they may have a student discount. Continental flies from Houston. You may wish to consider stopovers enroute. These are available with American, LACSA and TAN-SAHSA. Find out if it will cost extra and, if so, how much.

from Canada: While there are few charter flights from the US, many charter flights operate from Canada during the winter months for around C$600. Contact Go Travel (tel. 514-735-4526) in Montreal, Fiesta Wayfarer (tel. 416-498-5566) in Toronto, and Fiesta West (tel. 604-688-1102) in Vancouver. Charter fights are also now running into Liberia's Aeropuerto Llano Grande. **from Europe:** Iberia, KLM, Avianca/SAM all fly. If you are coming from this direction, you should be aware that many of the flights stop in the Caribbean enroute so they may be heavily booked. Ask about possible stopovers enroute. Costa Rica may also be reached by air from everywhere in the Central and South American region. Finally, if you wish to make a trip out of Costa Rica by air, you'll do well to purchase your ticket in advance: all tickets purchased in the country are subject to a 10% sales tax. **by bus:** Unless you have a damned hard ass and a hell of a lot of patience or plan on taking a month or so to complete the trip, this isn't really a viable alternative. It will cost you under US$100 for the total fare from Texas or San Diego. When you enter Costa Rica through Peñas Blancas, you may be asked if you've been taking malaria pills and, if so, you may be asked to produce them. There have been reports of travelers judged to be pro-Sandinista being refused entry. If you travel by TICA bus make sure that you get the correct passport back from the driver after he receives them from the immigration officer.

by sea: Unless you are willing to take one of the cruise ships—which occasionally dock at the port of Caldera near Puntarenas and near Limón for brief stopovers—there is no regularly scheduled alternative.

package tours: As they say, all that glitters is not gold. This cliché may be old but it remains pertinent when it comes to package tours. If you want to have everything taken care of, then package tours are the way to go. However, they do have at least two distinct disadvantages. Most decisions have already been made for you, which takes much of the thrill out of traveling; and you are more likely to be put up in a large characterless hotel (where the tour operators can get quantity discounts), rather than in a small inn (where you can get quality treatment). So think before you sign up. Also, read the fine print and see what's *really* included and what's not. Don't be taken in by useless freebies that gloss over the lack of paid meals, for example.

environmental and adventure tours: If you're pressed for time, and convenience is more important than money, you may want to sign up for one of these. It's possible to get any package you want in the US. One of the best nature expeditions is operated by International Expeditions who offer 10-day, all-inclusive tours departing from Miami. These explore the Monteverde, Puntarenas, and Tortuguero areas. A special three-day additional visit to Manuel Antonio is also available. Call 1–800–633–4734 or write 1776 Independence Court, Birmingham, AL 35216. Baja Expeditions (800–843–6967) is the US representative for Ríos Tropicales. Other companies include Biological Journeys (tel. 800–548–7555 and, in CA 707–839–0178, 1696 Ocean Drive, McKinleyville, CA 95521); Costa Rica Connection (tel. 805–543–8823, 958 Higuera St., San Luis Obispo, CA 93401); Geo Expeditions (tel. 800–351–5041, 209–532–0152, Box 3656, Sonora, CA 95370); Geostar (tel. 800–633–6633, 707–584–9552, 6050 Commerce Blvd., Ste. 110, Rohnert Pk., CA 94928); Journeys (tel. 800–345–4453, 206–365–0686, 3526 NE 155, Seattle WA 98155); Miller and Associates (tel. 509–996–3148, Box 819, Winthrop, WA 98862); Osprey Tours (tel. 508–645–9049, Box 23, West Tisbury, Martha's Vineyard, MA 02575).

senior citizen tours: Elderhostel, a sponsor of inexpensive tours, has a Costa Rican trip. Write 80 Boylston St., Ste. 400, Boston, MA 02116. For those who wish to explore the idea of retiring in Costa Rica, write Retirement Expedition Tours (tel. 209–577–4081), PO Box 6487, Modesto, CA 95355.

INTERNAL TRANSPORT

by air: Government-owned and subsidized, SANSA flies daily or several times weekly between San José and Tamarindo, Nosara, Samara, Quepos, Golfito, and Coto 47 near the border with Panama. Since fares are government-subsidized, rates are very reasonable, from about $8 to $18 one-way. During the tourist season, flights (which seat only 25–30 passengers) should be booked well in advance. If you don't have a booking, keep in mind that you can always try to fly standby. SANSA has a bad track record for reliability and it is not uncommon to find your flight cancelled without prior notice. Their office (tel. 21-9414) is just off Paseo de Colón on C. 24. Remember that SANSA considers confirmed reservations only those for which a cash payment has been received, and you must pay for your ticket the day before you leave. SANSA operates shuttle buses to and from the airport. During the tourist season Sportsfishing Costa Rica (38-2729, 38-2726, 37-5400) runs charter flights to Quepos daily for around $40. It's also possible to fly with Costa Rica Expeditions (tel. 22-0033) into Tortuguero. If you wish to charter a plane ($100 and up), call Aeronaves de Costa Rica (tel. 31-2541), VEASA (tel. 32-1010), Trans Costa Rica (tel. 32-0808), or Taxi Aereo (tel. 32-1579). These planes depart from the smaller Aeropuerto Tobías Bolaños near Pavas to the W of San José.

by train: Other than the stretch from Río Frío to Limón, which has been rebuilt and electrified, the nation's railway service is antiquated. The train system was designed to transport crops, not people, and train travel is both more expensive and time consuming than going by bus. Located at Av. 3, C. 17/19, the Atlantic Station (tel. 23-3311) has a train to Limón every morning. It takes five to eight hrs. to cover the 103-mile route. Ferrocarril Pacifica station (tel. 26-0011, Av. 20 at C. 2) runs to Puntarenas. Check with ICT or at the stations for current schedules. You'll want to bring along toilet paper for either run.

by bus: Buses run practically everywhere, though perhaps not always daily. There are comfortable and inexpensive runs on main highways to Puerto Limón, Golfito, Puntarenas, and Liberia. Travel times anywhere within the country are reasonable. It takes about eight hours from San José to Golfito for example. It's essential to know a bit of Spanish, but only a *bit* will go a long way. And remember not to flash money around and to keep a close watch on your things while in transit. Baggage can be a problem. Although some buses may have storage below, many do not—including the local buses. Overhead racks inside won't hold large backpacks or suitcases; it's preferable to carry as little as possible. If you're planning to travel on weekends or during three-day holidays, obtain tickets in advance, particularly to and from places such as Puntarenas, Manuel Antonio, the Caribbean coast, and beaches on the Nicoya Peninsula.

bus routes: There are over 700 bus routes covering virtually every hamlet, village, and town. Local buses link towns to each other, and long distance bus services link them to San José. They generally leave on the button, and the fare is collected on board. (Again, it is advisable to buy your ticket a few days in advance on major routes if you will be travelling on holidays or are on a tight schedule). The quality of the bus employed ranges from the huge white buses used on the San José-Puntarenas route to the geriatric Bluebirds found frequently in the countryside. On board, decorations near the driver may include painted murals of seascapes and pictures of Jesus. On the better roads—particularly along the smooth Inter-American Highway—travel is inexpensive and fast. But on the rougher rural roads fares and travel times escalate. You'll need to have patience! One problem with bus travel is that buses to more remote areas may leave only once or a few times per day. Your hotel, the ICT, and a bar or restaurant near the bus stop are all good sources for information on departures. Because schedules seldom change, the times in this book should be accurate. But if you're on a tight schedule or have an early departure you would do well to doublecheck.

hitching: Hitchhiking is slow but very possible and a good way to pass the time while waiting for buses in the boonies. In some places, where there are no buses, it may save you a taxi fare. In the rural areas, Costa Ricans with cars are generally conscious of the transport situation and, although there may not be many cars, a high percentage of those that do pass will stop for you.

by taxi: Generally reasonably priced, cabs are meterless—except in San José where the meters (*marías*) generally aren't used anyway—and the fare depends largely upon your ability to bargain in Spanish. But be sure to agree on one before getting into a cab. Cabs are easily identified by their red color. Especially if you have a group of people, taxis can also be a reasonable alternative to renting a car, but you should negotiate as well as ask around. **determining a fare:** Fares change like the weather. Factors include your apparent affluence, the driver's current psychological state, your own psychological state, your dress, and your pickup point or destination. If you are going to an expensive hotel, it's better just to give the nearest intersection. If you're unsure or the fare appears too high, an effective technique is to ask several drivers. If a San José driver refuses to use his meter, take his permit number and car license; the ICT office has the Ministry of Public Transport complaint forms. As the meter only goes up to 15 km, it's necessary to bargain for a further trip. Buses run until 10 or 11 in San José, but stop earlier in the smaller towns, after which you'll be dependent upon taxis. In the outback, many cabs are four-wheel drive. Finally, remember that the drivers are not tipped.

renting a car: Although renting a car may be an option you'll want to consider, you should know exactly what you're getting into. With one of the world's highest per capita accident rates, Costa Rica is not an easy place to drive in. Macho can be the rule here, and passing on narrow two-lane highways can be dangerous. Even on steep and winding grades, buses and trucks pass in both directions. In San José itself, the streets are narrow and one way; few parking lots or spaces are available. In defense of driving, however, it can truthfully be said that once you leave the San José area, the accident rate drops. Due to lower population and income levels, there are simply fewer cars. And, with over 29,000 km (18,020 mi.) of roads, there's plenty of territory to explore. You can use a valid US or International driver's license here for up to three months. A permit is necessary to drive a motorbike of up to 90cc. Cars may also be rented at the airport. You can expect to pay around $190/wk for a subcompact plus gas. Unless you have a credit card, you'll have to fork over a whopping deposit. The most useful vehicle, a four-wheel drive jeep, is the most expensive at around $50/day. Gas costs a bit more than US prices. A state-run monopoly, mandatory car insurance (a steep $8.50–$12/pd with $250 deductible) will be supplied by the rental company. Don't rent a four-wheel drive vehicle unless you really need it to get where you're going. As you should do everywhere, read the contract thoroughly—especially the fine print. Ask about unlimited mileage, free gas, late return penalties, and drop-off fees. Check the car over for dents and scratches and make sure that the agent notes any damage so you won't be charged later.

driving: Road hazards at night include pedestrians, holes, and livestock. Signs you should know the meaning of include *siga con precaution* (proceed with caution), *ceda el paso* (yield), *peligro* (danger), and *despacio* (slowly). Be sure to fill up at the main towns before heading out to the sticks where there may be no service stations. Also, while you'll find stations that are open 24 hours in San José, many in the countryside run from dawn to dusk. Bring a rag to wipe the inside windows in the rain. Unless otherwise posted, speed limits are usually 80 km (50 mph) on toll roads and highways. Speeders are subject to stiff fines, and you must also remember to use your seatbelt in the front or face a ticket. It's preferable to avoid driving in congested San José, and you may even wish to consider beginning your car rental elsewhere. **finding locations:** One way to find things is by using your odometer; another is to look out for the rather blaring ads for Delta cigarettes which have the names and pointers for major destinations on them. There are also signs denoting the entrance to various *playas* or beaches along both coasts. Your car gives you the advantage of driving in and exploring.

car trouble: Costa Rican law mandates that you must have flourescent triangles to place on the road in front and to the rear of your car in case of breakdown. Call Coopetaxi (tel. 35-9966) in this event. If you have an accident call 27-7150 or 27-8030 for a traffic cop. Wait for their approval before moving your car, and be sure to get the names and ID numbers of any witnesses. Sketch the area with the positions of the vehicles before and after the accident indicated. It is mandatory that you report the accident to the local municipality or Tribunal de Tránsito within eight days. Take a copy of this report—along with your driver's license, police report, insurance policy, and any other relevant information—to the INS (tel. 23-5800, 23-3446) at Av. 7 between C. 9/11. Finally, if a policeman stops you for speeding, don't pay the fine on the spot because this will go straight into his pocket. Insist on a citation which you will then have to go to court to pay.

rental agencies: For a full list check the yellow pages under "Alquiler de Automóviles." Some of the more prominent are ADA Rent-a-Car (tel. 33-6957), Budget (tel. 23-3284), Dollar (tel. 33-3339), Poás (tel. 21-2331), Viva (tel. 31-3341, 32-4333), Toyota (tel. 22-2250, 23-8979), Hertz (tel. 21-1818, 23-5959), Global (tel. 23-5325, 23-4056), Tropical (tel. 32-2111), Elegante (tel. 21-0136, 21-0284, 33-8605), Avis (tel. 32-9922, 42-1321). Many have branches at the airport. In Liberia to the N, Adventura Rent A Car (tel. 66-2349), El Bramadero, Liberia. Tropical also has a branch in the Hotel Karahé in Manuel Antonio.

Costa Rica distances in kms by road & (in parentheses) elevation above sea level in meters

	Alajuela (952)	Atenas (698)	Cartago (1435)	Ciudad Quesada (656)	Heredia (1190)	Liberia (144)	Limon (3)	Nicoya (123)	Paraiso (1405)	Paso Canoas (S.border) (128)	Peñas Blancas (N.border) (43)	Puerto Viejo (37)	Puntarenas (4)	Quepos (8)	San Ignacio Acosta (109)	San Isidro de El General (702)	San Jose (1161)	San Marcos Tarrazu (1429)	San Ramon (1057)	Santa Cruz (49)	Santiago Puriscal (1105)	Tilaran (564)	Turrialba (646)	Irazu Volcano (3432)
Atenas (698)	23																							
Cartago (1435)	45	64																						
Ciudad Quesada (656)	80	82	117																					
Heredia (1190)	12	35	33	87																				
Liberia (144)	201	169	238	221	209																			
Limon (3)	179	201	159	254	170	376																		
Nicoya (123)	304	262	345	314	288	77	455																	
Paraiso (1405)	50	72	7	125	41	247	140	326																
Paso Canoas (S.border) (128)	370	393	325	450	358	581	469	658	333															
Peñas Blancas (N.border) (43)	280	246	318	300	207	78	451	157	322	641														
Puerto Viejo (37)	98	120	120	173	86	295	256	374	127	446	370													
Puntarenas (4)	95	63	133	115	103	137	269	216	140	446	182	177												
Quepos (8)	140	124	163	176	145	198	299	277	170	428	243	233	61											
San Ignacio Acosta (109)	49	71	46	124	40	246	188	325	53	378	321	126	139	169										
San Isidro de El General (702)	154	176	114	229	145	351	262	430	122	215	426	232	245	79	140									
San Jose (1161)	20	42	23	95	11	217	159	296	30	349	292	47	110	140	29	134								
San Marcos Tarrazu (1429)	91	113	51	166	82	288	194	367	59	270	364	169	183	181	64	103	72							
San Ramon (1057)	44	22	82	64	52	160	218	239	89	408	238	127	53	114	88	193	59	130						
Santa Cruz (49)	257	224	296	278	265	56	431	23	303	621	134	177	193	254	302	407	272	334	216					
Santiago Puriscal (1105)	42	64	65	117	48	239	201	318	72	391	334	135	133	98	71	176	42	113	81	295				
Tilaran (564)	176	142	214	196	183	71	350	150	221	540	149	258	111	172	220	325	191	262	134	56	212			
Turrialba (646)	84	107	42	159	75	282	106	361	34	368	357	162	175	205	88	156	65	93	124	337	107	256		
Irazu Volcano (3432)	71	93	31	146	62	268	179	347	38	357	323	148	162	192	81	145	52	102	111	323	93	242	73	
Poas Volcano (2704)	40	63	77	119	46	227	226	320	90	406	303	72	134	180	89	193	56	117	84	297	82	216	120	108

TOURS

One option for visitors without a great deal of time or with an urge to savor a few different experiences is to take a tour or excursion. Most of these include hotel pickup, meals, and drop-off in their pricing. The advantage of tours is that you avoid crowded buses, you can cover a lot of territory, and your driver

will speak English (or your native tongue) and be very inform-
ative. The disadvantages include the added expense, the isolation from locals and the loss of flexibility. They do provide an
easy way to visit many of the national parks, reserves, and
wildlife refuges. Although most of the tours operate out of San
José, an increasing number are starting up in other areas of
the nation. In addition to those listed, large hotels may offer
their own tours for guests.

nature and adventure tours: It's very in to be green these
days among tour operators. So many people have jumped in to
the business of "ecotourism" so fast that many can not deliver
on their promises. One must choose carefully. Costa Rica Expeditions (tel. 22–0333) offers tours to all the major wildlife
sanctuaries in the country and operates Tortuga Lodge. With a
staff of more than 50, there's someone in the office from 5:30
AM to 9 PM in case you have a problem or wish to make a
booking. Costa Rica Sun Tours (tel. 55–3518, 55–3418) specializes in Arenal and the Tiskita Lodge, S of Golfito. Tours offered by Río Tropicales (tel. 33–6455) include a one-day raft
trip down the Río Corocobí, past birds and iguanas. Specializing in rafting and kayaking, Adventuras Naturales (tel. 33–
6455) offers packages which include trekking. Located W of
San José, Finca Ob-la-di, Ob-la-da (tel. 49–1179) offers tours on
horseback of this cattle ranch with a preserved forest full of
birds and monkeys. Specializing in groups, Horizontes (tel. 22–
2022) retails a large number of tours. Geotur (tel. 34–1867)
offers naturalist-led one-day tours of Carara Biological Reserve and Braulio Carrillo National Park. Caminos de la Selva
or Jungle Trails (tel. 55–3486) has an unusual variety of hiking and camping trips. Headquartered at Playa Tamarindo,
Papagayo Excursions (tel. 68–0859, 68–0652, 32–6854) operates cruises through mangrove swamps and to turtle nesting
sites.

other tours: Farming out their day tours through other
agents, Cielo Azul (tel. 32–7066) is one of the most prominent
companies. They feature tours of the highlands, Irazú, Poás,
Orosi, Lankester Gardens, Arenal, and Sarchi. Costs range
from $22 to $69 pp. Billed as being for visiting teachers and

students, the tours run by OTEC (tel. 22–0866) are only marginally cheaper than others. Swiss Travel (tel. 31–4055) offers a rail tour featuring a semi-private car with guide. Disembarking at Siquirres, you visit a banana plantation on the return. Other agencies to contact, which have both nature and general tours, include Cosmos Tours (tel. 33–3466), Tikal (tel. 23–2811), and TAM (tel. 23–5111). SANSA (tel. 33–5330) also has some package tours.

ACCOMMODATIONS

The nation has hundreds of hotels—everything from luxury resorts to simple hostelries. It all depends on what you want, and what you want you can find. *Típico* hotels can be found for a few dollars or less, and nearly every village has basic hotel rooms. If your Spanish is limited, it will be easier to make reservations on the E coast where nearly all the African Americans speak English. A 10% sales tax and 3% tourist tax are added. **making reservations:** Reservations should be made a month in advance during the dry season and three months in advance for Christmas and Easter. Be sure to reconfirm three days in advance. During the rest of the year, reservations are a good idea, but you generally can have your pick of rooms. Couples should state if they prefer twin or double beds. Rooms with a shared bath down the hall are the least expensive. Remember that most tourist-oriented hotels give a 20–30% discount during the low season. The major resorts and hotels have three or four sets of rates: winter, summer, shoulder, and (sometimes) Christmas. **terminology:** You will frequently encounter the "apartotel." This is an apartment hotel which has rooms with kitchen facilities. These are often suites and, in addition to daily, usually have weekly as well as monthly rates. Cabinas—literally cabins—are sometimes similar to motels and sometimes identical with apartment hotels. "Villas" and "chalets" are fancier cabinas. Found on the outskirts of San José, motels cater to the tryst trade. Finally, "pensión" and "hospedaje" are other names for inexpensive hotels. **pricing:** For the reader's convenience prices (generally inclusive of 13% tax) are listed in US dollars. They are subject to fluctuation and should be used only as a guideline. Wherever you go, there are likely to be one or more newer places not listed in this guide. Cabinas are generally more expensive for just one person, cheaper for two persons, and lower thereafter. Local hotels either charge double the single price for a couple or reduce the per person price slightly. Establishments for which no prices are listed are classified as follows: low budget ($2–10), inexpensive ($11–30), moderate ($31–50), expensive ($51–80), and luxury (over $80). It's a good idea to get the current rates from the tourist board; they can print them out if you request it at the Plaza de la Cultura office. If they don't list the rates, it's just that the hotel hasn't supplied them to the board, so use the address or phone number listed in the text to contact them directly. **reservations:** If you arrive without reservations, the ICT has offices to help you in the airport. Finally, while reservations may not be necessary for the large hotels except during the season, it would be prudent to reserve and send a deposit to the smaller establishments which do accept reservations so you can be certain of your booking. If you need to make reservations ahead, you should note that many of the coastal hotels have a San José number. It will be difficult to make reservations for the lower-priced hotels unless you can speak Spanish. However, the cheapest of these often do not take reservations in any case.

on a budget: In some of the less expensive establishments, "hot" water may mean an electrical device attached to the showerhead which warms the water. It's clever, and it does the trick. Among the difficulties you might encounter are blaring TVs, clucking chickens, mosquitoes, spiders, and cockroaches. Some of the rooms are dimly lit. In spite of this, the smaller hotels offer a genuine Tico experience, one which often brings you closer to the local people and their lives. Your neighbors will be ordinary, hardworking Costa Ricans, and not wealthy tourists on holiday. If you try it, you'll find that you can survive quite well without a/c—a fan or sometimes no fan will suffice. And, after you adjust to it, everything else just falls into place.

private nature reserves: These are one of the best opportunities you'll have to gain a deeper understanding of the ecology while simultaneously meeting residents. You can usually expect spartan accommodations, although some are fairly luxurious. Most are out of the way, but many provide transport either included in the rate or for an additional fee. They tend to be relatively expensive so they are not for low-budget travelers, although some (such as Rara Avis) do give a discount for IYHF card holders. All are described in the text.

camping: Camping is not only a practical alternative to hotels; it may well be that you have no choice. When you're visiting one of the national parks, the nearest place to stay may be many kilometers away. For camping at high elevations, a good bag and tent are required. Avoid staying in pastures which have ticks and chiggers. Although there are few organized camping areas more are being added in places such as Jacó and Moín along the Caribbean coast. If you decide to camp be sure that your things will be safe.

ENTERTAINMENT

Outside of San José, you may have to invent your own nightlife. At worst you might have to watch the stars overhead. Inside the city, there's generally plenty to do. Good sources are the *Tico Times,* Friday's issue of *La Nación,* and posters in front of the National Theater.

music and dance: The *Punta Guanacasteco,* the national dance, is performed to the accompaniment of the marimba and guitar. The national folk music is played on the *quijongo, ocarina,* and *chirimía*—wind instruments dating back to the pre-Columbian era. These are from Guanacaste Province and are not commonly seen. Modern dance performances take place at the Teatro Nacional as well as other venues from time to time. Discos abound everywhere as do jukebox-equipped bars. Many discos play endless *musica romantica,* mushy rock songs translated into Spanish. Watch as the couples cling to each other, tune after tune. With the distinct exception of San José, where they are basement-class prostitute pickup bars, a bar marked "Centro Social" connotes a community center with live music. **movies:** Most are dominated by the three themes of Kung fu, sex, and violence. Generally, the worst of American movies are shown with some finer films being shown in San José at such theaters as the Sala Garbo and at some of the cultural centers. Out in the boonies, theaters are generally very basic with entrance fees of less than $1. You can learn a lot about cultural attitudes by going to the movies and noting the audience reaction. **concerts:** There are a number of venues. Major groups seldom visit, but the National Symphony performs at Teatro Nacional as do some other local bands, including the local "new song" band Adrián Goizueta and Grupo Experimental.

gambling: Black jack and other games are found just about everywhere in and around San José. Some casinos also offer craps. Bingo is popular out in the provinces. The biggest and most widespread scam is the National Lottery.

VISAS, SERVICE, AND HEALTH

visas: American citizens may enter with a passport, driver's license, or voter's registration card and stay for 90 days, but they may not extend their visa for more than that if they do not have a passport. Canadians must have a passport only if traveling by a charter flight. All visitors should note that they will be expected to show sufficient funds and a return ticket.

for other nationalities: Citizens of the following nations do require passports but do not require visas for stays of up to 90 days: Great Britain, Germany, Spain, Argentina, Austria, Columbia, Denmark, South Korea, Japan, Netherlands, Finland, France, Italy, Israel, Norway, Roumania, and Luxembourg. Citizens of the following nations do not require visas for stays of up to 30 days: Honduras, Guatemala, Liechtenstein, Iceland, Sweden, Republic of Ireland, Switzerland, New Zealand, Brazil, Ecuador, Australia, Venezuela, Mexico, Monaco, and Belgium. All others must have visas.

extending your visa: If you wish to avoid the lines, language difficulties, and the general hassle, you can go to a travel agent and receive an exit permit, which will permit you to stay an extra 30 days. This must be done prior to your tourist card's expiration date, and you must bring along your passport, tourist card, three passport photos, and airline ticket. You should make a copy of the first few pages of your passport for use while the agent is obtaining the permit. You'll be charged a fee, but this will save you two trips to Immigration and a half day or so of standing in line. At the end of the permit's expiration, you will be required to leave the country for at least 72 hours. In order to extend it more than a month, you must do so at Immigration, although you may go through a travel agent to receive your exit permit before you leave. If you stay more than 92 days, a statement is required from the Ministerio de Haciendo showing that you owe no taxes. The travel agent may be able to get one of these as well. In any case, you'll be expected to show at least US$200 for each month you plan to extend. You may stay up to six months without departing so a 90-day extension is the maximum you will be granted. You should arrive at Immigration (located at C. 21, Av. 8 across from the Supreme Court) by 7:15 AM in the earlier part of the week. Go to the window labeled "Prorogas de Turismo" where you'll receive a form. Inquire as to the amount of revenue stamps you'll need and purchase those before going to the third (and hopefully final!) line. You'll receive a receipt for your passport which you'll have to come back for after several days.

bringing your pet: It's much simpler to leave Fido at home. If you want to persist, you should write far in advance of your visit to Jefe del Departamento de Zoonosis, Ministerio de Salud, 1000 San José, and ask for an importation form.

services and information: Tourist information centers are at the airport and in San José at the Plaza de la Cultura (tel. 22-1090). The service in the offices can range from excellent to execrable depending upon who is in charge and if they feel like abandoning their newspapers or not. Generally, they only give you what you ask for, so be sure to ask for all three maps which they may or may not have and for a look at the heavily edited and poorly photocopied sheets which give the lowdown on bus transport. You may borrow these and photocopy them in the film shop across the street. Although better maps are available, the giveaway maps (also on sale at bookshops) should be sufficient for ordinary use.

laundry: Although laundromats are scarce and incredibly expensive, your hotel can usually arrange to do laundry or hook you up with a launderer. Cheaper hotels have sinks (*pilas*) where you can do your laundry yourself. Located next to Spoon in Los Yoses to the E of downtown San José, Lava Más is one of the few self-service joints found in the country. Another (tel. 22-2407) is at Pavas near the US Embassy; take a bus from Coca Cola.

telephone service: Unlike some other nations, Costa Rica has a fairly reliable phone system, including a good supply of pay phones—although, as Costa Ricans love to telephone, there's almost always a line waiting for them. (To use a pay phone, wait for a dial tone *before* inserting your coins). Pay telephones take either the new or antiquated varieties of coins, so it's best to carry a supply of both varieties. Always in short supply, the two *colones* coins are being replaced by the five *colones* coins, leading one to suppose that the government has chosen to rectify the shortage by raising the price. Calls are limited to three minutes, after which you'll need to pay again. One species of machine has you place your coins on a rack to be digested as required; others will give you a signal, but be quick or face being cut off! No calls within the country require a prefix. Some villages (Cahuita and Puerto Viejo for example) have an exchange and operate largely by extensions. In areas where there are no regular public phones, shops, bars, and restaurants rent out their phone. It's best to ask the price before dialing to make sure that it is fair and not a *gringo* rate. Some hotels tack on a surcharge to the bill which allows you unlimited dialing within the country so, if your hotel has a phone in the room, ask about their policy when you check in. The number for local information is 113. For an English speaking operator, dial 116. When dialing the US or Canada direct from a local phone, call 001, 116, and the number. Other useful numbers are 112, time of day; 117, San José police; 118, fire department; 127, local police. For an AT&T overseas operater, dial 114. At the Radiográfica (C. 1, Av. 5) in San José, you can phone or wire abroad; either are very expensive. If you wish to make a credit card or collect call, you can reach AT&T operators, directly from USADirect phones at the airport, Radiográfica, and at the Holiday Inn, Av. 4, C. 5. The nation's area code is 011–506, a prefix which should be applied to all numbers listed in this book when dialing from abroad.

postal service: Window service at the main post office (Correos y Telegráphicos or Coretel, C. 2, Av. 1/3) runs from 7 to 6 weekdays and 7 to 2 on Sat. Other offices are located nationwide. The philatelic department is upstairs. Rates are inexpensive; your color postcard is likely to run you more than the stamp! Although, owing to the vagaries of the postal systems involved, it may take much longer, mail generally takes about five days to the US, Canada, or Europe. Sea mail (*marítimo*) generally runs about four to six weeks to North America. To ensure prompt delivery, mail from your hotel desk or a main post office and avoid enclosing anything other than a letter. You can have mail sent to you at your hotel or to *Lista De Correos* (General Delivery); the latter is at Window 17 in the main post office. Postal codes are placed *before* the city or town. In order to avoid both lugubrious bureaucracy and absolutely outrageous customs duties, avoid having anything sent to you except letters and perhaps a few snapshots. If you do receive a package, you may have to make two trips to the office way out in Zapote. Have your friends underline both "Costa Rica" and "Central America" to ensure that your letters won't languish in Puerto Rico! If you have American Express traveler's checks or card, you may have mail sent c/o Tan Travel Agency (tel. 33-0044), Apdo. 1864, San José. They're at Av. Central, C.1, 4F. **faxes:** Faxes may be sent via Radiográfica (tel. 23-1609). If your correspondent includes your hotel's phone number, they will notify you. Call 87-0513 or 87-0511 to see if you have received a fax.

broadcasting and media: There are four daily papers. The daily *La Nación* is a horrifically propogandistic tabloid said to be manipulated by right-wing US interests. Its vice-director is vice-president of the Free Costa Rica Movement (MRCL), a right-wing civic organization with an armed militia. The paper also published *Nicaragua Hoy*, a weekly *contra* newspaper produced by Pedro Joaquin Chamorro. The others, *La Prensa Libre*, and *La República* (originally founded by Figueres and his supporters in 1950), aren't much better and there have been allegations by former contra leader Edgar Chamorro and others that the CIA pays off reporters. There are four weekly newspapers including the *Esta Semana* (the best Spanish language source for news) and the equally fine *Universidad*, published by the University of Costa Rica. Journalist Martha Honey has called English language *Tico Times* "definitely the best newspaper in Central America." Their fine staff of investigative reporters includes David Dudenhoefer, Martha Bradt, Cyrus Reed, and Karen Cheney. All radio stations are privately owned, either by commercial interests or by religious broadcasters. Most stations play an amalgam of salsa and American rock and schlock. Radio Universidad, at 870 AM and 96.7 and 101.9 FM, specializes in classical music and educational programing. Radio Azul, 99 FM, plays chiefly jazz and "new age" music. Essential for anyone concerned about Central American politics and economics, *Mesoamerica* is published in San José's Barrio San Francisco. The library at the Friend's Peace Center sells copies. For a subscription in the US call 800-633-4931. Beaming to Nicaragua, Radio Impacto is run by the CIA, in violation of the law against foreign ownership of the media. Introduced in 1960, there are six TV stations. TV serves up a combination of the worst of American programing rendered into Spanish and bad local imitations of the worst of American programing. It is rather dismaying to see MTV in Spanish featuring videos of heavy metal bands from El Salvador! Cable Network News (CNN) and another cable service in English is available. A media censorship board is in operation; its effect is most apparent in movies. All journalists must be registered with the Colegio de Periodistas, a clear violation of the nation's obligations under the Human Rights Convention to which it is a signatory.

health: Costa Rican water is safe to drink, and this is perhaps the most sanitary of the Central American nations. Take basic precautions such as washing both your hands and pocketknife before peeling fruit. No immunizations are required. There are plenty of *farmacías* around should you require medicine, but most medications are imported (largely from Europe and the US) and are expensive. Costa Rica's health system is reputed to be among the world's best. Hospitals and other information are listed in the San José section. **snakebite:** In the extremely unlikely event you should be bitten by a snake, don't panic! Stay still and try to take note of its characteristics (size, color, pattern, and head shape). Nonpoisonous snake bites show two rows of teeth marks, but fang marks are lacking. Suck venom from the wound or push it out with your hands and apply a loose tourniquet. Walk back to the field station. **protection against insects:** Although scarce at higher altitudes, mosquitoes are prevalent in the lowlands. A mosquito net is a handy appurtenance, as are the mosquito coils (spirals) which keep the numbers down when you relax or sleep. *Pulperías* (general stores) will sell you one or two if that's all you need, but make sure you get a stand (*suporte*). Avoid inhaling the smoke. Dust your clothes and lower body with sulfur powder in order to stave off chiggers. Or dissolve locally-available *azufre sublimado* under your tongue; it gives your sweat an odor noxious to chiggers. Try antihistamine cream, Euthrax, or Caladryl to help soothe bites. You have to watch for ticks when you undress because they may not be evident otherwise. If you pull them straight off, you risk leaving their pincers stuck in you. Hold a lighted match or cigarette to the bite and squeeze the area to extract them. Gasoline, kerosene, or alcohol will encourage the tick to come out. Repellents are ineffective against sand gnats; use some antibiotic ointment and, as with all bites, avoid scratching or risk infection. In summary, prevention is the best cure. Take the precautions listed here, and wear adequate clothing.

MONEY AND SHOPPING

money: Monetary unit is the *colón* which is divided into 100 *céntimos*. Notes are issued in denominations of 50, 100, 500, and 1,000, while coins are minted in amounts of 1, 5, 10, 20 and 50 *colones*. Coins of 25 and 50 *céntimos* and five and ten *colones* notes are still in circulation, anachronistic holdovers from an era when a single *colón* was of tremendous value. The current exchange rate is US$1 = C 100. Given the frequent mini-devaluations, it is likely to reach 130 to the dollar in the near future. **changing money:** Most banks impose a service charge for travelers checks. Currency other than US$ can be exchanged only with difficulty. Canadian dollars and British Sterling can be exchanged at Banco Lyon, C. 2, Av. Central. German marks can be exchanged at the Banco Nacional in San José. Banks are generally open Mon. to Fri., 9–4; a few in San José are open later. It's desirable to carry at least some cash with you. Be sure to carry small bills (less than 100 *colo-*

nes) and coins when visiting villages where change may not be readily available for larger denominations. Exchange of up to US$50 in *colones* is permitted upon departure. You must produce an air ticket and identification to change your money back to foreign currency, and you lose around 2–3%; you can do so at the airport. Major credit cards are accepted by banks, established shops, and large restaurants. Black marketeers operate openly on Av. Central between Calles 2 and 4 and at many other locations. Changing on the black market brings only a slightly better rate. However, it's much faster than the banks, and traveler's checks frequently may be changed as well but at a lower rate. If you need to change on the black market and don't know where to go, just ask a resident expatriate. Often, if they're operating a business, they need cash for when they travel abroad or in order to send their profits back home.

credit cards: Although there are a large number of establishments (mostly high-priced) accepting credit cards, don't make them your chief source of cash. At the American Express office in San José (C. 1, Av. Central/1), you may write a personal check to purchase traveler's checks in dollars if you have one of their credit cards. If you are a guest at some select hotels, Visa and Mastercard can secure you cash advances in *colones* but not dollars. Located in the same building as Paprika Restaurant (Av. Central, C. 29/33), Credomatic accepts both Visa and Mastercard. To get here take the San Pedro bus and get off at Col. Sanders'. Located near the cathedral at Av. 4, C. 2, Banco Credito Agrícola de Cartago accepts only Visa. **note:** Be sure you investigate *all* of the charges before going this route.

shopping: Opening hours vary but stores are generally open 8–6 Mon. through Fri. with some stores closing from 12–2:30 in the afternoon. Most close down Sat. afternoons and are closed on Sundays. Aside from local handicrafts, there isn't much to buy that can't be found cheaper (or the same price) somewhere else. Many of the handicrafts are imported and then sold at inflated prices. As is the case with all luxury items, there's an import tax on photographic equipment and accessories so bring your own. Tee shirts make good souvenirs as do local coffee beans (about $1.65/lb).

souvenirs: Unique and inexpensive souvenirs include vanilla beans, vanilla extract, Café Rica (the national equivalent of Kahlua), and bags of coffee beans. Buy beans marked *puro,* indicating that no fillers or sugar has been added during the roasting process. *Palmito* (heart of palm) preserves and preserved *pejibaye* (a scrumptious palm fruit that tastes like a cross between a chestnut and a pumpkin) are good for your jaded and worldly friends. One souvenir that is functional during your visit is the rice bag-fashioned shopping bag; another is the traditional *campesino* sun hat made from cotton canvas. Souvenirs you won't want to bring out are things made from marguay, jaguar, or alligator skins—endangered species all.

bargaining: Although most of the stores have fixed prices, you can bargain in market stalls, and you should definitely do so with meterless taxi drivers.

American customs: Returning American citizens, under existing customs regulations, can lug back with them up to US$400 worth of duty-free goods provided the stay abroad exceeds 48 hours and that no part of the allowance has been used during the past 30 days. Items sent by post may be included in this tally, thus allowing shoppers to ship or have shipped goods like glass and china. Over that amount, purchases are dutied at a flat 10% on the next $1,000. Above $1,400, duty applied will vary. Joint declarations are permissible for members of a family traveling together. Thus, a couple traveling with two children will be allowed up to $3,200 in duty free goods. Undeclared gifts (one per day of up to $50 in value) may be sent to as many friends and relatives as you like. One fifth of liquor may be brought back as well as one carton of cigarettes. Plants in soil may not be brought to the US. If you're considering importing a large number of items, you'll want to consult "GSP and the Traveler," a booklet which outlines the goods admitted duty free to the US from Costa Rica. It's obtainable from the Department of the Treasury, US Customs Service, Washington, DC 20229.

Turrialba train station

Near Bribri

Canadian Customs: Canadian citizens may make an oral declaration four times per year to claim C$100 worth of exemptions which may include 200 cigarettes, 50 cigars, two pounds of tobacco, 40 fl. oz. of alcohol, and 24 12-oz. cans/bottles of beer. In order to claim this exemption, Canadians must have been out of the country for at least 48 hours. A Canadian who's been away for at least seven days may make a written declaration once a year and claim C$300 worth of exemptions. After a trip of 48 hours or longer, Canadians receive a special duty rate of 20% on the value of goods up to C$300 in excess of the C$100 or C$300 exemption they claim. This excess cannot be applied to liquor or cigarettes. Goods claimed under the C$300 exemption may follow, but merchandise claimed under all other exemptions must be accompanied.

British customs: Each person over the age of 17 may bring in one liter of alcohol or two of champagne, port, sherry or vermouth plus two liters of table wine; 200 cigarettes or 50 cigars or 250 grams of tobacco; 250 cc of toilet water; 50 gms (two fluid ounces) of perfume; and up to £28 of other goods.

German customs: Residents may bring back 200 cigarettes, 50 cigars, 100 cigarillos, or 250 grams of tobacco; two liters of alcoholic beverages not exceeding 44 proof or one liter of alcohol over 44 proof; and two liters of wine; and up to DM300 of other items.

LIFE, LANGUAGE, AND STUDY

living in Costa Rica: Many American retirees have opted to live in Costa Rica. *Pensionados* possess rights identical with citizenship except they cannot work or vote. Despite these defi-

Cathedral, Cartago

ciencies, they do have advantages over the locals—such as being able to bring their household goods once and import a car (valued under US$16,000) once every five years at reduced tax. They can sell the old one at that time. Life is not a bed of roses here; *pensionados* complain of the complex bureaucracy and the frequent switches in government policy towards them. Living in Costa Rica is a tremendous opportunity for retirees, not to isolate oneself in a "tropical paradise" but to open new horizons—learning a new language and becoming immersed in a foreign culture by volunteering one's skills. You may qualify if you can offer proof of a guaranteed US$600/mo. income. For information contact the Departamento de Jubilados, Instituto Costarricense de Turismo, Apto. 777, (Av. 4, C. 5) San José, tel. 23–1733, ext. 264. Located next to the Jubilados office on the ground floor of the ICT building is the Asociación de Pensionados y Rentistas de Costa Rica (address: Apdo. 6368, San José). Held monthly on the second Tues. at the Irazú Hotel, the Newcomer's Seminar, part hard sell and part question-and-answer session, provides valuable information. Another valuable resource is the book *Living in Costa Rica,* published by the US Government Women's Association, an organization composed of Embassy wives. Yet another source of information is the *Costa Rica Report,* a monthly independent newsletter. Subscribe by sending US$42 to Apdo. 6283, San José. If you do want to come, it would be better to stage a dry run of six months to a year so you can be sure that you've really made the right decision. Finally, you'll need to hire a local lawyer to implement the process; a great deal of red ink is involved.

volunteering: This may be the best way to *really* experience the country. Opportunities range from sea turtle banding to journalism. For those with an interest in regional politics, an excellent opportunity is a six-month internship for qualified Spanish-speaking college students and graduates at *Mesoamerica,* an outstanding monthly that covers regional politics. Participants gain valuable experience in professional journalism. It's possible to support yourself by teaching English (about $3/hr) but you must be available at least half-time. Send a resumé along with recommendations and the months you could be available to ICAS, Apdo. 300, 10002 San José, Costa Rica. Another good opportunity if you can speak Spanish is to volunteer in a national park. For information, contact Stanley Arguedas, tel. 33–5055. Write Asociación de Voluntarias de Parques Nacionales, Servicio de Parques Nacionales, Apdo. 10104, 1000 San José. Begin planning at least three months in advance. Rara Avis (see description in "Meseta Central" chapter) also needs qualified volunteer guides on occasion. Contact Amos Bien (tel. 53–0844) at Apdo. 8105, 1000 San José, Costa Rica. If you have six months and some skills to offer in a relevant field (agriculture, aquaculture, forestry, ecology, photography, etc.) and want to live in the Talamancan countryside, then ANAI might have a volunteer position. ANAI is involved with the concept and practice of "Earth Stewardship" in the lowland tropics, attempting to resolve the conflict between conservation and development in rural communities. Volunteers are expected to have reasonable conversational ability in Spanish, have their own insurance, and provide their own transportation. ANAI can provide housing and limited assistance with food. Write Apdo. 902, Puerto Limón 7300, Costa Rica. Or, from May to Dec., write Dr. William O. McLarney, 1176 Bryson City Road, Franklin, NC 28734, tel. (704) 524–8369. If the sea and sea turtles interest you a fantastic opportunity is to volunteer at the Caribbean Conservation Corporation's Green Turtle Research Center at Tortuguero National Park. Sponsored by the Audubon Society, 10- and 17-day packages are available and range in price from a low of $1,422 to a high of $1,971 depending upon the program (either "nesting ecology and physiology of the leatherback turtle" or "tagging of the Atlantic green turtle"), length of stay, and number of participants; it is also possible to arrange for a longer stay. The fee is so high because you are helping fund the program, and a substantial portion of the amount may be tax deductible. A limited number of positions are also available for research assistants who receive no salary but are granted room and board. For more information contact the Massachusetts Audubon Society (800–289–9504, 617–259–9500), Natural History Travel, Lincoln, MA 01773. The University of California at Berkeley (tel. 415–642–6586) also sends volunteers into the field in the company of researchers to locations that include Lomas Barbudal. Write UREP, University of California, Berkeley, CA 94720. The Monteverde Institute coordinates a limited number of international volunteer service projects which usually center around farming or building with added courses such as Spanish, biology, or workshops on regional issues. Call 61–1253 or write Tomás Guidon or Polly Morrison, MVI, Apdo. 10165, 1000 San José. Volunteers are also always needed at the reserve itself. Lodging but not food is provided. Write Monteverde Cloud Forest Reserve, Apdo. 8–3870, 1000 San José.

language: The more Spanish you speak the better! It would be dishonest to pretend that without basic "travel Spanish" you can travel by bus around the country, negotiate meals in local (*comida típico*) restaurants, and stay in lower priced accommodation. Even if you don't speak more than a few words, be sure to use them. The more you speak, the more you'll learn, and you won't learn *unless* you speak. If you regard the country as an intensive language laboratory, your Spanish will improve remarkably within a short time. But if you're going in without any language ability at all, don't despair. Sign language is an effective means of communication when the situation arises; another possibility is a writing pad for numbers and prices. **note:** While Costa Rican Spanish is more in accord with that found in Spain than others, its pronunication most resembles Guatemalan Spanish.

studying Spanish: There are a number of language schools, but study here is much more expensive than in countries such as Guatemala. If you plan to study here, you'll need at least a few months to make any significant progress. Costs run from $2–$5 ph, and $7 ph for private lessons. **language schools:** Most of these are in and around San José. Running a Spanish program geared towards those concerned with social and environmental issues, ICADS (tel. 25–0508) discusses issues such as agriculture, social justice, and refugees. Write PO Box 145450, Coral Gables, FL 33114 or Apdo. 3, 2070, Sabanilla, San José. Headquartered in Los Yoses to the E with a branch in the center of the city, the Centro Cultural Costarricense

Norteamericano (tel. 25–9433, ext. 56; Apdo. 1489, 1000 San José) charges US$130 for classes running two months, two hours per day. Geared towards missionaries, ILISA (tel. 25–2495) accepts others for its intensive courses on a space available basis. Write Apdo. 1001, 2050 San Pedro. In the US, call (818) 843–1226. Also running a study farm in Santa Ana to the W of San José, Centro Linguistica Conversa (tel. 28–6922, 21–7649) offers from 6–15 hours of instruction per week. Write Apdo, 17, Centro Colón, San José. Offering four to six hours per day, two to four week courses, INTENSA (tel. 24–6309) can be reached at Apdo. 8110, 1000 San José. ILISA (Latin American Institute of Languages) offers two to four week intensive classes. Write Apdo. 1001, 2050 San José; call 25–2495, 25–6713 or toll free in the US 1–800–344–MEGA, 818–843–1226 in CA. Forester Institute Internacional (tel. 25–3155, 25–0135) has classes ranging in length from a week to a month. Write Apdo. 6945, 1000 San José, or tel. (619) 792–5693. Instituto de Lengua Español (tel. 27–7366) has five week courses beginning in Jan., June, and Sept. Write Apdo. 100, 2350 San José. Offering two to four week programs along with a three day mini survival course ($75), Instituto Universal de Idiomas (tel. 57–0441, 23–9662) is at Apdo. 219, 2120 San Francisco de Guadalupe. Offering special packages out at Cariari Country Club, Lisatec (tel. 39–2225) is at Apdo. 228, San Antonio de Belen. Preferring students who can commit themselves for four months, Communicacion Transcontinental (tel. 21–3364) is at Apdo. 8501, 1000 San José. With both group and individual lessons, IALC (tel. 25-4313) has a one week minimum. Write Apdo. 200, 1001 San José.

study seminars: In order to give English-speaking persons first hand experience with and a better understanding of the people and issues of Central America, the Institute for Central American Studies (ICAS, tel. 27–9928) offers 12-day seminars which generally provide background on each of the Central American nations and visits to political and other institutions in Costa Rica and Nicaragua. For RT airfare from Miami, hostel or roominghouse accommodations, meals, local transport, and program, the cost is $1,150 ($1,000 for students). Airport taxes are not included. For information write Apdo. 300, San José, Costa Rica. The Monteverde Institute hosts groups of university students during its summer programs in tropical biology. Call 61-1253 or write Tomás Guidon or Polly Morrison, MVI, Apdo. 10165, 1000 San José. Offering its students the opportunity to meet policymakers from all sides of the political spectrum during its course on Central America, the Central American Institute for International Affairs (ICAI, tel. 55-0859) also offers courses in Spanish, art, and Costa Rican education and society. Write Apdo. 3316, San José. The Organization for Tropical Studies (OTS, tel. 36-6696) offers two month courses at their research stations as well as logistical support for doctoral dissertations. Write PO Box DM, Duke Station, Durham, NC 27706, tel. (919) 684-5774. Offering structured internships in Costa Rica or Nicaragua, the Institute for Central American Development Studies (ICADS, tel. 25-0508) discusses issues such as agriculture, social justice, and refugees. Write PO Box 145450 Coral Gables, FL 33114 or Apdo. 3, 2070 Sabanilla, San José. Work is also a form of study, and the Council on International Exchange (CIEE) sponsors a work-travel program. Call (212) 661-1414 or write 205 E. 42nd St., NY, NY 10017.

university study: For longer term study, the University for Peace (tel. 49-1072) offers two-year Masters in Communications for Peace, Ecology and Natural Resources, and Human Rights degrees. Write Apdo. 199, 1250 San José. One innovative program is offered through Friend's World College's Latin American Regional Center (tel. 25-0289), Apdo. 8946, 1000 San José or Plover Lande, Huntington, NY 11743. Working on their own, students are awarded credit through their journals. Although it is primarily geared towards students attending several midwestern colleges, any student may apply to enter the Associated Colleges of the Midwest (ACM) program. While the fall semester focuses on language study and the social sciences, the spring deals with field research in the physical or social sciences. Write 18 S Michigan Ave., Ste. 1010, Chicago, IL 60603. Offering one to three semester courses, the University of Kansas welcomes students of sophomore level or higher at any US college or university. Write Office of Studies

Abroad, 204 Lippincot Hall, Lawrence, KS 66045. The University of Costa Rica (tel. 24–3660) offers "special student" status for foreigners who pay double the local rates. Auditors (*oyente*) are also welcome. During the winter break (Dec. to March) a number of *cursos libres* are offered for the price of a small registration fee. Contact Oficina de Asuntos Internacionales, Ciudad Universitaria Rodrigo Facio, San José.

CONDUCT

No matter how fluent your Spanish is, never believe all the directions you are given. Sometimes, in a misguided attempt to please, local people will steer you wrong. It's better to ask a few people and get a consensus. As Costa Ricans also consider themselves to be "Americans," it would be polite to refer to yourself as a "*norteamericano*" if you are a US citizen. Currently, despite the straitened circumstances of the average Tico (low wages, high interest rates, high inflation), the nation is a relative paradise for visitors. Unlike countries such as Mexico, where open season has been declared upon *touristas*, here you will find yourself treated as a welcome guest. Help keep it that way by showing respect and courtesy in your dealings with locals and exercising a sense of fairness in your dealings. Remember that every visitor has an impact, and your behavior will make a difference. Sadly, you will meet many foreigners here—real estate salesmen, other budding entrepreneurs, *pensionados* turned into alcoholics and the like—who have no real affinity with the country and might well be happier residing somewhere else. Keep in mind that Latin cultural mores prevail here. Men and women alike tend to dress conservatively. If you want to be accepted and respected—and avoid being called a *puta*—dress respectably. Skirts are appropriate attire for women in small, conservative villages. Bathing suits are unsuitable on main streets as is revealing female attire. Unlike other Central American nations, however, skimpy bathing suits *are* acceptable on Costa Rican beaches. And despite all of the conservatism, it is definitely acceptable to kiss and cuddle in public, as any visitor to San José will note immediately. Finally, if you want to be loved and respected by the police, you should carry your passport. In this "democracy," carrying of passports and ID cards is mandatory, and the police may stop you at any time and ask to see identification without any justification whatsoever. But if you don't have it on you, unless you look like you might be a wetback from the N or S, they probably won't bother you. It's a sad fact but you'll see the worst American influence everywhere. Poor people will squander precious funds on overpriced meals at McDonalds, a sporty pair of Reebocks, or Levis—all in lieu of less expensive Costa Rican products. If you have the chance to steer them right, do it! **drugs:** All drugs—from marijuana to cocaine—are treated as narcotics, with the exception of alcohol, coffee, tobacco and their ilk. Sentences of eight years or longer are not unusual.

theft: Although Costa Rica is being marketed as a "peaceful paradise," any glance around at the painted steel bars, barbed wire, and the signs warning of attack dogs show that thievery is endemic. There's been a dramatic increase in violent crime and mugging. Although the Ticos will blame Nicaraguans or Panamanians for all of the thievery, this, of course, is nonsense. Thievery is present, but it has yet to reach the desparate level of Peru, where a camera grabbed from around the neck of a tourist represents a year's income. Nevertheless, you should not have any problems if you take adequate precautions. The very best prevention is being aware that you might be a victim. By all means especially avoid the slum areas of San José, don't flash money or possessions around and, in general, keep a low profile—avoid looking affluent. Keep track of your possessions; things like expensive sunglasses are very popular. Don't leave anything unattended on the beach, and keep off the deserted beaches at night. "Holy" Week, which the *ladrones* do not regard as sacrosant, is the most dangerous time for thievery. Avoid carrying anything in your back pockets. Women should carry purses that can be secured under your upper arm. Gangs have trademark tricks. One is to create a distraction and steal your bag. Another is to spill a bit of ice cream on your back and solicitously wipe it up while fleecing you at the same time. Refuse politely if offered candy or a soft drink on a bus; there have been cases of tourists being drugged and waking up hours later without their possessions. Never, never leave anything in an unoccupied vehicle, not even in a trunk; there are reports of thieves cleaning out vehicles in broad daylight. In front of major hotels and around the Museo Nacional are notorious areas for break-ins. Even if they see a theft or mugging happen, Costa Ricans are reluctant to get involved because of the complications that might ensue. Other things to avoid are: contact with drug dealers, getting drunk in public, or walking in a secluded area at night. Overly friendly Ticos (and foreigners as well) who hang out in tourist areas often may have an ulterior motive. Remember that locals who form sexual liaisons with foreigners often do so with pecuniary gain in mind. And, if you give one of them access to your hotel room, it can be a bit sticky if you have to go to the police later and make a charge. It's useful to photocopy your passport and keep it separately along with the numbers of your travelers checks and any credit cards. A useful precaution is to secure any unnecessary valuables in the hotel safe; a more effective precaution is to leave them at home.

women traveling alone: Costa Rican men are not quite as chauvinist as their neighbors. But, perhaps because of their Spanish pedigree, the males are much more verbally aggressive and persistent than in, say, Guatemala. Some women maintain that they appear to be "always in heat." Their favorite activity in life appears to be to *piropear* (compliment) females, hopefully making a *conquista* of a *gringa.* Expect to be called *mi amor* (my love), *guapa* (cute), and other, sometimes less endearing, epithets. Eclipsing even politics and soccer in popularity, flirting is the national sport. If you see a man staring at you intently, don't be alarmed; he's just practicing *dando cuerdo* (making eyes). Married or not, a Tico male will profess to love you with the greatest passion in mankind's history. Don't buy it! On the Caribbean coast, there are a number of "beach boys" available for rent should you be in the mood. But be warned that places like Cahuita are superb breeding grounds for AIDS because one woman is replaced by another—over and over. So proceed with caution.

men traveling alone: Costa Rican women have been mythologized for their great beauty and their good standing as *chineadoras,* women who will take care of men as if they were babies. Of course, this is nonsense. But if you don't think that a number of *gringos* buy the myth, check the classified section of the *Tico Times.* Prostitution is legal in Costa Rica. Although it will not guarantee that a hooker does not have AIDS or some other disease, your chances of safety might be better if you insist on seeing their *carnet de salud,* a health card issued by the government which must be updated regularly. Avoid being rolled in set up situations, many of which take place around Parque Morazán which might be better called Hooker Central. A favorite technique is for a tart to come up to you and give you a big bear hug while her accomplice grabs your wallet from your back pocket. If you see a young femme disrobing in the moonlight, be aware that she has two burly accomplices hidden in the bushes. Many other hookers have been known to roll their Johns while they sleep, or have an accomplice steal your wallet or anything else handy. So be careful during the *timo del amor.*

traveling with children: Costa Ricans love children, and the high health standards are a positive consideration. If you want to bring an infant with you, note that disposable diapers are very expensive and not readily available. The environmentally conscious, however, will wish to use cloth. Although many restaurants have highchairs and booster seats, car seats are unavailable, so if you plan on renting a vehicle, you'll either have to bring one along or do without. If your children are under 18 and stay more than 90 days, they'll require permission from the Patronato Office (C. 19, Av. 6) if you want them to leave with you! Both parents must be present in order to secure the permit. If you're a single parent traveling alone, you must have the permission of the other notarized by the nearest Costa Rican consul prior to your arrival.

environmental conduct: Respect the natural environment. Take nothing and remember that corals are easily broken. Exercise caution while snorkeling, scuba diving, or anchoring a boat. Dispose of plastics properly. Remember that six pack rings, plastic bags, and fishing lines can cause injury or prove fatal to sea turtles, fish, and birds. Unable to regurgitate anything they swallow, turtles may mistake plastic bags for jellyfish or choke on fishing lines. Birds may starve to death after becoming entangled in lines, nets, and plastic rings. Remember that the national parks were created to preserve the environment, and refrain from carrying off plants, rocks, animals, or other materials. Those interested in preserving the environment or in gaining a further appreciation would do well to contact the environmental organizations listed in this book.

riptides: Especially because of the dearth of lifeguards, these are a major environmental hazard, causing 80% of all drownings. If you are caught in one, yelling and waving your hands is the surest way to drown. Conserve your energy and try to swim in a parallel direction over to where the waves are breaking and ride them to shore. The best move is to avoid swimming at dangerous beaches. A good rule of thumb is: the larger the wave, the stronger the rip. Some dangerous beaches are Puntarenas's Playa Barranca and Playa Doña Ana, sections of Jacó's Beach, the beach outside Manuel Antonio National Park, Playa Espadilla Sur inside the same park, Limón's Playa Bonita, and the section of the beach near the entrance to Cahuita National Park.

OTHER PRACTICALITIES

what to take: Bring as little as possible, i.e. bring only what you need. It's easy just to wash clothes in the sink and thus save lugging around a week's laundry. Remember, simple is best. Set your priorities according to your needs. With a light pack or bag, you can breeze through from one region to another easily. Confining yourself to carry-on luggage also saves waiting at the airport. And, if a second bag of luggage gets lost, you at least have the essentials you need until it turns up. If you do pack a lot of clothes, you could leave things at your hotel and pick them up later. When packing, it's preferable to take dark, loose clothing. If you're going to wear shorts, they should be long and loose. **protectives:** Avon's Skin-So-Soft bath oil, when diluted 50% with water, serves as an excellent sand flea repellent. Sunscreen should have an 8–15 level "PABA" or greater. A flashlight is essential, and you might want to bring two, a larger one and one to fit in your handbag or daypack. Feminine hygiene items are rarely found outside of San José; bring a good supply. Likewise, all prescription medicines, creams and ointments, and other items should be brought with you. **others:** Books are double US prices so you'll probably want to stock up before arrival. It's a good idea to have toilet paper with you, as the least expensive hotels as well as park restrooms may not supply it. Film is very expensive so be sure to bring a good supply. Plastic trash bags and an assortment of different sized baggies will also come in handy. High-topped rubber boots (*botas de hule*) are an essential investment (around $8) after your arrival. If you have unusually large feet, though, it would be a good idea to bring your own. **budget travel:** If you're a budget traveler, be sure to bring along earpugs, some rope for a clothesline, towel and washcloth, toilet paper, cup, small mirror, a universal plug for the sink, and a cotton sheet. A smaller pack is preferable because a large one will not fit on the overhead rack above the bus seats. **hikers and backpackers:** If nature is your focus, you'll want to bring a rain parka, walking shoes or hiking boots, a day pack, canteen, hat, binoculars, and insect repellent as well as a bird book or two. Loose cotton trousers are recommened; jeans take a long time to dry. **anglers:** Necessities include sleeved shirts and pants, a wide-brimmed hat, and effective sun protection. For the Caribbean coast raingear is necessary, even during the dry season. Although lodges can generally arrange rentals, it's better to bring your own equipment. Bring a 20 lb. or stronger line for saltwater fishing.

measurements: The metric system is used, and gasoline and milk are both sold by the liter. While road distances are given in kilometers, road speed signs and car speedometers use miles per hour. Land elevations are expressed in meters. In addition to metric, traditional units are in use. Traditional measurements include the *libra* (0.46 kg., 1.014 lbs), *arroba* (10.59 kg, 25.35 lbs), *quintal* (46 kg., 101.40 lbs), *fanega* (4 hectoliters, 11.35 bushels), *quartillo* (3.71 kg, 7 lbs), *carga* (816.4 kg., 1,800 lbs), *manzana* (2.82 hectares, 7 acres), and the *caballeria* (42.5 hectares, 111.68 acres). The *vara* (about 100 yds.) is often used to describe distances. Although Costa Rica operates on Central Standard Time, one can accurately say that time here is measured in *ahorita*, which can be defined as the uncertain and uncharted period after which an official will return to his office or a bus will leave. Electric current is 110 volts AC. **conversions:** A meter equals three feet and three inches. A kilometer equals .62 miles (about $5/9$ of a mile); a square km is equal to about $3/8$ of a square mile.

photography: Film is expensive here so you might want to bring your own. Kodachrome KR 36, ASA 64, is the best all around slide film. For prints 100 or 200 ASA is preferred, while 1000 ASA is just the thing underwater. For underwater shots use a polarizing filter to cut down on glare; a flash should be used in deep water. Avoid photographs between 10 and 2 when there are harsh shadows. Photograph landscapes while keeping the sun to your rear. Set your camera a stop or a stop and a half down when photographing beaches in order to prevent overexposure from glare. A sunshade is a useful addition. Keep your camera and film out of the heat. Silica gel packets are useful for staving off mildew. If you're intending to shoot animals in their environment, the ideal would be to bring two camera bodies (loaded with ASA 64 and ASA 1000 film) along with 300 mm zoom and regular lenses. Animal photography is a chancy proposition owing to distances and dense vegetation. You can't hesitate or the animal may be gone! Replace your batteries before a trip or bring a spare set. Finally, remember not to subject your exposed film of ASA 400 or greater to the X-ray machines at the airport: hand carry them through. Because local developing is very expensive and of generally poor quality, it's better to take your film home for developing.

visiting the national parks: Many consider these treasures to be the nation's greatest attraction for visitors. A total 9% of the land is with the National Park System, and nearly all volcanic summits are set within biological preserves or the 14 national parks. Although the Park Service should be the best-equipped government agency, it is actually the worst off. Some 350 employees must manage more than 400,000 visitors on a budget that has been increased only minimally year after year. No permission is now required to visit the parks and biological reserves unless you are planning to conduct research. Hours are generally 8–4 daily. Foreign visitors to the parks are charged $1 per visit, twice the fee charged Ticos and residents. An annual pass is available at $10 for Ticos and residents and $20 for visitors. If you do need a permit, you should stop in at Park Service Headquarters, Av. 9, Calle 17/19, San José, tel. 23–2398. Otherwise, if you need more information, you must go to the information office at the rear of Parque Bolivar. Office hours are Mon. to Fri. 8–11:30 and 12:15–3; closed on Mon. Radio communication with the other parks, reserves and refuges is available 24 hours so you can contact them with regard to overnight space, availability of horses and/or guides. Call 33–4070. Bilingual staff here can get you the latest scoop on road conditions, etc. At the parks themselves, personnel may only speak Spanish. As staff and space is limited, it is essential for them to know when to expect visitors and to anticipate what their needs will be in terms of meals, camping spaces, bunkrooms, guides, or horses—all of which may or may not be available. They may be able to help with transportation, alloting you transport on the park vehicles. The Park Service Guide is in Spanish. For many of the parks, you'll have to bring your own food, and it may be difficult to get to others without a car. If you take a bus, you may be let off 10–15 km from a park entrance. (The most accurate current transportation information is included in each park description). Wildlife checklists and maps are sold at the CIDA office at San José's national zoo. Another alternative may be to visit the parks with a tour. (See "adventure tours" and the "getting there" sections of individual national parks for listings). **wildlife refuges:** For info on the *refugios* call the Vida Silvestre at 33–8112 or 21–9533. **seeing wildlife:** Because their survival mechanisms are geared towards differing needs and circumstances, Costa Rica's wildlife differs dramatically from that found on East Africa's open plains. While the latter depend upon strength, speed, and size, Costa Rica's depend upon camouflage for survival, which means that they are smaller and more difficult to see. Whether you're visiting the reserve on your own, with a group, or on a group tour, it is essential to maintain quiet. The quieter you are, the more you will see, and you will see what you deserve to see. Early morning and late afternoon are the best times for viewing wildlife. The best way to see wildlife, if you are really serious about it, is to camp. During the dry season, the animals come down to drink at waterholes during the early morning and late afternoon.

foundations: If you would like to help conservation in Costa Rica, there are a number of organizations which welcome donations. Write the National Parks Association or the Neotropical Foundation (tel. 33–0033) at Apdo. 236, 1002 San José. Working to expand the Monteverde Biological Preserve, helping implement Arenal National Park, and providing community education, among other projects, the Monteverde Conservation League accepts donations at Apdo. 10165, 1000 San José. You can also direct donations to them for the Children's Rainforest, or direct to the Children's Rainforest, PO Box 936, Lewiston, MA 04240. In Britain write Children's Tropical Forests, UK, The Old Rectory, Market Deeping, Peterborough PE6 8DA, England. The Costa Rica Association for the Protection of Nature (ASCONA, tel. 22–2288, 22–2296) is at Apdo. 8–3790, 1000 San José. A watchdog group whose members patrol protected areas on weekends in search of illegal logging,

APREFLORAS (tel. 87–0540) is at Apdo. 8–4330, 1000 San José. Working to protect Lomas Barbudal, the Amigos de Lomas Barbudal (tel. 415–526–4115) is at 691 Colusa Av., Berkeley, CA 94707. Arbofilia (tel. 36–7145) is involved with ecological regeneration. Donations for them can be sent via The Audubon Society of Portland, 5151 NW Cornell Rd., Portland, OR 92710. Another worthy organization to support is the Nature Conservancy, which buys land and sets it aside in debt-for-nature swaps. Send tax-deductible contributions to Costa Rica Program, The Nature Conservancy, 1785 Mass. Ave. NW, Washington, DC 20036. If you believe that elevating the quality of social and economic life is a positive step towards ensuring the continued protection of the rainforest, then you may wish to support KuKula (tel. 58–4058, 58–3085), a volunteer organization based in Limón, which attends to the needs of street kids with projects including environmental educational camping excursions, medical and dental referrals, attention to individual needs, and more. Write Apdo. 463, 7300 Limón. If your interests run towards supporting local highbrow culture, you might wish to donate funds to the financially strapped Youth Symphony and other worthy projects. Write Ars Musica (tel. 33–9890), Apdo. 1035, San José.

WHAT TO TAKE

Clothing

socks and shoes
underwear
sandals, thongs, or windsurfing thongs
T-shirts, shirts (or blouses)
skirts/pants, shorts
swimsuit
hat
light jacket/sweater

Toiletries

soap
shampoo
towel, washcloth
toothpaste/toothbrush
comb/brush
prescription medicines
chapstick/other essential toiletries
insect repellent
suntan lotion/sunscreen
shaving kit
toilet paper
nail clippers
hand lotion
small mirror

Other Items

passport/identification
driver's license
travelers checks
moneybelt
address book
notebook
Spanish-English dictionary
pens/pencils
books, maps
watch
camera/film
flashlight/batteries
snorkeling equipment
earplugs
compass
extra glasses
umbrella/poncho

rubber boots
laundry bag
laundry soap/detergent
matches/lighter
frisbee/sports equipment
cooking supplies (if necessary)

COSTA RICA NATIONAL TOURIST BUREAU (ITC) OFFICES

San José

Plaza de la Cultura
Avenidas Central/2, Calle 5
Tel. 22–1090
23–1733, x277
42–1820 (airport office)

Miami

1101 Brickell Avenue
BIV Tower, Suite 801
Miami, FL 33131
Tel. (305) 358–2150
(800) 327–7033

Los Angeles

3540 Wilshire Blvd.
LA, CA 90010
Tel. (213) 382–8080

SAN JOSÉ

Once a sleepy backwater, San José today is a mixture of boldly intruding billboards advertising Kentucky Fried and Coke, shanty houses on hillside *tugurios,* and 10-speed bicyclists in spandex, who roam the streets in the company of Mercedes and Volvos. Within a single generation San José has been transformed from a quiet town into a crowded, bustling metropolis, one which has already engulfed neighboring suburbs and threatens to swallow the neighboring cities of Cartago, Alajuela, and Heredia, in the process of creating one giant megalopolis. Forecasts are that the greater San José metropolitan area will have over two million inhabitants by the end of this decade. With some 660–700,000 people, 30% of the nation lives here. Indeed, compared to the slow-paced provincial towns, San José's traffic-clogged streets appear overpoweringly tumultuous. Noisy and polluted, San José has few parks, and its traditional character has been lost in the new nondescript North American-style architecture. Fast food emporiums—like Archi's Fried Chicken and Billy Boy Hamburgers—dot the mish-mash architectural landscape. Schizophrenia is the name of the game in big cities these days. And San José is no exception. This is a surprisingly eclectic city where you can expect the unexpected, from drive-through ice cream parlors to wild after-hours dancing to merengue at the Pizza Hut downtown. Between the signs and the bronze plaques on buildings, one might think that the city is actually named Oscar Arias. Despite the city's size however, it still retains some of the characteristics of a collection of villages—a city created by agriculture rather than industry, with pastoral surroundings still

1. Coca Cola Bus Terminal
2. Buses for Guanacaste
3. Buses for Liberia and Jacó
4. Buses for Alajuela
   via the airport
5. Parque La Merced,
   Bus for Poás
6. Metropolitan Cathedral,
   Bus for Heredia via La Uruca
7. Central Market
8. Buses for Puntarenas,
   Tilarán, Río Frío,
   and Monteverde
9. Old Penitentiary
10. Teatro Melico Salazar
11. Parque Central
12. Bus to Sixaola (via Cahuita)
13. Bus to Heredia (via Tíbas)
14. Vishnu Restaurant
15. Gran Hotel, Nutrisoda
16. National Theater
17. Cultural Plaza
    (Gold Museum, Tourism
    Information Office)
18. Amstel Hotel, hostess bar area
19. Esmaralda, Ticalinda
20. Parque Morazán
21. Aurola Holiday Inn
22. Parque España
23. INS Building (Jade Museum)
24. Don Carlos Hotel
25. Parque Bolivar (Zoo)
26. Parque Nacional
27. National Library,
    Contemporary Art Museum
28. Bus to Limón
29. Toruma Youth Hostel
30. Democracy Plaza, busses to
    Cartago and Turrialba
31. National Museum
32. Criminology Museum
33. Shakti Restaurant
34. Buses to San Isidro and Golfito
35. Train to Puntarenas
36. El Pueblo Shopping Complex

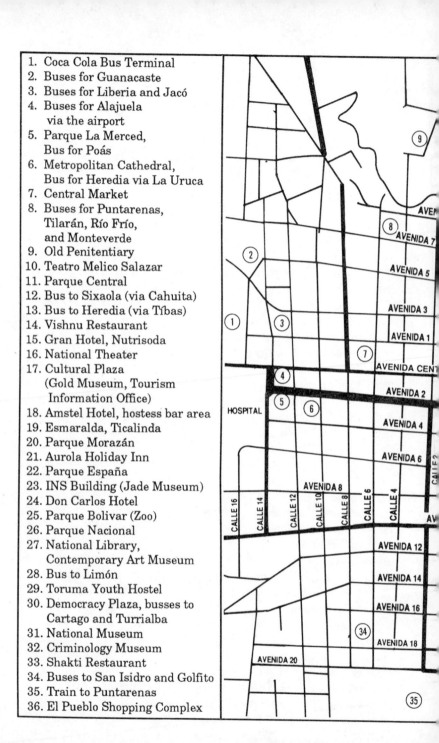

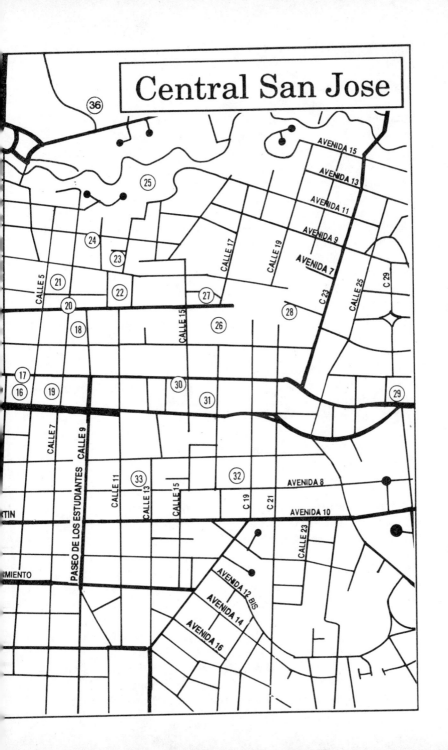

Central San Jose

visible from many areas. It still is a small town at its heart. Believe it or not, many Joséfinos, as residents of the capital are known, still shop at the neighborhood *pulpería*, hang out at *sodas* and bars, and greet each other by name. And it does have its saving graces. A cool city, the daily temperature averages around 22°–25°C (70°F). There are a variety of cinemas, theaters, clubs, restaurants, bars, museums, and the whole gamut of services.

layout: Avenida Central, the W end of which has been turned into an outdoor pedestrian mall, divides the downtown. This is a place to promenade and window shop. The wide variety of quality, expensive imported goods in its stores astonishes visitors arriving from other Central American nations. A continuation of Avenida Central, the broad, bustling, and busy Paseo Colón is another area of interest. What one might call the "Champs Elysées" of San José, this area has seen a number of its elegant houses disappear, to be replaced with the likes of fast food emporiums and car dealerships. One traditional-style home, the Casa de Leones, vanished within a three-day interval. The street terminates in La Sabana, formerly the site of the national airport which has evolved into the nation's largest urban park. Surrounding the city farther out are the *barrios* (neighborhoods) such as Bellavista, Sabana Norte, Sabana Sur; still further out, are the *Area Metropolitanas* (municipalities) which are extensions of the city.

getting around: It's easy enough to do with a little practice. Equipped with turnstyles and quite often with wooden seats, slow but reasonably frequent city buses are priced from just five *colones* and up. The fare is marked near the door, and they are identified in the front windshield both by number and destination. The driver will make change. Many either depart from or pass by the vicinity of Parque Central. Smaller (and therefore speedier) microbuses also run. Once the site of a now vanished Coca Cola bottling facility, "Coca Cola," as this rough neighborhood is still known, is the locus for buses to the suburbs and outlying towns. It's always preferable to board here rather than at the later stops, when it may be difficult or impossible to get a seat. Buses from here run to outlying towns like Ciudad Colón, Santa Ana, Escazú, Sarchí, Naranjo, Orotina and Quepos. Buses for most destinations to the W (including Guanacaste) are nearby. **routing:** There are innumerable bus routes within the city. Two of the most convenient routes are the Sabana Cemetario and the Cemetario Sabana buses which run in parallel ellipses in opposite directions and on different streets around the Sabana and into town. Because of their circuitous routing, however, it may be faster to walk. The Estadio Sabana runs from the stadium to the Parque Central and back. For Los Yoses or San Pedro, the San Pedro bus can drop you off a block from the Atlantic RR station or right near the church and park in the center of the university area. The C. Blanco bus runs to El Pueblo. If you wish to take a bus late at night (from Los Yoses to Parque Central for example), it is better to take the first bus that comes along, even if it is a suburban bus and you have to pay more. (Fare are determined by the length of the route).

on foot: One might expect from looking at the map that San José is a large city. Actually it is more like a metropolis compressed into Lilliputian format. It's easy to walk around the central part of the city. The blocks are small and you can cover a considerable amount of distance in 20 min. by foot. However, be extremely cautious when crossing streets. Drivers appear to regard their fellow humans as squishy things to be run over, and they actually appear to *speed up* when they see you coming! Watch the cars, not the stoplights because, as far as the drivers are concerned, traffic lights might as well be permanent Christmas decorations. **finding locations:** Laid out in a grid, *calles* run E to W and *avenidas* run N to S. Numbering begins in all directions from Avenida Central. Even-numbered *calles* run to the W; odd-numbered *calles* run to the E. Odd-numbered *avenidas* run to the N of Avenida Central; even-numbered ones run to the S. You can usually find street numbers on the corners of buildings rather than on street signs. However, many streets are poorly marked. Buildings themselves, however, are not numbered, and addresses are expressed in *varas*—units of slightly less than a 100 yards—or in units of 100 meters (*cien meter*). Either are the approximate

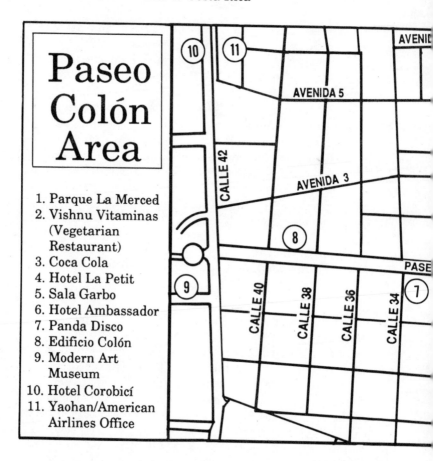

Paseo Colón Area

1. Parque La Merced
2. Vishnu Vitaminas (Vegetarian Restaurant)
3. Coca Cola
4. Hotel La Petit
5. Sala Garbo
6. Hotel Ambassador
7. Panda Disco
8. Edificio Colón
9. Modern Art Museum
10. Hotel Corobicí
11. Yaohan/American Airlines Office

equivalent of a block, though an average block is actually shorter. An address given as "Av. 7, C. 9/11" indicates that the building faces either side of Avenida 7 on the block between Calles 9 and 11. Directions are also given from known landmarks, which can make things harder to find. Businesses, restaurants, etc. are advertised in terms of meters from a famous landmark.

by taxi: An average trip costs around US $2 or less. Although the taxis theoretically have meters (called "Marías"), they are normally either broken or drivers maintain they are, so price

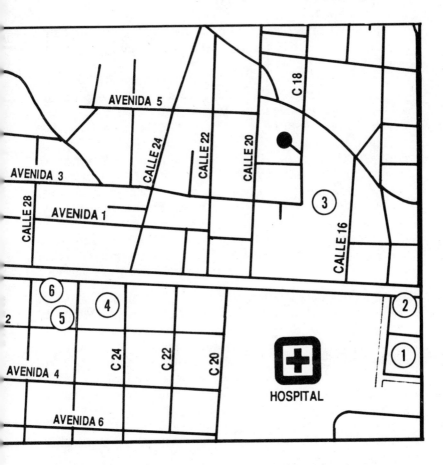

negotiations are mandatory! Be aware that taxi drivers normally attempt to charge tourists from five to ten times the correct fare. One way to approximate your fare is to estimate it in terms of nine blocks per km and count the first km as 60 US cents with 25 cents per km thereafter. You should note that there is a 20% surcharge after 10 PM. The bright red cabs are equipped with roof lights. It's difficult to find a taxi on weekend evenings so plan accordingly.

arriving by air: All flights enter the country through Juan Santamaría International Airport, 17 km W of San José. You may bring in up to US$100 in goods for friends. If you intend to stay for more than 90 days, you should have a passport which is a prerequisite in order to apply for an extension. The tourist information counter is just before customs. The bank is open Mon to Fri. 6:30 to 6, weekends and holidays from 7–1. A small shop sells powdered *café puro* as well as the current *Tico Times,* the *New York Times,* and other local papers. Other facilities include a post office and a duty-free shop. No baggage storage facilities are available. If the bank is closed, it may be possible to change US$ bills with someone at the tourist bureau. If you have limited luggage, the San José-Alajuela bus stop is just across from the entrance. It is about 25 cents to the terminal at Av. 2 and C. 12 via Paseo Colón. A cab to the city will cost you about US$8—twice as much as you might normally pay for a similar distance to and from a different location. A *colectivo,* if you can locate one, will run you about $2.

history: Expanding from the initial settlement of Cartago, a group of farmers founded Villa Nueva de la Boca del Monte in 1737. Some time afterward, locals got tired of dealing with such a long title, and the name was changed to San José, after the town's patron saint. The original settlement was expanded by the arrival of Spaniards and creole smugglers, the latter having been expelled from Cartago as punishment for dealing in contraband.

DOWNTOWN SIGHTS

While there is not a great deal of spectacular interest here, the visitor will find it rewarding to spend at least half a day walking around town. The place to begin is in the Parque Central, bounded by Calles Central and 2 and Av. 2 and 4. The perfect place to escape from the surrounding hustle and bustle, this small park is great for hanging out during the day. It's also important as a bus terminal.

Catedral Metropolitana: Colored off-white and not particularly spectacular, the cathedral is more notable for the structure attached to its rear. The administration building represents a merger between 19th C San José style and that of Europe; its stone-cased windows and pediments draw from the traditions of Renaissance Italy. At the corner of C. Central on the N side of the square, the Teatro Melico Salazar features fluted Corinthian columns, balconies, and pediments with stuccoed relief sculptures.

Teatro Nacional: One of the few buildings constructed before the beginning of this century, the Belgian-designed National Theater was financed by *cafetaleros* (coffee barons) and finished in 1897. Often billed as a miniature version of either Paris or Milan opera house, it replicates neither, and its rust-colored roof is typically Costa Rican. The impetus for its construction came after a European opera company, featuring the famed singer Angela Pelati, played in Guatemala in 1890 but turned down a San José date due to the lack of a suitable venue. Planned by Belgian architects, its metal framework was the work of Belgian craftsmen. Ornamented in baroque decorations gilded with 22.5 karat gold, its Great Hall of Spectacles seats 1,040. The refreshment area features changing exhibits by local artists. Decorated in pink marble, the main lobby features two sculptures by Pietro Capurro representing comedy and tragedy. "Heroes of Misery," the sculpture in the atrium, is the work of Costa Rican artist Juan Ramon Bonilla. The Carrara marble grand staircase leads up to the foyer which has paintings along with a mural showing the nation's major exports. The ceiling fresco, painted by Italian Arturo Fontana and illuminated by an 85-light chandelier, depicts unclad celestial deities. Another of his paintings, in the Presidential Box which is set dead center in the balcony directly over the entrance, depicts Justice and the Nation. In its foyer, a three-part fresco by Vespasiano Bignami represents Dawn, Day, and Night. Replicas of the originals, the furniture in the room to the rear is fashioned from mahogany and has been gold leafed. Originally fashioned from European pine, the floor was replaced with a selection of the 10 varieties of local hardwoods in 1940. One of the theater's unique features was the manual winch which once raised the floor to stage level—an operation performed by 12 men in just under an hour—allowing it to be used as a ballroom. Its Renaissance-style facade features statuary by Pietry Bulgarelli, which represent Music, Fame, and Dance. Statues by Adriatico Feoli of Beethoven and Calderon de la Barca, a 17th C playwright and poet, sit in niches on either side of the entrance. The building can be visited on your own, day or night ($1 admission), but if you have the chance, don't miss one of the performances, held here almost daily. Outside the theater, the plays of the street progress as vendors flog their wares and an evangelical preacher thumps his bible against his head as he prognosticates the disasters to come.

Plaza de la Cultura: Situated along Av. Central between C. 3 and C. 5 right beside the Teatro Nacional, this multilevel outdoor cultural plaza features underground exhibit halls. While you're here, be sure to head down the stairs and stop by the underground Instituto Costarricense de Turismo (ICT), the tourist information center located near the corner of Av. Central and C. 5. **museums:** Right next door to the ICT is the entrance to the two museums. First enter the Museo Numismatica. It features Indian artifacts, old coins, banknotes, and a 1000 *colón* gold piece issued in 1970—which gives you an idea of how far and how fast the currency has fallen. (Open Tues. to Sun., 10–5). Next door, a small exhibit hall features works from the Central Bank's art collection. Entered through thick vault doors set at the base of a beautiful winding marble staircase, the Museo de Oro displays one of the world's finest collections of gold-crafted art—over 1,600 pieces in all weighing 24,000 troy ounces—making it the hemisphere's second largest collection. It's almost surrealistically spooky and quiet with beautiful displays and immaculately polished parquet floors. Gold pieces featuring people, iguanas, quetzals, frogs, as well as jewelry and bells are displayed inside plexiglass cases. As you leave through the vault door at the end, you come upon what might well be a hydroponic garden used in an interstellar craft. Given the spiralling marble staircase, the roof high overhead composed of triangular concrete blocks, the mechanical whir of the a/c, and the occasional "bing" of the elevator, one might expect laser-gun toting androids to come trotting down the stairs at any moment. If you need a quick escape from San José for whatever reason, this otherworldly environment is the place! It's open weekdays from 9–5.

Museo de Jade: Misleadingly named, this small jewel of a museum is really a full fledged introduction to the cultures of Costa Rica's indigenous peoples. There are musical instruments, bows and arrows, an aerial photo of the Guayabo archaeological site, ceramic ocarinas, flints, anthropomorphically-shaped *metales* (grinding stones) and others with elaborately carved undersides, a disk with Mayan script on its underside, fantastic female ceramic figurines (from AD 700–1100), and a large, two-piece incense burner with a marvelous *lagarto* (lizard) carved on the lid. In sum total, the quality of both the imagery and the technique puts most contemporary art to shame. After some finely crafted carved jade pieces showing South American influences, there's a sitting room with a great view of the N. Give your feet, brain, and eyes a brief rest here because you'll need it for what's to come. Next is a room displaying ceramic and gold objects. Then, the displays change with room after room of anthropomorphically-shaped jade scrapers and other objects from the Pacific coast, many of which show a Mayan influence. Work from the central and Atlantic areas is also on display. The last room shows some enormous clay phalluses along with phallic ocarinas, masturbating clay men, ceramic hermaphrodite and female fertility figures, and a group of wild-eyed, frantically clutching copulating clay couples. Finally, out in the hall there's a replica of a 14th C Tang Dynasty ceramic horse, a gift from the Chinese Embassy. Located on the 11th Fl., INS (Instituto Nacional de Seguros; Institute for National Security) C. 11, Av. 7, tel. 23–58–00. Open Mon.–Fri., 9–3. And be sure to check out the views before you leave; to the S is the Edificio Metálico (Metal Building), an incongruous green pre-fab building designed by French architect Victor Balatard.

vicinity of Museo de Jade: Also known as the Parque de la Expresión, the atmosphere of the Parque España (next to the INS, between Av. 5 and 7 at C. 11) is accentuated by the transplanted tropical trees. Artists sell here on Sunday. Across C. 11 is the Spanish-style Casa Amarilla, home of the nation's foreign ministry. Stroll through the traditional neighborhoods to the N where you'll find old tin-roofed homes of brick and wood.

Parque Zoológico Simón Bolivar: Set at the N edge of the downtown area, off Av. 11, this rather run-down, dank, and dilapidated animal prison appears to have been deliberately designed to torture its inmates. The only animals that appear to be content are the monkeys who swing about joyfully in their concrete enclosure. The cats and many of the other animals appear to be crying "Ay Bendido!" Sights like this make one question whether the nation's much-touted concern for nature and preservation comes from its heart or if this is a national image cultivated in order to capture ecodollars. If you do come, be sure to stop at the park information office in the rear, although they generally have minimal info in English. Open. Tues. to Fri. 8:30–3:30, Sat., Sun., and holidays, 9–4:30. Just down Av. 11 to the W of the "zoo" are a handmade chocolate shop and the offices of Amnistía Internacional. If you walk along C. 11 you can reach a park by climbing the steps by the guardia civil post and the RR tracks, continuing along through Barrio Aranjuez, and taking a L two blocks after the tracks. Here are basketball courts and a soccer field.

Museo Nacional: Housed in the Bellavista Fortress, a former army headquarters and barracks, the National Museum of Costa Rica displays pre-Columbian artifacts, period religious garb and dress, and other items from the colonial era. Visible bullet marks from the 1948 civil war on the building's exterior make it a living monument to recent history. The entrance features a small gift shop, a courtyard containing prehistoric basalt balls, and a cannon. The Sala Doris Stone's exhibits includes a mastadon tooth, displays of Mesoamerican-style ceramics to the L and South American to the R, and anthropomorphic *metales,* as well as other beautiful artwork. The Sala Arqueología exhibits miniature brass and gold artifacts including jewelry. During the reign of not-so-modest Oscar Arias, the Sala Colonial had been transformed into a living tribute to the president and his noble Nobel. It may now display colonial era pieces. Other rooms show colonial furniture, presidential portraits and statuary, historical photos, and a collection of gigantic stick figures representing cultural groups who have added to the nation's ethnic fabric. There's also a fine collection of folk art, most of which was imported in colonial times from Mexico and Guatemala as Costa Rica has always had a minimal number of artisans. The most engaging of these is a fantastic, brightly colored Guatemalan cabinet *creche* with a crowned Virgin in its center. The devil—whose face indicates that he may vomit at any instant—lies at the bottom level. (C. 17, Av. 2/Central; tel. 22–1229, 21–0295.) Open Tues. to Sat. 8:30–5, Sun. and holidays, 9–5. Students with ID free.

vicinity of the Museo Nacional: While you're in the area, you may wish to check out the Plaza de la Democracía (Plaza of Democracy) which cost US$1.5 billion to construct, and the Moorish-style cream-colored legislature building. Set to the N is the Parque Nacional which centers around an allegorical statue featuring the five Latin American nations driving out William Walker (see "History"). Of the "parks" downtown, this is the only one which truly deserves the name. Across from the park, the imposing Biblioteca Nacional (National Library) features a mural of the sun on the outside; Galería Nacional de Arte Contemporáneo (GANAC), a branch of the modern art museum with rotating exhibits on the W side, is open Mon. to Fri. 10–5, closed 1–1:45 for lunch.

Museo de la Criminología: Set inside the Hall of Justice at Av. 6, C. 17, this combination crime museum and museum of judicial history (open 1–4 on Mon.,Wed., and Fri.) displays weapons used in violent crimes, counterfeit lottery tickets and money (including US$), pictures of magic mushrooms, drug paraphernalia, photos of severed hands, and jars containing items like an embalmed hand severed with a machete, an illegally aborted fetus, and severed feet. Be sure to eat your lunch first.

other sights: The newest museum is a science museum in the old Central Penitentiary (Penitenciaría) to the N of downtown San José on C. 4 N of Av. 9. Check with the ICT for hours. Divided by C. 7 and Av. 3 into four individual gardens, compact Parque Morazán features a pseudo Japanese-style section in the NE. The "Temple of Music," which once featured concerts, stands in the park's center. The entirety of this small park is now overshadowed by the immense Aurola Holiday Inn with its reflecting glass panes. On C. 2 and Av. 2/4, the Post Office Museum is open Mon. to Fri., 8–5. The National Liquor Factory (tel. 23–6244) can be toured after 4 PM weekdays. Delineated by Av. 2 and 4 and Calles 12 and 14, Parque Carrillo features a 4-foot in diameter pre-Columbian stone sphere from Palmar Sur. Another imposing relic, the steam engine of the Northern Railway stands on a spur in front of Ferrocarril Pacifica station on Av. 20 at C. 2. You might also wish to visit the Museum of Printing, in the Imprenta Nacional in suburban La Uruca. Open Mon. to Fri. from 9 to 3:30. A Children's Museum is also under development in Ciudad Colón on a tract donated by the UN through the University of Peace.

OUTLYING SIGHTS

Parque Metropolitano (La Sabana): Set at the opposite end of the wealthy Paseo de Colón district is La Sabana, the city's largest park, which was formerly the site of the national airport. The lake here was drained for the airport and then restored later. Sports facilities include a gym, pool, and stadium. On a typical Sunday afternoon, you'll find sports (soccer, soft-

Lake Arenal

ball, tennis, and basketball), picnickers, cyclists, and even a revivalist group.

Museo de Arte Costarricense: Housed in what was formerly the airport control tower, the Costa Rican Museum of Art stands on C. 42, at the E side of La Sabana. This Spanish-style building houses everything from pre-Columbian to modern art. Included in its collection are portraits, woodcuts, antique painted wooden sculptured busts, and antique ink drawings of the Gulf of Nicoya and a festival in Guanacaste. There's also the wooden sculpture "Los Amantes" by Juan Manuel Sanchez, paintings, woodcuts, and a giant agricultural mural by Francisco Amighetti, the feminist portraits of Max Jiménez, and a sculptured wooden chair by Juan Luis Rodriguez. The museum is divided into sections such as *abstracción y figuracíon* and *nuevas tendencias.* The latter features works like Rafael Ottón Solis's "Homenaje a Monseñor Romero" and a batik on paper by Anabel Martén. Although the area is small, the robust collection is incredibly diverse, and the quality of its varied sculptures is outstanding. Postcards and tee shirts are for sale by the entrance. Open Tues. through Sun., 8–5. Take any Sabana bus from Av. 3, C. Central/2, or from the Parque Central.

Museo de Ciencias Naturales: Opened in 1959, the Natural Sciences Museum (tel. 32–6427) is located in Collegio La Salle, a school set at the SW extremity of Sabana Park. You can either walk from the art museum or take the Estadio Sabana bus from near Parque Central. Stuffed animals is the word here with over 1,000 birds as well as monkeys, and other forest dwellers. Ring the buzzer at the R and the curator will come to the door, collect the small admission fee, and switch on all the lights for you. The first room to the R has a small archaeological collection. A pleasant place to sit and read, the courtyard has a whale skeleton. One room displays various bottles containing sea urchins, octupi, human fetuses, and bats. There are shells, shells, and more shells; rocks, rocks, and more rocks. Other rooms feature dioramas so poorly conceived and executed that they are almost comedic at times. Check out the chimp holding the plastic pineapple, and the spaced out orang-

Río Colorado, near Liberia

utan clutching his plastic pear. Then, there's the fierce looking mamma opposum with the kiddies riding shotgun on top, and the two-headed baby ox. Finally, the *conejo domestico* has such a wild expression and tensely poised posture that he appears to have hopped straight from the pages of Richard Adams' novel *Watership Down.* If you do come, you'll undoubtedly have fun picking the most obscenely stuffed animal. Open Tues. to Fri., 8–3, Sat. 8–12.

Museo de Entomología Located downstairs in the Facultade de Artes Musicales (music department) of the Universitas de Costa Rica in Sabanilla Montes de Oca, a suburb E of San José, Central America's sole public collection of insects features a wonderful display of butterflies, including the turquoise-colored *morpho amathonte.* There are also some dioramas, Hercules and elephant beetles, and the totally cute *megaloblatta rufiles,* a four-inch cockroach. To get here take the San Pedro bus near the Teatro Nacional on Av. 2 between Calles 5 and 7; get off when you see the park with the church on your L. Open Mon. to Fri., 1–5; researchers welcome anytime; tel. 25–5555. While you're in the area you might want to visit the small, somewhat funky campus and the surrounding area which has a number of restaurants including vegetarian-macrobiotic La Mazorca.

ACCOMMODATION

You can find any type of hotel in this area—from fleabags to luxury suites. You have the option of staying directly downtown or of basing yourself farther out and commuting.

luxury accommodation: The two best known luxury hotels are the Sheraton Herradura and the Cariari. Located five min. from the airport and 20 min. from downtown, the Herradura's facilities include a/c, satellite TV, restaurant, tennis, golf, and a small orchid garden. Call 39–0033 or write Apdo. 7–1880, 1000 San José. Telephone toll free: 800–325–3535, USA; 800–268–9330, E Canada; or 800–268–9393, W Canada. The framed photos on walls of the Cariari Hotel (tel. 39–0022) attest to visits by luminaries such as Colonel Harlan Sanders, Ronald Reagan, Warren Beatty, George Schultz, Jimmy Carter, and Henry Kissinger. This resort and country club complex features a/c, color TV, pool, sauna, Jacuzzi, shops, and casino. For an additional fee, you may use the golf course, pool, tennis and basketball courts, and gym. In the US, telephone 800 CARIARI or (exc. FL) 800–325–1337; after second dial tone dial 221 or write Apdo. 737, Centro Colón, San José. Overlooking Parque Bolívar, the service-oriented Hotel L'Ambiance's rates include continental breakfast. This hotel has six-rooms and one suite, set in a Spanish-style home, with a restaurant, a/c, and private TV. Call 22–6702, 23–1598 or write Apdo. 1040, 2050 San Pedro. The Corobicí (tel. 32–8122) features a/c, restaurant, pool, casino, and spa. It is located at the end of Paseo Colón right at the beginning of La Sabana. In the US, telephone 800 CARIARI or (exc. FL) 800–325–1337; after second tone dial 221. Or write Apdo. 2443, 1000 San José. Located across from Parque Morazán, the 20-room Aurola Holiday Inn (tel. 33–7233) is the city's most imposing hotel. Its features include restaurant, pool, a/c, cable TV, parking, and spa. Write Apdo. 7802, 1000 San José or call 800–Holiday in the US.

expensive accommodation: Acclaimed by all who have stayed there, 80-room Hotel Bougainvillea (tel. 33–6622) has a restaurant, a/c, pool, Jacuzzi, and parking. Its cousin, Bougainvillea Santo Domingo (tel. 36–8822), is set on a 10-acre estate about 15 min. from San José. Its facilities include restaurant, satellite TV, tennis, pool, jogging trail, and shuttle bus. A bed and breakfast set in a restored coffee plantation home, Hotel Santo Tomas (tel. 55–0448, 22–3946) is behind the Aurola Holiday Inn on Av. 7. Centrally located on the Plaza de la Cultura, the Gran Hotel Costa Rica (tel. 21–4000) has cable TV, casino, restaurant, a/c, and parking. Write Apdo. 527,

1000 San José. Located in a quiet neighborhood near La Sabana, Hotel Torremolinos (tel. 22–9129) has suites and full suites with cable TV, pool, sauna, massage, and a/c (full suites only). Located on C. 4 between Av. Central/2, Hotel Royal Dutch (tel. 22–1414) features restaurant, TV, and a/c. Write Apdo. 4258, 1000 San José. On C. Central between Av. 3/5, Hotel Europa (tel. 22–1222) has cable TV, pool and restaurant. Write Apdo. 72, San José or call 800–223–6764 in the US. The 330-room Hotel Irazú (tel. 32–4811) has a pool, casino, restaurant, spa, and cable TV. Write Apdo, 962, 1000 San José or call toll free: 800–223–0888, US; 800–268–7041 E Canada; 800–663–9582 in W Canada. Located on Av. Central between C. 7/9, the 120-room Hotel Presidente (tel. 22–3022) features restaurant, cable TV, a/c, casino, and some kitchen-equipped suites. Write Apdo. 2922, 1000 San José. Featuring a/c, cable TV, casino, and sauna, the businessman-oriented Balmoral (tel. 21–7826) is at Av. Central, C. 7/9. Write Apdo. 3344, 1000 San José. Located on the SW side of la Sabana, the Tennis Club (tel. 32–1266) features a pool, tennis, sauna, gym, and skating rink. Write Apdo. 4964, San José.

moderate accommodation: One of the most popular places to stay is the centrally located Amstel (C. 7, Av. 1/3) which has friendly staff, comfortable rooms with a/c, bath, communal cable TV, and a fine restaurant. Call 22–4622 or write Apdo. 4192, San José. The former home of President-Dictator Tomás Guardia (1870–82), Hotel Don Carlos (tel. 21–6707) is on C. 9 between Av. 7/9. It features a restaurant, cable TV, and gym. With some a/c rooms, the Gran Via (tel. 22–7737) is at Av. Central and C. 13. Write Apdo 1433, San José. Featuring a restaurant, the Plaza (tel. 22–5533) is at Av. Central, C. 2/4. The centrally located (C. Central/Av. Central) Chinese-influenced Hotel Royal Garden (tel. 57–0022, 57–0023) can be contacted at Apdo. 3493, 1000 San José. Featuring comfortable one- and two-bedroom units, Apartotel Castilla (tel. 21–2080) is on C. 24, Av. 2/4. Write Apdo. 4699, San José. In Los Yoses, Apartotel El Conquistador (tel. 25–3022) can be contacted at Apdo. 303 2050 San Pedro, and Apartotel Lamm (tel. 21–4290) can be reached at Apdo. 2729, 1000 San José. Others include Los Yoses (tel. 25-0033, Apdo, 1597, 1000 San José), the Napoleón near La Sabana (tel. 23-3252, Apdo. 86340, San José), Ramgo near the Tennis Club (tel. 32-3823, Apdo. 1441, 1000 San José), and the San José (tel. 21-6684, Av. 2, C. 17/19).

inexpensive accommodation: On the N side of the University of Costa Rica in San Pedro, D'Galah Hotel (tel. 34-1743, 53-7539) has a coffee shop, sauna, and some rooms with kitchenettes. Write Apdo. 85,2350 San José. Set in the vicinity of Parque Morazán on C. 9 between Av. 1/3, Pensión Costa Rica Inn (tel. 22-5203) has attractive rooms with bath, $16 s, $20 d; there's a 10% reduction for weekly rental. You can make reservations in the US by phoning (318) 263-2059 or by writing Apdo. 10282, 1000 San José. Located on C. 6 between Av. Central/2, Hotel Diplomat (tel. 21-8133, 21-8744) charges from $13 s and $20 d. Write Apdo. 6606, 1000 San José. The Petit Hotel has singles with private bath for $14, doubles $18. Shared bathrooms run from $9. Facilities include free coffee, communal TV, and kitchen privileges. In the Coca Cola area are Hotel Alameda (tel. 21-3045, 21-63330, Av. Central, C. 12/14, Apdo. 680, San José), and Cacts (tel. 21-2928, Av. 3, C. 28/30, Apdo. 379, 1005 San José). The Musoc (tel. 22-9437), next to the Coca Cola terminal (at C. 16, Av. 1/30) is noisy but very popular. Located on C. 6 between Av. Central and Av. 2, the centrally located Diplomat (tel. 21-8133) is popular. Others include the Fortuna (tel. 23-5344, Av. 6, C. 2/4, the Galilea (tel. 33-6925, Av. Central, C. 11/13), the Ritz (tel. 22-4103, C. Central, Av. 8-10), the Talamanca (tel. 33-5033, Av. 2, C. 8/10), and the Astoria (tel. 21-2174, Av. 7, C. 7/9).

low-budget accommodation: There's no dearth of cheap places to stay in town. A very basic but hospitable place to stay with lots of guests from the *gringo* trail, Ticalinda is at Av. 2, C. 5, #553. Look for the door right next to Esmeralda's. The Principe (tel. 22-7983, Av. 6, C. Central/2) is both cheap and very popular with travelers. Another good place is Pensión Americana, C. 2, Av. 1. A good place to base yourself if the train or bus to Limón is on your itinerary, the Bella Vista (tel.

23–0095, Av. Central, C. 19/21) is next to Dennie's Restaurant. Also try the Boruca (tel. 23–0016, C. 14, Av. 1/3), the Capital (tel. 21–8497, C. 4, Av. 3/5), Central (tel. 21–2767, Av. 3, C. 4/6), Marlyn (tel. 33–3212, C. 4, Av. 7/9), the Morazán (tel. 21–9083, Av. 3, C. 11/15), the Otoya (C. Central, Av. 5/7), the Roma (tel. 23–2179, C. 14, Av. 1), the Johnson (C. 8 and Av. Central). Hotel Cocorí (tel. 33–0081, C. 16 Av. 3 near Hospital San Juan de Dios), Pensión Centro Continental (tel. 33–1731, Av. 8/10 and C. Central), Hotel Colón (C. 4, Av. 1, #150 N), Gran CentroAmerico (tel. 21–3362, Av. 2, C. 8), and Hotel Riolto, C. 2, Av. 5.

others: A quiet and secluded oasis attractive to those who want access to the peace movement, Casa Ridgeway, in the Quaker-established Centro Por La Paz, offers accommodation: $5 pp in a small dorm room, $8 s, and $16 d. There's an excellent lending library, kitchen privileges, hot water, and the location (Av. 6B, C. 15) can't be beat. Although budget travelers can find better values pricewise elsewhere, it is highly recommended. Toruma Youth Hostel stands on the N side of Av. Central in the eastern suburb of Los Yoses. Tell a taxi driver to let you off at *"Albergue Juvenil Toruma cerca de Pollos Fritos Kentucky"* or you can take the San Pedro bus which also passes by. Here, high-ceilinged dorms hold 6–20. It's open 24 hours, and you can stay as long as you wish. However, at over $3 pp, it's the same price as staying in an inexpensive pensíon on your own, and you have a shower schedule to contend with on top of the lack of privacy. One distinct advantage of staying here is that you do get to meet a lot of people.

accommodation near San José: If you wish to avoid the hustle of the urban areas you might stay at any of the lodgings suggested under the towns listed in the "Meseta Central" section. An "American-operated" bed and breakfast, Casa María (tel. 28–2270) is located 800 yards E of the Palacio Municipal in Escazú. Modeled after a US Civil War era mansion and billed as the ultimate in luxury, the Tara (tel. 28–9651) is surrounded by 38,000 square feet of grounds. It has swimming pool, tennis court, and health club. Write Apdo. 1459, Escazú 1250. Complete with washing machine, cable TV, a/c, pool, sauna, and restaurant, Apartotel María Alexander is also in Escazú. Write Apdo. 3756, 1000 San José. Two hotels in San Antonio de Escazú are the inexpensive Pico Blanco (tel. 28–1908, Apdo. 900, Escazú) and the Posada Pegasus (tel. 28–4196, Apdo. 370, Escazú). Both are mountain getaways. Apartotel La Perla (tel. 32–6153) is in La Uruca. Located 2 km from the attractive fruit growing town of Atenas along a country road, Tranquilidad (tel. 46–5460) is a bed and breakfast featuring a pool and nearby waterfall.

FOOD

hotel dining: The Amstel (tel. 22–4622, C. 7, Av. 1/3) is well known for its reasonably priced and tasty dishes. Another good place is the Hotel Bougainvillea. The Hotel Balmoral's Restaurante Altamira serves Spanish cuisine. The Hotel Cariari features a Sunday brunch from 11:30 to 3.

budget dining: Churrería Manolo Chocolatería (Av. Central, C. 2) is good for breakfast; Bella Vista (Av. Central, C. 19/21) specializes in Limón-style fare. *Sodas* are the way to go both for price and local color. One of the best is Soda Palace (C. 2, Av. 2) where money changers are; good coffee. Fu Su Ku (C. 2, Av. 2) has Korean food. Also try Chicharronera Nacional (Av. 1, C. 3/5). For attractive outdoor cafeteria-style dining, try Recesos (Av. 2 and 4 on C. 21), just near the Museo Nacional. Soda Tico has a cheap breakfast along with a $1 lunch between OTEC and Parque Morazán. Another reasonably priced place is Soda Amón, near the Hotel Aurora in Barrio Amón. Also try El Escorial (Av. 1, C. 5/7), Finistere-Food World (Av. Central/C. 7), Soda La Casita (Av. 1, C. Central/1), Soda Central (Av. 1, C. 3/5). Located on Sabana Sur, Bar/Restaurante La Forestita serves *típico* food. Set across from the E side of La Sabana, large Soda Tapia serves reasonably priced local food on tables both inside and out on the sidewalk. For real low-budget dining try the Mercado Central, the market, an excellent place to sample low-cost traditional Tico food, especially *cevice*.

gourmet cuisine: For French food, expensive L'Ile-de France (tel. 22–4241, C. 7, Av. Central/2) has high quality food and service. Il Tula is in Escazú and Maybo is in San Pedro. La Mallorquina (tel. 23–7624) in Paseo Colón (C. 28/30) specializes in Spanish and French cuisine. With an elegantly expensive colonial-style atmosphere, La Masia de Triquell (tel. 21–5073, C. 40, Av. 2) serves Spanish food as do Casino Español (C. 7, Av. Central/1), El Escorial (Av. 1, C. 5/7) and the less expensive Casa España (6F, Banco de San José, C. Central/Av. 3./5). La Bastille (Paseo Colón/C. 30) serves gourmet-quality continental cuisine. W of the ICT building in San Pedro, La Galería, Kudamm, and Villa Franken all offer German food. Chalet Suizo (av.1, C. 5/7) features a pan-European menu. Located across from the Outdoor Club in Curridabat, Via Veneto (tel. 34–2898) serves Italian food in an elegant atmosphere. Ana (Paseo Colón, C. 24/26) features unpretentious Italian food. Also try Piccolo Roma (Av. 2, C. 24). Specializing in the Middle East, Beirut (tel. 57–1808) is one block N of Kentucky Fried on Paseo Colón.

Chinese and Asian food: These include San Pedro's Nueva China (across from Banco Popular), Tin-Jo, and Ave. Fénix—all of which serve Mandarin; neighboring Don Wang serves Taiwanese. The Royal Garden Hotel's restaurant serves Cantonese fare. Located on the E side of the ICE building, Flor del Loto serves up Hunan and Szechuan Chinese specialities. Near the outdoor club in Curridabat, moderately-priced Lai Yuin (tel. 53–5055) specializes in Chinese seafood. Located N of La Sabana, Mariscos del Oriente also features Chinese-style seafood. Definitely for those with weighty wallets, the Sakura, in the Herradura, specializes in Japanese cuisine. The medium-priced Arirang in Edificio Colón (Paseo Colón, C. 24/26) is the sole Korean restaurant.

seafood: With branches near Hotel Irazú in San José 2000 shopping center and at Plaza del Sol shopping center, the medium-priced Fuente de los Mariscos is well known. Another famous seafood restaurant is Rias Bajas in El Pueblo. Lobster's Inn (Paseo Colón/C. 24) serves up guess what? Bar Peru Tico, just around the corner from the Hotel Bellavista, has excellent seafood at moderate prices. With a blue-and-white marquee and plenty of parking, Mariquería La Princesa Marina (open 10:30–11:30 daily on the W side of the Sabana) offers reasonably priced seafood. La Cocina de Leña at El Pueblo features local specialties such as *mondongo* and *olla de carne.*

vegetarian dining: There are a large number of vegetarian restaurants, most of which feature simple but delicious fare with brown rice as a base. Specializing in raw food, La Nutrisoda (tel. 55–3959) is in the bottom of Los Arcadas. Hospitable Hungarian emigrant Joe here offers daily specials, tabouli salad, avocado and humus sandwiches, and handmade sugarless fruit ices. Open Mon. to Fri., 11–7. Just up the street at C. 3, Avenidas Central/1, Soda Vishnu serves vaguely Indian-style vegetarian food and great fruit salads with ice cream. Try their sandwiches and soyburgers. Another (and often tastier) branch is Vishnu Vitaminas (tel. 23–0294). Open Mon. to Sat. 8–8; 9–6 Sun. Open Mon. to Fri. from 8–4, Don Sol is 150 feet E of the Casa Amarilla, the Foreign Ministry, on Av. 7. This is a convenient place to eat either before or after visiting the Jade Museum in the INS building. The author's favorite for the food, atmosphere, and price is Shakti (tel. 22–9096, open 11–6:30). Besides the daily specials ($1.65) it features a wide variety of dishes including salad, *bistec vegetariano,* herbal teas, granola, and five kinds of spaghetti. For other restaurants check under "San Pedro" below.

fast food: Expensive compared to the better quality meals you can find in any *soda*. The city appears to specialize in fast food. Representations of Ronald McDonald are so omnipresent one might think that he, not Calderón, is president! You will find McDonald's at Av. Central C. 5/7, across from the Cultural Plaza, and at C. 4, Av. Central/1); Pollo Kentucky (Av. 2, C. 6 and Av. Central C. 2); Pizza Hut (Av. 1, C. 3/5, C. 4 Av. Central/2, and at Paseo Colón). Burger King is reportedly on the way and Wendy's can't be far behind. There are innumerable clones—such as Archi's and Woopy's. Don't find them; they'll find you.

cafés, baked goods and other delicacies: A popular outdoor café for people watching, Parisien Café is on the ground floor of the Gran Hotel Costa Rica (C. 3, Av. 2). The National Theater café across the way features artwork, marble tabletops, and classical chamber music. This is undoubtedly the plushest place in the country to sip coffee. Other small, good coffee shops include Las Cuartetas (C. 2/Av. 3/5), Manolo's (Av. Central, C. Central/1 and Av. Central, C. 9/11), and Spoon (Av. Central, C. 5/7). A few blocks from the Hotel Amstel, Asociación Macrobiotica has baked goods. To the N at Av. 7 and C. 3A, Govinda sells loaves of wholewheat bread for $1. Repositería Fina Coppelia along Paseo Colón offers hamburgers, fruit salad and baked goods. Set off C. 40 just down from the Iberia office, Bar/Restaurante Bembec has tables set outside and high quality pastries. Located next to Super K Mart on Sabana Sur, the delicatessen Prísa sells cheese, dried banana packets, and other delicacies. Repositería Samara is farther down the road.

Los Yoses food: Good coffee shops here include Azufrán, Spoon, Giacomín, Café Ruisenor. Dine at Restáurant La Galería (tel. 34–0850) or Paprika (tel. 25–8971, Av. Central, C. 29/33). Located in the shopping center next to Cancún, reasonably-priced Valerio's (tel.25–0838) features pizza, lasagna, and desserts.

San Pedro food: This lively student-oriented area offers a wide range of reasonable restaurants. El Pomodoro pizza is next to the church at the university. Also specializing in pizza, La Casa del Angel serves cinnamon-flavored coffee. La Mazorca (tel. 24–8069) is perhaps the nation's best known vegetarian restaurant; its cozy café atmosphere makes you feel as if you could be in Cambridge, MA or Berkeley, CA. Located in Centro Commercial de la C. Real, Ambrosia serves a mixture of vegetarian and non-vegetarian cuisine. Le Bistro serves french food. For high class dining, try expensive Greta's (tel.

53–3107) or La Petite Provence (tel. 55–1559, Av. Central, C. 27).

outlying dining: Restaurant Típico Los Americas (tel. 59–0773) is to the S in San Miguel de Desamparados alongside Iglesia San Miguel. Its menu includes *chicharronnes, mondongo,* and *tamales.*

ENTERTAINMENT

There's always something to do here. If you get a chance, check out Canto America. Led by Manuel Monestel, this band features a fusion of salsa with calypso, reggae, and even rumba. Visitors should be aware that the red light district begins at the W. of C. 8. Avoid the area around Cine Libano, Av. 7, C. 10–14, and the three to four block area S. of Av. 4 at C. 4.

classical music: The National Symphony Orchestra performs most weekends from April to Nov. at the National Theater. Featuring chamber music, the "Una Hora de Musica" is also held here once or twice a month during the same period. Near the Hotel Bougainvillea, Chavetas Tavern has a classical music variety program every Mon. night. Many of the cultural centers also have concerts.

dance: The Compañía Nacional de Danza holds two to four performances per year. College troupes of reknown are the Danza Una of the National University and the UCR's Danza Universitaría. The Instituto Technical also has a folkloric dance troupe. Other groups include Cedanza, Codanza, Danza Contemporánea, Danza Libre, and Diquis Tiquis. Composed of teenagers, San Luis Gonzaga Amateur Troupe is one of the oldest performing companies. Danacart is out in neighboring Cartago.

theater: In addition to the papers, check the listings on the board in front of the Teatro Nacional. Don't miss a performance at the National Theater if you can help it. Even though most of the plays are presented in Spanish, with the exception of those presented by the Little Theater Group at the American cultural center, no language ability is necessary to enjoy performances by the opera, symphony, and dance (Compañía Nacional de Danza) companies. The National Theater Company often takes a satirical bent in their performances. Performances are listed in *La Nación* and here are the addresses: Teatro de la Aduana (C. 25, Av. 3/5); Teatro del Angel (Av. Central, C13/15); Teatro Bellas Artes (E side of the UCR campus at San Pedro); Teatro Carpa (Av. Central, C29); Sala de la C. 15 (Av. 2, C. 15); Teatro Chaplin (Av. 9, C 1/3); Teatro Laurence Olivier (Av. 2, C. 28) Teatro La Mascara (C. 13, Av. 2/4); Teatro Melico Salazar (Av. 2, C. Central/2); Teatro Tiempo (C. 13, Av. Central/2); Teatro Vargas Calvo (C. 3/5, Av. 2).

around El Pueblo: Popular with "los plasticos," the area around this imitation Spanish-style shopping center is one of the liveliest in the nation. Cocoloco has two dance floors, one a small *salsa* disco and the other a more dimly lit room, playing more intimate music. Live bands play here midweek. More conventional La Plaza is an attractive disco and salsa/merengue club. Dark and steamy Infinito features three different discos (rock, Latin, and salsa). Other bars include Amaretta and Bar Boquitas which has an intimate atmosphere. Jerry Morgan's Piano Bar has a glittery interior. Salón Musical de Lety features cabaret entertainment. Momentos is romantic.

other discos: Located near the middle of Paseo Colón, Club Panda is a large disco with video screen and no cover; you sometimes see rich white American kids tooling daddy's Benz into the driveway. Hot and sweaty Disco Salsa 54 (C. 3 Av. 1/3) plays a lot of romantic music. El Tunel de Tiempo (Av. Central, C. 11/13) has a head-spinning, light-spiralling entrance. Set on

C. 7 off Av. 1, La Torre is a mostly gay high energy disco. One of the best around, Dynasty Discoteque, at Centro Comercial del Sur which is about 10 blocks S of the Teatro Nacional, plays reggae, calypso, rap, funk, and soul. Take the Desamparados bus from the N side of the Parque Central. SUS is in outlying Sabanilla.

bars: In a converted century-old sea captain's house, Key Largo is the city's most notorious bar and teems with craftily winking hookers (first price $100) who aspire to being high-class. There's a live band, caged toucans, and a back-room restaurant. Similar but less high-class bars like Happy Days, New York, and Nashville South are nearby. The Charleston (C. 9, Av. 2/4) is a video bar which attempts to create a Charleston-like atmosphere. American-owned yuppie bar, Risa's is at C. 1, Av. Central. Or try Los Murales (Gran Hotel) and Las Palmas (Aurola Holiday Inn). El Tablado is next to Toruma. Monday night is open-mike, and the other nights vary. Near the Cine Magaly which in turn is near the Toruma YH, El Cuartel de la Boca del Monte, with white walls and prints, is attractive and one of the classiest places around; it also features live music. Open 24 hours a day, Chelles (at Av. Central, C. 9). is a landmark—a great spot for people watching. A version with booths, Chelles Taberna is around the corner. Dennie's (Av. Central, C. 19/21) features live music and Caribbean food. Bar Peru Tico is around the corner from the Hotel Bellavista. With rooms furnished in 50s and 60s styles, the Liverpool, a small bar 600 yards N of La Granja in Barrio Mexico, specializes in rock and roll, blues, and oldies. San Pedro's Bar Rock showcases heavy metal. Out in San Pedro on C. Central across from the Banco Anglo, Club Crocodilio—complete with large video and a crocodile hanging over the bar—is popular with university students. Located in San Pedro, Baleares frequently features *Nueva Cancion* (new song) folk music. Across from Casey's Used Books, Los Arcos is a dark and intimate makeout bar. Some of the city's strip joints are in the area centering around C. 2, Av. 8. Pious television evangelical types will find Club 700, the local branch of the 700 club, on C. 1.

mariachi: This has become such a national institution that many Ticos believe that they invented it! Centrally located La Esmeralda (Av. 2, C. 5/7) is lively and open 24 hours except on Sun. Next to the Barrio México church, Bar México features mariachis. As it's in a bad neighborhood, take a bus (C. 6, Av. Central) or hop a cab.

cinema: First-run films cost around $1.50 in mostly-comfortable theaters. Theaters include the Magaly (Av. Central, C. 23), the Colón 1 and 2 (Centro Colón on Paseo Colón), California (C. 23, Av. 1), Capri 1 and 2 (Av. Central, C. 9), Cine Omni (C. 3, Av. Central/1), and Cinema Real (C. 11, Av. 6/8). Art films are shown at the Sala Garbo next to Teatro Laurence Olivier, Av. 2, C. 28, near Paseo Colón. Check the ads in *La Nación* for times.

gambling: Casino locations include the Cariari, Corobicí, Aurola Holiday Inn, Irazú, and Balmoral Hotels. Another popular spot is Club Colonial, on Av. 1 at C. 9.

events and festivals: The Copa del Café, a week-long tennis tournament, draws an international collection of talented teenagers. In the Carrera de la Paz, a footrace held in March, around a thousand people run from San José's National Gymnasium to the campus of the University for Peace in Villa Colón. Featuring 500-plus species, the National Orchid Show, a weekend-long festival takes place in the Colegio de Medicos y Cirujanos headquarters in Sabana Sur every March. Taking place on the second Sunday in March, National Oxcart Day celebrates the *boyero* (oxcart driver) and the *carreta* (the wooden-wheeled painted cart); the locus for the celebration is in San Antonio de Escazú outside of San José. The nation's cattlemen assemble at the Bonanza Fairgrounds on the airport highway for the Bonanza Cattle Show every March. Featured are prize bulls, bullfights, rodeos, horseraces, and mechanical bulls. Taking place the same month, the Crafts Fair on the Plaza de la Cultura features 150–200 local artisans exhibiting their wares. In San José's Plaza de la Democracía, an annual three-day Festival of Native American handicrafts in April is followed by the celebration of Earth Day. Many events are held in and around San José during Easter Holy Week from Wed. noon through Sun. During University Week taking place around the beginning of May, University of Costa Rica students crown a queen and participate in sports events and a parade. Many local bands also perform on campus. On May 15, the Día del Boyero ("Day of the Oxcart Driver") is held in San Antonio de Escazú near San José. Activities include parades featuring brightly colored oxcarts, the blessing of animals and crops by the local priest. On San Juan Day, May 17, around 1,500 run the Carrera de San Juan, 22.5 km from El Alto de Ochomongo (near Cartago) to San Juan de Tibás, N of San José. Celebrating International Black People's Day and taking place in San José every August, the cultural week Semana Afro-Costarricense's highlights are lectures, panel discussions, and displays. At 6 PM on Sept. 15, the nation's Independence Day (which is also that of all Central America), the Freedom Torch, relayed by a chain of student runners stretching all the way from Guatemala, arrives in San José, and Ticos join in singing the national anthem. That evening schoolchildren march in *farole* (lantern) parades carrying handmade lanterns along the route. Sponsored by the Asociación Canófila Costarricense every Nov., the International Dog Show features a splendid assortment of dogs. Held in San José the same month, during the International Theater Festival a variety of theater groups perform plays, puppet shows, and street theater.

year end fiestas: Commencing with the distribution of the *aguinaldo*, the annual bonus given to salaried workers, the city's liveliest time is during December, when the sidewalks are crowded with *chinamos* stalls which sell toys, nativity creche paraphernalia, and fruit such as apples and grapes. Merchants are open for extended hours, and the streets get wilder and wilder as the month progresses. During the last week of December and extending through the beginning of January, bullfights are held at the Zapote ring daily. The *topé*, a procession of horses, departs from Paseo Colón, proceeds along Av. Central and ends at Plaza Viquez. Finally, a dance in Parque Central welcomes the New Year.

OTHER PRACTICALITIES

health spas: If you're missing your workout, Spa Corobicí next to the hotel of the same name, has Nautilus, aerobics, and massages; it offers temporary memberships. Affiliated with the Corobicí, Los Cipreses is a "sports medicine" center in Curridabat with three basketball courts, three swimming pools, a half-sized soccer field, and a gym. Near the Indoor Club in Curridabat, Fisicultura de Oriente (tel. 53–9014) specializes in massages. Facilities here include pool, sauna, Jacuzzi, and weight room. Finally, for a low-calorie, diet-oriented vacation contact Lisa Ohlenbusch (tel. 39–2225) at La Estopa.

organizations and clubs: There are innumerable clubs in San José. The US citizens in Costa Rica for Peace (tel. 33–6168), off C. 15 on Av. 6B, meet Mon. eves. Hash House Harriers (tel. 28–0769) run on Monday at 5 PM. Promoting partnership between Costa Rica and Oregon, Partners of the Americas (tel. 59–4326) is at Apdo. 219, 2400 San José. Located 1,200 feet N and 300 feet W of the Parque Morazán's pavilion, the Krishnamurti Information Center (tel. 48–4172, 24–3360) holds bi-weekly meetings on Wed.

embassies: The US Embassy (tel. 22–5566) is out in the W suburb of Pavas. The Canadian High Commission (tel. 23–0446) is at Edif Cronos 60, Av. Central. The UK's address is Edificio Centro Colón 110, tel. 21–5566. The Federal Republic of Germany (tel. 21–5811) is at C. 36, Av. 3A. The Swiss Consulate (tel. 21–4829) is at 4th Fl., Centro Colón, Paseo Colón. For others consult the telephone directory's yellow pages under "Embajadas y Consulados."

health: English-speaking doctors and 24-hour service can be found at Clínica Americana (tel. 22–1010), Av. 14, Calles Central/1, at the Clínica Bíblica (tel. 23–5422), C. 1, Av. 14/16, and at Clínica Católica in Guadalupe. Since charges are uniform if you are not covered by the social security system and the care at these is superior, it's better to go to these private hospitals. While US insurance coverage isn't accepted, credit cards are, and you can have your company reimburse you later. In case of an emergency, go to any public hospital; the nearest one to downtown is Hospital San Juan de Díos (tel. 22–0166), Av. Central and C. 16. To call a Red Cross ambulance, phone 21–5818.

shopping: Apropox (C. 3, Av. Central/1) manufactures quality clothing. What they don't have in stock, they will make to order. Arte Libros Regalso, next to Dankha Botique (Av. 5, C. 3), sells second hand goods plus English books for 75 cents. Centrally located, Galerías Plaza de Cultura is a general department store at Av. Central C. 5/7. Others are to the W along Av. Central. A good place for high-quality leatherwork is at the chain Artesanías Melety, the most centrally located of which is at Av. 1, C. 1/3. Other depots for leather include Galería del Cuero (Av. 1, C. 5) and Del Río. C. 9. Lower quality but more affordable goods are found at Industrias Pesapop, C. 3, Av. 1/3. For silver ornaments, try La Casa del Indio, Av. 2, C. 5/7.

crafts and souvenirs: Selling finely crafted but steeply priced wooden bowls among other items, La Galería is at C. 1, Av. Central/1. Mercado Nacional de Artesanías, the National Handicraft Market (C. 11, Av. 2/4), offers souvenirs similar to those found in hotel stores as does CANAPI, an artisans' guild at C. 11, Av. 2b. Specializing in crafts such as pottery and gourds carved by Indians, ANDA is on Av. Central between C. 5/7. Next to the Melico Salazar Theater on Av. 2 between C. Central/2, Arte Rica has an unusual assortment of craft items. On C. 9 at Av. 9, the Hotel Don Carlos also has a gift shop with a good selection. Magia is at C. 5 between Av. 1/3, and La Casona is on C. Central between Av. Central/1. Located behind Iglesia La Soledad, Casa del Artesano (C. 11, Av. 4/6) is another craft center. Also check out the weekend market in front of the National Theater. Furniture makers include Barry Biesanz, tel. 28–1811, in Escazú and Jay Morrison, tel. 28–6697, Santa Ana. Moravia, a NE suburb, is well known for its leather crafts including belts, wallets, briefcases, and purses.

Sarchí is famous for its *carreta,* painted ox carts, both full-size and in miniature, and other souvenirs.

shopping centers: Set up as an imitation colonial village—complete with tile roofs, walls of stucco and whitewashed brick, wrought iron lamps, and narrow streets—is Centro Commercial (El Pueblo Shopping Center). The nighttime is the right time for boogeying here. Take the C. Blancos bus (Av. 5, C. 1/3), a cab, or walk. Less tasteful, the Centro Commercial is a few km S of Av. Central. The National Museum's shop sometimes has examples of indigenous weaving. Hammocks, paintings, and pottery are sold in front of the Gran Hotel Costa Rica on the Cultural Plaza. Another outdoor vending area is at the stalls on the E side of C. Central, just N of Av. Central. A shop along the S side of the Sabana sells baskets, ornate mats, and ceramics.

camping supplies: For camping equipment, Aro Ltd. (Av. 18, C. 13) sells camping gas refillable cartridges. Ferretería El Clavo (C. 6, Av. 8) has *gasolina blanca* (kerosene). Other stores with outdoor gear include Carlos Luís (Av. Central, C. 2/4) and Palacio del Deporte (C. 2, Av. 2/4).

markets: Mercado Central is at C. 6., Av. 1. Here, you can buy fresh spices (sold in 10 and 25 gm bags), fruits and vegetables, and there's also a stall selling honey and natural herbs. Herbs are also available in bulk at La Avena Hierba S on Paseo de los Estudiantes. A block N, at C. 8 between Av. 3 and 5, is the Borbón which specializes in vegetables. Another market is at the Coca Cola bus terminal at C. 16, between Av. 1 and 3. Held to the W of Plaza Viquez (C. 7/9, Av. 16/20) on Sat. AM a *fería del agricultor* (farmer's market) offers goods ranging from homemade wholewheat bread and pastries to fruits. Fresh organic produce is sold by Club Vida Natural, 300 feet S of San Pedro's Restaurant La Nueva China. Call 24–8713 or 73–6079 for information. For hardware items try Ferretería Glazman, Av. 5, C. 6/8.

food shopping: In addition to the above-mentioned markets, there are a number of places to buy food items. King of the supermarkets is Mas X Menos chain; there's a branch on Paseo Colón across from the Ambassador Hotel. Its chief competitor is the Automercado chain (closed Suns.). Set at the end of Paseo Colón on C. 42, Yaohan offers a wide selection. Sample highly inflated prices are Campbell's Cream of Mushroom Soup $1.65/can, tuna *sashimi* $12.30/kg, tofu $1.76/pkg., sugar 76 cents/two kg., Kodacolor Gold 100 36 film, $5.31/pkg., can of Old Milwaukee beer 94 cents. The place is huge and has commando-mentality security guards with walkie talkies patrolling. In case you have an interest in the nation that controls this supermarket as well as the Corobicí, Herradura, and Irazú hotels, SANSA airlines, and a lot of other properties, the Centro Información Japones is on the level above. Cafe Moka sells beans along with peanuts on Av. Central near C. 10.

drugstores: Located at Av. 4 between C. Central and 1, Clínica Biblica's dispensary is open 24 hrs. a day. The Farmacía Cartin is on the east side of the Central Market. The Farmacía del Este is across from Banco popular in San Pedro. The Farmacía del Oeste is across from the US Embassy.

information and services: The ICT has its information offices in the underground portion of the Cultural Plaza at C. 5 (tel. 22-1090) and at the airport. Also known as Coretel (Correos y Telégrafos), the main post office (Correo Central) is on C. 2, Av. 1/3. Window service runs from 7 to 6 weekdays and from 7 to 2 on Sat. You can have mail sent via Post Restante here. Accepting mail directed to traveler's check and card holders, American Express is at 4F, T.A.M. Travel, C. 1, Av. Central/1. For banking on Sat. AM try the bank across from the Amstel Hotel on Av. 1, C. 7. Although it may not be hard to find a pay phone in the city, it can be exasperating to try and find one which both works and for which you have the correct coinage. Try hotel lobbies or outside the ICE building at C. 1, Av. 2. In case you need to change your reservation, the American Airlines office (tel. 55-1607, 55-1911) is in the Centro Cars Building, Sabana Este, which is the enormous reflecting glass VW car sales building next to Yaohan. For laundry and dry cleaning try Centro Commercial, 7:30 AM to 8 PM; another launderer is on Paseo Colón near Restaurante Bastille (to the W of downtown); Lavantia Doña Ana (closed Sun.) is 125m (400 ft.) to the E of Plaza Gonzales near the Ministry of Public Transport to the SE; and yet another is in the Centro Commercial on the N side of the San Pedro road to the E of Los Yoses. To get here take the San Pedro bus on Av. 2 and ask the driver to let you off.

libraries and cultural centers: Best for periodicals and books in English is the US-sponsored Centro Cultural Costarricense Norteamericano (Costa Rican-American Cultural Center, tel. 25-9433) which is in eastern San José on C. Negritos. You'll have to pay a membership fee if you wish to borrow books. Set on C. 21 just off Av. Central on the E side of the Parque Nacional, the Centro Cultural de Mexico (open Mon. to Fri, 3–5), has a small library, and the Instituto Costarricense Sovietico (ICCS) shows films. Another library is at the Biblioteca National (Av. 3 at C. 15) which has a newspaper room featuring foreign journals such as *The People's Korea*. Another is the one at the University of Costa Rica in San Pedro. Alianza Franco Costarricense, Av. 7, C. 5, has French newspapers and shows films every Thurs. evening. The Instituto Goethe highlights German culture; the San Pedro bus passes right by.

maps and bookstores: Librería Lehmann, Av. Central, C. 1/3 and Librería Universal, Av. Central, C. Central/1, have good map sections as well as a fine selection of books. Located in the Arcadas Mall at Av. 1, Calles Central/2, Librería Quijote has a smaller selection of English books including some used ones. The Bookshop (Av. 1, C. 1/3) has an excellent supply of maps as well as travel guides. To find inexpensive used books in an unforgettable atmosphere, go to Casey's Book Exchange, C. Central, Av. 7/9. Staufer Books is down the street from the Cultural Center. The National Geographic Institute of the Ministry of Public Works, Av. 20, C. 9/11, sells maps and a variety of geographic publications. Open Mon.-Fri. from 8:30–3:30, the Barrio La Cruz bus from Parque Central comes here. The Ministry of Transport (Av. 18, C. 9) has street maps of towns and topographic maps. French and Italian magazines are available at Librería Francesa/Libería Italiana, C. 3, Av. 1 Central.

FROM SAN JOSÉ

A number of day excursions can be made. If your time is limited, you may wish to make a short train trip and return by bus. Good day trips include Volcano Poás, Orosi Valley, Aserrí, San Antonio de Escazú, Alajuela, Volcano Irazú, Ojo de Agua, Cartago, Heredia, or Santiago Puriscal.

by rail: Leaving from the Ferrocarril Pacifica station (tel. 26–0011) on Av. 20 at C. 2., the train to Puntarenas (3.5 hrs.) passes through Orotina, a market town that is the focal point for many of those boarding the train. Sit on the L in order to see Barranca gorge. Take the Pasa Ancho bus from Parque Central. Check with ICT or at the stations for current schedules.

by bus: Especially during weekends and holidays, it's preferable to buy your ticket the day before and arrive an hour before departure. The following buses run from or stop near "Coca Cola" Liberia, Av. 2, C. 14; Nicoya, C. 14, Av. 5; Puntarenas and Puerto Viejo de Sarapiquí (in the La Selva area), C. 12, Av. 7/9; Santa Cruz, C. 16, Av. 1/3; Zarcero, C. 16, Av. 3. The bus for Alajuela leaves from Av. 2, C. 14; Cañas from C. 16, Av. 1/3; Cartago and Turrialba from C. 13, Av. Central/2; Golfito from near the Pacific RR at Av. 18, C. 4; Guápiles at C. 12, Av. 7/9; Limón from near the Atlantic RR at Av. 3, C. 19/21; San Isidro at C. 15, Av. 7/9; Tílaran at C. 12, Av. 9/11; and Zona Sur, from Av. 11, C. 4. For other destinations see the "getting there:" section under the specific entry. **note:** A four billion *colón* project to construct three large bus terminals in the metropolitan area is underway, so you should check upon arrival to see if it has been completed. If so, although the departure times are unlikely to change, you will have to check with the ICT for the new departure points of selected lines.

VICINITY OF SAN JOSÉ

Parque del Este: Situed in the hills above San Pedro in San Rafael de Montes de Oca, this park has a jogging and exercise trail, pool, soccer field, basketball courts, playgrounds, picnic tables, a nature trail, and great views. It's open daily except Mon. until 4. Take the San Ramón de Tres Ríos bus from Av. 2, C. 5/7.

Moravia: A handicraft center 7 km NE of San José, the shops in this slow-paced small town feature everything from furniture to leather work. Its most famous shop is Caballo Blanco, set on one corner of the plaza. Others include La Rueda and El Potro. Eat at Soda San Martín. Take the bus from Av. 3, C. 3/5 or the microbus from Av. 7, C. 6 and disembark at the main stop, two blocks before the main square.

Coronado: This country town features a Gothic-style church and good views of San José. Club Mediterráneo (tel. 29–0661) is the local gourmet restaurant. Situated one km before the town on the R hand side, the Instituto Clodomiro Picando researches snakes and processes venom into antivenin serum. Held every Fri. afternoon from 1:30 to 3:30, the "milking" demonstration is something no serpent lover will choose to miss. It begins with the milking: snake after snake is pinned down with a hook, then picked up firmly but carefully. After prying open its jaws, the snake's fangs are pressed against the netting at the slender neck of the large metal venom collection cannister. After the sickly colored milk is expelled, the process is repeated again and again. A small *terciopelo* snake is also fed to a *zopilota,* which is immune to its venom, and which slowly crushes, and then eats it. One of the smallest but certainly the most frightening snake is the *culebra del mar,* found on the Pacific coast from California to Chile, for which there is no serum available. Fortunately, only 10 people have been bitten by it during the past 10 years. The *biblo la diablo* and the *lora* are small, green poisonous snakes. Found in Guanacaste, the *cascabel* rattler is less aggressive than the *terciopelo.* Then, there's the coral snake with its distinctive red, yellow, and black coloring; the false coral which alternates red, black, and yellow; a boa constrictor which hisses and snaps; and the aggressive bushmaster or *matabuey.* The afternoon's high point comes with the display of two Asiatic cobras. Mice are crushed to death with giant tweezers and fed to the snakes to munch on. Then, in case you came late, there's another display of milking. Open 8–12, 1–4, Mon. to Fri. To get here take a bus from Moravia or from Av. 5, C. 3/5. On the way back, if you choose to walk, it's a pleasant stroll down to Moravia, less than an hour away.

Aserí: Situated 10 km past the working class suburbs of Desamparados and San Rafael, Aserí—its clean country atmosphere and whitewashed church with its broken clock—provides a welcome break from the polluted urban environment. Check out the large religious statuary by the altar. Take a bus here from C. 2, Av. 6/8.

Ciudad Colón: This area has the Finca Ob-La-Di Ob-La-Da (tel. 49–1179) which offers nature tours on horseback with a trip to a waterfall. The campus of the University for Peace is also here.

Reserva Guayabo: To get to this indigenous reserve, take the Santiago Purcisal bus from Coca Cola, C. 16, Av. 1/3. Leaving approximately every 45 min. and taking about an hour, the trip proceeds through rolling countryside, climbing up with hairpin turns and spectacular drops. Located at km 30, this chilly reserve is home of the Quitirrsí Indians who are noted for their basketweaving ability. Purcial, at the end of the line, is mainly of note for its seismic activity: it was the epicenter for thousands of tremors during 1990.

San Antonio de Escazú: Brightly painted oxcarts ply the streets of this Mediterranean-flavored mountain town which features a church, colorful adobe houses with outdoor ovens, and views of Volcano Barva, and San José. Eat at Hotel Mirador Pico Blanco or Tiquicia, both of which command legendary views. Take a bus from C. 16, Av. Central/1. If you only want to go as far as the preceding town of Escazú, noted for its expatriate community, board a bus at Av. 1, Calles 16/18.

Lomas de Ayarco: This affluent neighborhood on the way to Cartago has some of the nation's most opulent dwellings. Robert Vesco's former mansion has room for 25 cars in its enclosed driveway. The incredible extravagance of these houses contrasts dramatically with the rural poverty so evident elsewhere. It's as though the rich were spitting in the face of the nation's poor who struggle so diligently to eke out a living.

Grecia: This pineapple cultivation and sugar processing center has a church roofed in dark red painted metal. Stay at Cabaña Los Cipreses, Cabinas Los Trapiches, or low-budget Pensión Quirós.

Sarchí: In the nation's most famous crafts center, family-run workshops make painted oxcarts using traditional designs, which have been passed on for generations. The compulsion to paint rules the denizens here to the point that even the bus stops and garbage cans are decorated! In addition to the real McCoy, souvenirs—including napkin holders, salad bowls, and jewelry—are also made for the tourist market. Visit the Joaquín Chaverri factory and sales outlet. Before leaving town, be sure to note the bi-towered, multi-windowed church. To get here take the hourly Grecia bus from Coca Cola and connect there with the Alajuela–Sarchí bus. This is preferable to going to Alajuela and then changing.

Ojo de Agua: Meaning literally "Eye of Water," 6,000 gallons of water per minute gush out here, filling three big swimming pools. Bordering are tennis courts and a lake with rowboats. You'll have plenty of chances to meet locals here on weekends. A few km S of Alajuela and to the SE of the airport, Ojo de Agua can be reached by bus from Alajuela, Heredia, or from Av. 1, C. 18/20 in San José, about every half-hour on weekdays and every 15 min. on weekends.

La Garita: Just 20 min. from San José, here is the nation's closest equivalent to Disneyland. Open Tues. to Sun. and 1.5 km to the L of the Fiesta de Maíz, Bosque Encantado (tel. 48–7050) is a lake surrounded by a castle and storybook characters. About 3.5 km to the R after the Atenas turnoff is the Zoo-Ave, an exotic bird collection; 50 cents admission. A restaurant featuring the entire range of native corn dishes, La Fiesta de Maíz is open Thurs. to Sun. and is about 2.5 km on the L after the Atenas turnoff. Free samples are offered. Take the hourly Atenas bus or the La Garita bus, both from Coca Cola, to get here. If you're driving, get off at the Grecia exit.

THE MESETA
CENTRAL

This, the nation's principal area, represents to Costa Ricans an accentuated version of what the Tokai region is to Japan or the Boston-Washington corridor is to the US. Although it is also densely populated and contains the nation's capital, every other dimension—size, industrialization, and degree of pollution—is on a smaller scale. This 32 by 80 km (20 by 50 mi.) "plateau"—which in reality is more a series of valleys intersected by rolling hills—still retains a primarily agricultural base. Much of the land has been shaped by the innumerable volcanic eruptions which, over the eons, have also given the soil its fertility. In addition to the locus of San José, it also includes the towns of Heredia, Alajuela, Cartago, and Turrialba as well as many smaller villages. Although it is sometimes referred to as the "Switzerland of Central America," the area is Swiss only in its orderliness and not in its wealth or climate. Verdant and shimmering fields of sugarcane grow in the E. Elsewhere the ever-present coffee colors the landscape in shades that vary from shiny green to green and red according to the season. Acres of plastic-covered houseplants and flowers are another feature on the landscape; these are for export. Factories are interspersed with pastures and coffee plant-covered hills. You'll see the occasional sugar processing plant, macadamia plantations, a man hacking sugar cane, and teams of men and women picking coffee. However, not all is pastoral paradise. During the rainy season dark grey clouds loom men-

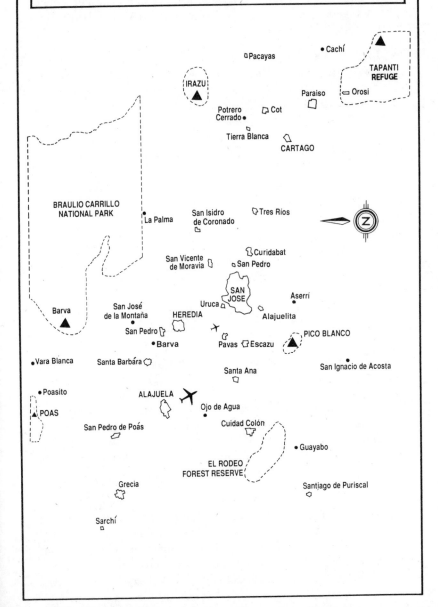

The Meseta Central

- Cachí
- ▲ TAPANTI REFUGE
- ◻ Pacayas
- ▲ IRAZU
- Paraiso ◻
- ◻ Orosi
- Potrero Cerrado • ◻ Cot
- ◻ Tierra Blanca
- ◻ CARTAGO
- BRAULIO CARRILLO NATIONAL PARK
- • La Palma
- San Isidro de Coronado ◻
- ◻ Tres Ríos
- ◎ Z
- ◻ Curidabat
- San Vicente de Moravia ◻
- ◻ San Pedro
- SAN JOSE
- Aserrí •
- Barva ▲
- San José de la Montaña
- HEREDIA ◻
- Uruca ◻
- Alajelita ◻
- San Pedro ◻
- ✈
- Pavas ◻ Escazu
- PICO BLANCO ▲
- • Barva
- •Vara Blanca
- Santa Barbára ◻
- Santa Ana ◻
- San Ignacio de Acosta •
- • Poasito
- ALAJUELA ◻
- ✈
- ▲ POAS
- Ojo de Agua •
- Cuidad Colón ◻
- San Pedro de Poás ◻
- • Guayabo
- EL RODEO FOREST RESERVE
- Grecia ◻
- Santiago de Puriscal ◻
- Sarchí ◻

acingly over hills, and deforestation is always appalingly evident, with treeless plots edging up to the tops of hills. **note:** For organizational convenience, areas on the periphery (but not geographically part of) the Meseta Central are also included in this section.

exploring: As local wags have it, outside of San José there is a nation called Costa Rica. And the Meseta Central region is one of the best places to begin seeing it. Here are three charming provincial capitals (Alajuela, Cartago, and Heredia), dramatic volcanos, winding roads and rivers, hot springs, old churches, and much more. If you have only time to do a few things you'll have to choose carefully. Buses are generally plentiful, and the area is perfect for day or overnight trips. The more adventurous you are here, the more memorable experiences you'll have to take back home with you.

ALAJUELA

This pleasant town located near the airport, just a 23 km (17 mi.) ride W of the capital, was founded in 1790. It is noted as a center for sugar processing, cattle marketing, and small industry. As in other towns, the street signs feature advertising, and every part is accessible on foot. **getting there:** Take a microbus from Av. 2, C. 12/14; they leave every 15 min. until midnight and then hourly on the hour. To get here by car, take "la pista" (the Cañas highway) and follow the turnoff near the airport.

sights: The charming bandstand-equipped plaza resembles a cross between a garden and a forest. In its trees reside a number of three-toed sloths. On its borders are solidly constructed buildings from the era when coffee dominated the local economy. One of these is the teacher's training college. It shares the building with the Museo de Juan Santamaría (open 2–9 daily) which deals with the war against William Walker. A remodeled colonial-style *carcel* (jail) dating from 1874, the museum is more of interest for its ambience than its content, and it's a pleasant place to sit. With a dome-shaped roof of bright red corrugated metal, the white-columned cathedral stands in front of the park. Its interior is more ornate and spacious than those in other towns, and it has large religious statuary— including a very realistic Jesus nailed to the cross and bleeding which is to the L of the altar. There's also an image of the Black Virgin along with a small, wall-mounted cabinet filled with arms, legs, and other body parts in case you missed the displays in the cathedral in Cartago. Although it doesn't show it now, the cupola, which has its balconies and curtains painted on, cracked in half during the March 1990 quake. Some of the town's other buildings suffered fissures. To get to Iglesia La Agonía, walk along the edge of the square, passing the circular red corrugated roof cupola of the church which contrasts sharply with the ultra-modern reflective glass bank directly across the street, and continue down until you see the immense structure on the R. If it's closed ask at the shop to get in. Inside, there's a Renaissance-like portrait of Our Mother of Perpetual Sorrow, a brown Christ suspended above the altar, and a number of large murals. One statue depicts a priest holding a cross with a miniature Jesus on it as a skull and flowers rest at his feet. The town's other park, a block to the N at C. 2, Av. 3, is named after Juan Santamaría, and his statue is across the way.

festivals and events: Held in Alajeula in April, the Día de Juan Santamaría commemorates Costa Rica's only national hero and the town's pride and joy. There is a parade with marching bands and majorettes. Held in July, the Mango Festival, the highlight of Alejuela's year, offers nine days of parades, music, outdoor food markets, and arts and crafts fairs.

accommodations: Near the plaza, Hotel Alajuela (tel. 41-1241) is moderately priced (from US$9 s or US$13 d); they also have a few furnished apartments. Less expensive hotels include the El Real (C. 8, Av. 1/Central), the Moderno (down the street across the RR tracks), and the El Tucano (tel. 48–7192) at Turrucales. In La Garita the Villa Comfort Geriatric Hotel is a senior citizen's establishment featuring landscaped grounds and recreation facilities, with special diets and 24-hour medical care.

food and shopping: Best restaurant is the Cencerro, up-stairs on Av. Central across from the plaza. La Jarra, at C. 2 and Av. 2, upstairs and a block S from the square, is less expensive. You can also try Bar Marisquería Evelyn, to the R of the *museo* and down towards the square, or La Troja, across the street from the museo and down. It has a sophisticated art and jazz atmosphere; a good place to bring a hot date. Open daily, the central market is a fascinating place to explore as well as to eat. There's also a giant outdoor market every Sat. AM. Although considered to be a farmer's market, it's actually run by the ubiquitous middlemen, the bane of Costa Rica's marketplace economy. Every type of vegetable and fruit imaginable is for sale. Huge trucks at the rear unload and sell bananas, enormous Japanese-style pumpkins are sawed up, and young boys sell bundles of garlic with all of the enthusiasm of country preachers. Most of the produce is sold in one long row of stalls each topped with multicolored, beach-ball-like umbrellas. A block and a half W of the plaza on Av. Central, ItalPan is one of many bakeries selling baked goods. There's not much to buy in town here (save for some remarkably tacky souvenirs), but if you're in the market for a casket, there's a great place just 100 feet L of the *museo*.

events and festivals: Soccer games are held most Suns. at the stadium. La Guacima has car and motorcycle races every weekend.

information and services: A former country club, Campestre del Sol (tel. 42–0077) features swimming pools, gymnasium, dance hall; open Tues. through Sun., 8–4.

from Alajuela: W of town along the highway to Atenas, the Zoológico de Aves Tropicales, a bird zoo, is located across from a *"vivero"* or tropical plant farm. Open 9–5 daily, admission is charged. A special bus leaves at 8 AM on Sun. from the S side of the church for Poás. At La Garita, there's a hydroelectric dam, a number of plant nurseries, and an amusement park featuring animal sculptures, a pool, and a lake.

PARQUE NACIONAL VOLCÁN POÁS (POAS VOLCANO)

With a breadth of a mile and a depth of 1000 feet, Poás is the world's largest geyser-type crater and is protected in a 13,835-acre national park. Located 23 mi. from Alajuela and 37 mi. from San José, Poás last erupted in 1978 but is still boiling and steaming. As you progress towards its 8,871-ft. summit, the weather becomes cloudier and cooler and coffee plantations give way to pastures filled with dairy cattle and terraced potato patches.

getting there: A bus runs from the SE corner of Parque Merced in San José at 8:30 on Sundays and holidays; be there by 7:30 to assure a seat. The ride, in an exquisitely funky "Bluebird" brand bus, takes 2.5 hrs. (including a 20 min. rest stop where you can breakfast briefly). The bus arrives at 11 and returns at 2:30. Another bus leaves at 9 AM from the SE corner of the plaza in Alajuela. An alternative is to take an hourly bus from Alajuela's Parque de Cemetario to San Pedro de Poás, and then take a taxi RT (about $20 RT) from there, or go by bus to Poasita, 6 mi. from the crater. Along with some snacks or a box lunch, you should bring a sweater or jacket and rain gear all year round. If you're driving, take the expressway to Alajuela and then proceed via San Pedro de Poás and Poasito. Another route is to go through Heredia, Barva, Los Cartagos, and Poasito.

orientation: The first thing you find at the crater is the visitor's center. At 11 and 1 it has a slide show in Spanish about the National Parks. A road leads up to the two lookout points over the volcano. If you've never seen an active volcano before, you're in for an amazing sight! The lake on the bottom has somewhat muddy waters which change colors depending upon the degree of volcanic activity. From the road leading to the crater there's a short trail to Botos Lake, highlighted by a number of *sombrilla de pobre* (poor people's umbrella) plants and dwarf trees. Once believed to have a whirlpool which would suck unwary swimmers through a passage into the active crater, this lake is fed entirely by rainwater, and it hosts algae, shrimp, and various species of frogs and toads. Its greenish color is due to the presence of sulfur in colloidal state. There is no access down to the lake, and there is only one other trail: the Sendero Escalonia runs from the picnic tables past wooden trail markers inscribed with poetic paeans to the environs.

history: Out of a total of five craters formed, Lake Botos was number three in the line; the present active crater was number five. Although the first European, Mata Guevara, reached the crater at an unknown date, its first mention in a written document was in 1783, and a priest named Arias, arriving in 1815 from Alajuela, baptized it with the name Juan de Dios. The other names, Poás and Votos or Botos, by which the crater has been known are thought to be the names of indigenous tribes that lived in the area. Curiously, a tourist hotel was built less than a mile from the crater in 1915; it closed in 1924, and no trace remains today. Eruptions occurred in 1888, 1904, 1905, 1910, and 1952–54. Aftr things settled down, a cone of ash and debris had formed at the site of the lake which had refilled with water by 1967 and hasn't changed much since. Comprising 13,138 acres, the Parque Nacional Volcán Poás was established on Jan. 30, 1971. Since 1989, it has again become increasingly active, and the sulfur gas and steam ejected have caused acid rain, resulting in the destruction of 75% of Grecia's 1989 coffee crop and causing skin and respiratory problems.

*Iguana, Palo Verde
National Park*

Playa Hermosa

Birds on Isla de Pájaro, Río Tempisque, Palo Verde National Park

Marenco sunset (Sergio Miranda)

Isla del Caño (Sergio Miranda)

festivals and events: Held Mar. 15, the nationwide celebration of Farmer's Day is headquartered in Tierra Blanca (whose farmers celebrate deliverance from a plague of locusts in 1877). It is a day devoted to the farmer's patron saint, San Isidro, a humble 12th C. Spanish farmer. On Mar. 19, San José Day, local families traditionally visit Volcan Poás for a hike and picnic.

accommodations: Set next to the farm El Cortijo at Vara Blanca up in the hills at 6,000 feet and billed as a "bed and breakfast" accommodating up to 15 people, Poás Volcano Lodge was originally built by an English family, and incorporates elements of Welsh farmhouses, English cottages, and American architecture into its design. There are areas of protected forest within the farm. For more information call 55-3486 or write Jungle Trails, Apdo. 2413-1000, San José, Costa Rica.

food: It's best to bring your own as there's usually little or nothing for sale at the crater. About 10 miles above Alajuela, Chubascos has tables set amidst an outdoor garden. Specialties include large *casados*, strawberry and blackberry shakes, and cheesecake.

vicinity of Poás: Open 9-3:30, Tues. to Sun., the Fraijanes Lake Recreation Park, about a half-hour down the road from the summit, has paths through cypress and pine groves, a lagoon, exercise course, and basketball courts. Famous La Paz falls are at Vara Blanca just after the Poás turnoff.

HEREDIA

Another in the line of provincial capitals this university town and coffee growing center of 30,000 sits at the foot of extinct

Volcano Barva, 11 km (7 mi.) from San José. Nicknamed "La Ciudad de las Flores," Heredia is one of the most peaceful and relaxing towns in the nation. To get here take one of the frequent buses from C. 1, Av. 7/9 (via Tibás), from Av. 2, C. 12 (via La Uruca), or from the terminal in Alajuela.

sights: Dating from 1797, the squat, solid, and imposing church appears to ruminate about days of yore from its spot on the plaza; its low contours were designed to resist earthquake damage. The bells in this old church were brought from Cuzco, Peru in the colonial era. Supplicants gather in the morning to pray. Inside there are numerous large statues including one to the L of the altar which has the Virgin Mary standing on a white neon crescent moon and surrounded by white neon stars of David. There's also a full-length statue of Jesus who's brown skinned, dreadlocked, clothed in a velvet gown, and penned-in (presumably) for protection. In addition to several other old colonial-style buildings, El Fortín, a Spanish-style fort tower that has become the town's emblem, borders the central plaza to its L. On the N side of the park is the Casa de la Cultura which features art exhibits.

accommodation: Right in town stay at low budget Hotel Verano (tel. 37–1616, C. 4, Av. 6) or at the even cheaper Colonial (Av. 4, C. 4/6). Camping is permitted at Bosque de la Hoja, three mi. from San Rafael de Heredia. A full 12 mi. N of San José, the village of San José de la Montaña offers accommodation in the cool hills. Try the Hotel de Montaña El Pórtico (tel. 37–6022; 21–2039 in San José) NW of town, or the inexpensive Cabañas de Montaña Cypresal (tel. 37–4466). Nearby are the ivy-covered, fireplace-equipped, and moderately priced, Cabañas Las Ardillas (tel. 21–4294, 22–8134). Inexpensive and tasteful El Pórtico (tel. 37–6022), up the road, has heated rooms along with pool, Jacuzzi, and restaurant. Located in Parque Residencial del Monte, Monte de la Cruz, Heredia, Hotel Chalet Tikal (tel. 39–7070) has 10 two-story chalets with hot water, trout fishing, conference rooms, French cuisine, and a surrounding cloud forest with waterfalls. Write Apdo. 7812, 1000 San José. Located half a mile off the road from Barva to Alajuela and just short of a mile from the town of Santa Barbara de Heredia, expensive Finca Rosa Country Inn (tel. 39–9392) set at 4,265 ft., features four suites and one master suite, each with its own design theme, as well as a complete range of services—all supplemented by nature trails and gardens with fruit trees. Write Apdo. 41–3009, Santa Barbara de Heredia, Costa Rica.

food and entertainment: Set 1500 feet E of Pop's ice cream on the plaza, Café Plaza features cuisine as diverse as lasagna, pastries, expresso coffee, and stuffed croissants. Mercado Florense is 900 feet S and 150 feet W of the Church. Student bars near the university include El Bulevar and La Choza.

vicinity of Heredia: The Attiro coffee mill, on the outskirts of town, is one of several *beneficios* nearby. On the outskirts of San Pedro de Barva (tel. 37–1915), the Centro de Investigaciones de Cafe features a small coffee museum with coffee production antiquities including a display of grinders and carved wooden statues of coffee workers in action. Open weekdays until 3. Take the Santa Bárbara por Barrio Jesús bus from Av. 1, C. 1/3 in Heredia. Up on the street just past El Fortín to the L (C. 1, Av. 1/3) is the stop for Barva. Situated a few miles to the N, Barva's grassy plaza features low, thick-walled buildings with red-tiled roofs and a baroque-style 19th C. church; it has been declared the nation's first historic town. Get here from Heredia. From here you can also continue on by bus to San Pedro de Barva and the coffee museum. When you return to Heredia, be sure to note the house shaped like a miniature castle just before town on the R.

Monte de La Cruz: This is still one of the most traditional areas in the Meseta Central. Three miles from San Rafael de Heredia, Bosque de la Hoja is one and a half miles down a forest road. There's not much in the way of facilities here except for the Bar las Chorreras, but the hiking trails traverse forests and meadows. Back on the main road, El Castillo is a stately country club. The $5 admission entitles you to use the pool, gym, ice-skating rink, BBQ pits, and to ride on the go-carts and the miniature train. Look for it on the R, a few hundred yards after the sign for Residencial El Castillo. The turnoff for Monte de la Cruz is another half mile. To the L is Hotel Chalet Tirol (gourmet food) which has several great hiking trails in their private cloud forest reserve, including one with a grove of waterfalls. There's also a restaurant (open 10–11) at Monte de la Cruz. **getting there:** Take an hourly (8–8) bus from the Mercado Florense; the buses at 9, 12, and 4 proceed to 6/10 of a mile before Monte de la Cruz. By car take the San Isidro exit to the L approximately eight miles down the Guápiles highway and continue until you reach San Isidro where you turn R in front of the church and continue one and a half miles to Concepción and then on to San Rafael where you turn R at the church.

PARQUE NACIONAL BRAULIO CARRILLO (BRAULIO CARRILLO NATIONAL PARK)

The only national park near San José, Braulio Carrillo begins seven miles from San José enroute to Guápiles and encompasses elevations ranging from eastern lowlands (1500 feet) up to the summit of 9,534 ft. Volcán Barva. If you are going to the Atlantic Coast, it is virtually inevitable that you will pass through this park. The only national park divided by a highway, as you drive, the surrounding greenery is often enveloped in mist resembling that seen in Chinese landscape paintings. Rainfall averages 110–150 inches annually, and it rains almost daily between March and October; the park's E slope is generally overcast when it isn't raining.

history: The story of this park is tied to people attending to the lessons of history, a historically significant occurrence in and of itself. After the idea of a highway surfaced in 1973, environmentalists, fearing a repeat of the indiscriminate deforestation which had followed the openings of other new roads in the past, argued for the establishment of this park. It was inaugurated in April 1978, and the Limón highway opened to traffic in 1987. Under the US AID-funded Foresta project, the park has received funds for more trails and view points and a visitor's center.

flora and fauna: Covering 108,969 acres, 84% of the park's surface is primeval forest, 11% is used for ranching and farming, and 5% is secondary forest. There are over 500 species of birds; the magnificent quetzal resides on Volcán Barva as well as on other high peaks.

getting there: Take the hourly Guápiles-bound bus from C. 12, Av. 9. An impressive way to enter the park is by Volcán Barva through the road leading to Sacaramento de San José de la Montaña. In addition to the ranger stations at either Zurquí or Quebrada Gonzales, it's possible to enter the park near La Virgen off the road to Puerto Viejo de la Sarapiquí if you have a 4WD. If you want to climb Barva, Geotur's tours include a visit to a banana and a *cacao* plantation enroute to Limón where you lunch and enjoy the beach before returning. Call 34–1867. Jungle Trails (tel. 55–3486) also operates hiking tours here.

hiking: Inquire at the ranger station concerning trails and current conditions. There are two trails accessible from the highway. One, before the tunnel, is sheer and arduous; the other, the Sendero Botello, 11 mi. after the tunnel and 1.5 mi. before the Quebrada Gonzales station at the park's far end, is less difficult. Both are muddy. You're most likely to spot birds along these trails. There's also a four-day hike from Barva to Puerto Viejo de Sarapiquí with shelters available along the way. Enroute you descend from 9,514 ft. to 112 ft. **climbing Barva:** From Heredia take a 6 AM San José de la Montaña-Paso Llano bus from behind Heredia's Mercado Central. Watch for signs at Paso Llano (Porrosati) leading to the entrance, 4 mi. to the L. Sacramento is 4 mi. farther, and from there it is approximately 2 mi. to the top of Volcán Barva (9,534 ft.). Its main lake has a 600-foot diameter. The Danta, another lake, is nearby. Be sure to bring a compass, rubber boots, warm clothing and food—no matter how nice the weather is! Although they were planning only a day hike around the crater, three German hikers were lost in rain and fog for 11 days here. Plan to make it back in time for the 5 PM bus. **the banana highway:** As the RR to Limón ran only as far as Carrillo, 30 miles from San José, capitalist entrepreneur extraordinaire Minor Keith built a highway through here in 1881 to connect the capital with the terminal. Fallen into disrepair since completion of the railway line, it now makes a wonderful day hike. Take a bus (Av. 3, C. 3/5) to San Jerónimo de Moravia and then a road to the N; in less than an hour, at the "Alto de Palma" area, you'll come to the old stone pavement which you can follow along for about 6 miles until you reach the park boundary; entrance is prohibited here.

CARTAGO

Located 14 mi. E of San José in the Valle de Guarco, this once-impoverished village founded in 1523, is the nation's oldest settlement. Since the 1800s Cartago has also been known as la Ciudad de las Brumas, the "city of fog." A former nickname is la Ciudad del Lodo, the city of mud. If you arrive on a rainy day, you'll soon see why. A nickname for the inhabitants is *pateros* (potato people), probably because potatoes are such an important crop in this province.

getting there: Buses run from San José about every 20 minutes. They leave from near the Plaza de la Democracía. Be sure to get the *directo* bus.

sights: Cartago does not have as many old buildings nor the atmosphere one might expect in a city of its age largely because earthquakes (in 1841 and 1910), along with raining ash and debris from Volcán Irazú, have destroyed most of its old buildings. If you are coming by bus, you might want to get out at the town's center where you'll see Las Ruinas. Iglesia de Convento, the parish church of La Parroquia, the first dedicated to Santiago (St. James), was severely damaged by earthquakes, and, after the 1910 quake—perhaps owing to the legend that the Creator had cursed the church owing to its priest's murder of his brother—it was deemed not to be worthwhile to rebuild it. Today, it's a walled park complete with trees, a pond, shrubs, and benches—all of which combine to afford a more attractive park than any found in San José. The plaza built in front which has a statue of the opera tenor Manuel Salazar Zuniga is a great place to relax a while and birdwatch. **the cathedral:** A few blocks away to the E, this is the town's main attraction. An example of what some have called a Byzantine-style church and others an architectural mishmash, the Basilica de Nuestra Señora de Los Angeles (Basilica of Our Lady of the Angels), the nation's patron saint, houses a statuette of the Black Virgin holding the infant Christ. Legend has it that on Aug. 2, 1635 a young girl named Juana Periera found a small statuette of the Virgin Mary perched on a rock beside a stream while strolling in a forest. Taking the statuette home, she placed it in her collection. Passing the same point the next afternoon, she discovered another identical statuette at the same location. Returning home, she found that the first statuette had vanished, and she placed the new one where it had stood. After this happened three days in a row, she went to the priest who, after having the identical experience, decided to build a shrine at the site. Today the rock is found in the church's basement and thousands credit the stream's water with miraculous powers to heal injuries, handicaps, and even enable supplicants to survive surgery. Arriving supplicants have donated miniature trinkets resembling the body parts requiring healing, and there are fingers, arms, hearts, stomachs, eyes, legs, livers, lungs, and feet in cases all over the church; many of them are silver medallions. You could spend hours gazing at the collection. Trophies are the gift of grateful sports teams who allegedly owed their victories to the Virgin's intervention, and there are photos of children next to written testimony extolling the Virgin's healing powers; there's even a geisha doll and a pair of carved wooden oxen being led by a *campesino*. Statuary abounds, and there are also some beautiful confession booths. At the rear to the L of the altar is a collection of life-sized statues, some with desperately unhappy faces. Downstairs, reduced and weathered by years of attention and chiseling, is the original stone, topped with a replica of the Virgin which is done up in an elaborate gold case. The original, crudely fashioned from a granite-like stone, is rarely removed from its cabinet set above the altar. Stolen several times, it has always been returned. Holy water, from the stream which still runs alongside, is available in a shed at the back; you must pay 50 cents for a container. Across the street in a diagonal from the R of the cathedral's entrance, you'll see a shop, "Venta de Objetos Religiosos," which sells hands, feet, eyes, and other paraphernalia at reasonable prices. Finally, if you have time, you may want to see the art exhibits at the Casa de la Ciudad in Edificio Pirie.

practicalities: If you're looking for comfortable hotels, there are none to be found. If all you want is an inexpensive place to sleep so that you can head up to the top of Irazú the next morning, that can be found near the railway station and the market. Try The Casa Blanca in Barrio Asia, and less expensive Pensión El Brumoso, or the Valencia. Most of the others rent rooms by the hour for obvious purposes, so if you don't mind creaking springs and frantic gasps coming from the room next door. . . . Bars and restaurants cluster around the basilica. Pizza y hamburguesas Maui is on the N side of the park in front of the cathedral; a large restaurant is behind it. One of the most attractive places to dine is Salón Paris, which features Venetian and bullfight scenes, and is opposite one corner of the market on the main street. Located near the bus station, the large and bustling market, featuring yet another replica of the Virgin, has lunch counters galore. Watch the mother and daughter team in one shop making *tortillas*. You also might find any kind of odd souvenir in its innumerable shops.

festivals and events: The Virgin of Los Angeles, held on August 1, is Cartago's largest festival; thousands arrive for this.

vicinity of Cartago: Set 5 miles to the SE of Cartago, Jardín Lankester, the Lankester Gardens (named after their founder British expatriate Dr. Charles Lankester who founded them in the 1940s), possesses one of the nation's finest orchid collections. Although the over 800 species found here bloom throughout the year, the blossoms are at their peak in March. Also featured are fruit trees, groves of bamboo, aloe, hardwoods, bromeliads and other species. Unfortunately, they're all identified in Latin, so unless you're a botanist it might as well be Greek to you. Guided tours are offered on the half hour from 8:30–3:30 daily. Although you can come through on your own, an employee will tag along behind to make sure you keep to the route and don't pick anything. To get there, take the Paraíso bus from the Cartago terminal and get off at the Ricalit factory and the distinctive and unforgettable dog training school sign, then walk just over a quarter-mile down the side road to the S leading to the entrance. If you want to head outwards and onwards after your visit take a bus marked "Orosi" (see Valle de Orosi section below). If you're driving, you'll want to check out the spectacular view from the *mirador* (lookout point) a few miles past Paraíso enroute to the S. Also near Paraíso is the Auto-vivero del Río, a combined greenhouse and miniature zoo which sells colored volcanic stones, plants, and rabbits. For transport to Irazú, see the Irazú section. Finally, on the way back to San José, the Nuestra Señora de Pilar Religious Art Museum is on the S side of the Church of Tres Ríos.

route of the saints: This road to the S takes one along to villages like Santa María de Dota, San Marcos de Tarrazú, San Pablo de León Cortés, and San Cristobal Sur. In the vicinity is also La Lucha where Don Pepe Figueres had his famous farm. At Cañon del Guarco, km 58 on the Interamerican, a road leads seven km downhill to Copey and then another seven down to Santa María where there are some low-budget hotels. From Santa María buses return at 6, 9, 2, and 4. This makes a great day trip.

San Geraldo de Dota: At km 80 on the Interamerican, the entrance to this village is quite a bit farther S. The interior of these cloud forests has been acclaimed as the best place in the nation to see a quetzal. Stay at Cabinas Chacón (tel. 71–1732) for $20 pp, meals included. Transportation from the junction (nine km on a bad road) is available.

PARQUE NACIONAL VOLCÁN IRAZÚ (IRAZÚ VOLCANO)

Rising to 11,260 ft., Irazú is one of the few volcanoes that may be viewed up close with ease. And, should the day be clear, both the Atlantic and Pacific are visible from its summit. A lumbering menace that has devastated Cartago on more than one occasion, its presence has also had a beneficial effect: the very ash that wreaks devastation is also responsible for the soil's fecundity.

orientation: This mountain is the birthplace of the Chirripó, Reventación, Sarapiquí, and Grande de Tárcoles rivers. It has shot billows of steam up as high as 1,640 ft. and volcanic debris up to 984 ft. With a rusty, mineral-colored lake at its bottom, Diego de la Haya is approximately 2,270 ft. wide and 328 ft. deep; its NW slope features active fumaroles. Measuring 3,445 ft. in diameter, the principal crater is 820–984 ft. deep. **note:** Although the crater walls may appear to be safe, it is actually quite dangerous to descend to either crater's bottom.

flora and fauna: The vegetation is adapted to high altitude and low temperatures. Wildlife here is scarce but there are forest cats, porcupines, coyotes, and a variety of birds including the mountain robin and the volcano junco, a chunky sparrow.

history: Although there are many possible explanations for the volcano's name, the most likely one is that it derives from *Iztarú,* an Indian word meaning "mountain of tremors and thunder." Although it has held various names, it has been known solely by this alias since 1854. The mountain's first recorded eruption occurred in 1723. The newly formed crater was the present-day Diego de la Haya. The next eruption was in 1775, and it also erupted in 1822, perhaps in celebration of Costa Rica's independence that year. The area was established as a 5,700-acre park in 1955. From 1963–65, the eruptions traumatized the region, affecting farming in San José, Alajuela, and Heredia provinces. In 1963, 300 houses were destroyed, and the next eruption, the following year, poured five inches of ash on San José. An estimated 250 million *colones* in agricultural revenues were lost as a consequence.

getting there: Unfortunately, there is no public bus service all the way to the top. The closest you can get is to Tierra Blanca or Linda Vista. From there you must hike, hitch, or grab a taxi. The bus to Linda Vista (8.5 km, 13.7 mi., from the crater) leaves Mon. and Thurs. at 5:45 AM from Cartago, arriving at 8 and returning at 12:45 to arrive back in Cartago at 2. Ask in Cartago about buses as far as Tierra Blanca. Another alternative is to take a taxi from Cartago, about $15 RT after bargaining. It's preferable to visit in the dry season, and it would be a good idea to bring food with you. Another convenient way to get there is with Cielo Azul (tel. 32–7066) which has half- or full-day tours. Full-day tours include Orosi Valley.

sights enroute: On the way from Cartago, you will pass many dairy farms, potato patches, and the immaculate towns of Potrero Cerrado and Tierra Blanca, "White Land"—so named either because of the ash or because of the fecundity of the soil. After the town of Cot, you come next to Potrero Cerrado ("Closed Field"), then you pass a TB sanatorium converted into a juvenile reform school. Prusia was destroyed by an eruption, and the surrounding area has been reforested by the Guardia Civil. Now known as Area Recreativa Jiménez Oreamuno, it's reached by a short but steep hike. There are picnic tables and trails.

accommodation: Stay at the Hotel de Montaña Gestoria Irazú (tel. 53–0827), 20 km (12.4 mi.) from Cartago and 12 km (7.5 mi.) from the crater, for under US$10. Another alternative is to overnight in Cartago. The only place to eat, other than at the none-too-good hotel just mentioned, is at the Linda Vista, a somewhat pricey basic restaurant featuring an incredible display of name cards, *cedulas,* and foreign banknotes.

VALLE DE OROSI (OROSI VALLEY)

This spectacularly scenic area makes a great day trip from San José, providing a good opportunity for an escape from the urban sprawl into the countryside by car or bus.

getting there: To go by bus, take a Cachí bus to Cartago and then ask to be let off at Ujarrás. You can then walk half an hour to Charrara (on Suns., the bus goes all the way at 8, 11, and 12). Cielo Azul offers your choice of two tours: one in which you visit Irazú in the morning and Orosi in the afternoon, and another in which you can just visit Orosi.

festivals and events: Held mid-March, the Ujarrás pilgrimage, a procession from Paraíso to the ruined church in Ujarrás, commemorates the rescue of Ujarrás by the *Virgen* from floods. Her graven image returns along with the crowd for the occasion.

mirador: There are two scenic overlooks in the region. Featuring a garden-like setting, Mirador de Orosi, a facility constructed by the ICT, has some of the most magnificent views in the nation. Take the path to your L; Irazú and Turrialba peaks will be directly in front, and, as you continue along, you'll see Orosi on the side with coffee plantations in the foreground. Dammed at its lower end by the Cachí Dam, the Río Rentavazón winds and wends its way down the valley.

Orosi and vicinity: With the nation's oldest active church, Orosi, a village in which Indians were once forcibly resettled, is a pleasant, well manicured town. It has several *balnearios,* public baths, and hot springs. Be sure to visit the restored church. Built between 1743 and 1786 and located next to the soccer field, it has whitewashed walls of sun-dried bricks, paved brick floors, a red tile roof supported by eight square cedar columns set on stone, and religious statuary thought to be the work of Mexican and Guatemalan artists. Next door, the monastery has been converted into a museum housing a collection of religious art. There's a Christ in a coffin, elaborate candelabras, clerical robes, and a bleeding wooden Christ along with other statuary. (Open daily, 9–12, 1–5, ten cents admission). On the lake's N side, another ICT facility offers a swimming pool, picnic area, restaurant, playing fields, boat launching area, and campground.

Refugio Nacional de Fauna Silvestre Tapantí: The side road leading to the Río Macho hydroelectric plant, two km after Orosi, leads 12 km (no bus available; taxi about $3.50 OW) to the 12,577-acre Tapantí forest reserve which offers nature trails, a good stream for trout fishing (with a permit) and a lookout point. It's open 6–4 so birders can get an early start. Inside, you might see quetzal, olingo, or kinkajou. It rains a tremendous amount in this area, especially between May and October, so you'll want to be well prepared. As compensation for the weather, there are approximately 150 streams and rivers running through. Fishing is permitted in designated areas. There's a small exhibit room at the entrance and nearby trails, with a *mirador* overlooking a waterfall. To enter the reserve from its S extremity, known as the Reserva Forestal Río Macho, get information from the *pulpería* owner in La Trinidad de Dota, 1.5 hrs. S of San José on the Inter-American Highway.

Las Chesperitos is next to the ranger station there, and you can stay at inexpensive La Georgina a half-hour away. The refuge is open from 6 to 4 daily.

Palomo: Accessible by either a footbridge from Orosi (which exacts a maintenance toll on Sundays) or a sturdier suspension bridge two km farther on, the chief feature here is the inexpensive Motel Río (tel. 73–3128, 73–3057), with a swimming pool and restaurant specializing in fresh fish. Some of the inexpensive units are equipped with kitchenettes. Most buses end here so if you wish to visit Cachí dam eight km away, you must either walk, hitch, or backtrack to Cartago where you catch a bus via Ujarrás.

La Casa del Soñador: Built by master woodcarver and retired university professor, Macedonio Quesada Volorin, this primitive yet ornate wooden "House of the Dreamer," built late in 1989, rises on boulders by the side of the road right next to the Río Naranjo. The carved female silhouettes gazing out from the windows as you approach represent gossiping women. The shutters pull down to match the outline when the window is closed. The feeling of his work appears to evoke not only Costa Rica and Latin America but also native American art along with Dayak and Japanese Buddhist monk primitive woodcarvings. Along the side is a carving of the Last Supper, and along the back side a representation of the Children's Last Supper. The carved door immediately adjacent has a dog, mother, and child which represents the love of mother for her child and the love of the dog for the child. Inside are carved nativity creches and other woodwork, much of which is made from coffee roots, tirra, cerro royal, and pilon woods. Macedonio's one small bedroom and other workspace is upstairs. He's teaching disadvantaged locals to carve, and his assistants are constantly chiseling away downstairs. Cachí Dam, just down the road, was constructed during the mid-1960s for 182 million *colones*. Check in the marsh across the road to spot waterbirds.

Ujarrás: Past Cachí dam 1.5 km to the W down a side road. Now a historic shrine, the ruins of Ujarrás church, built in 1681–93 and abandoned in 1833 after a flood forced the village to relocate on higher ground, are set in beautifully maintained grounds with flowers, birds, and a stand of bamboo. Coffee plantations and a reforested pine grove border the grounds. According to legend, a Huetar Indian found a wooden box in a river which he brought to Ujarrás. From here no one could move it farther. When opened, it was found to contain a statue of the Virgin, and a church was built on the spot. This very Virgin was credited with repelling an invasion by the pirate Henry Morgan and his brigands who were turned back in 1666 from their attempt to sack Cartago by an outnumbered band of colonial militia. Today she resides in Paraíso, where all of the inhabitants of the time relocated. She is now known as Virgen de Candelaria and has been declared Patron Saint of the *guardias*. A fiesta is still held here in mid-March. The cross on the grounds was found in a nearby canyon. Eat at Restaurante Típico Ujarrás. Featuring a pool, basketball courts, boating on the lake, picnic tables, and a restaurant, the Lacustre Charrara recreation area is two km off the main road down a spur from the Ujarrás road. On weekends and holidays the bus goes all the way instead of dropping you off at the turnoff. Closed on Mon. The Ujarrás lookout point is located six km from the Charrara turnoff towards Paraíso. Nearby is the Veil de la Novio (Bridal Veil) waterfall. According to legend, a group of family and friends arrived here to celebrate a wedding. The horse went berserk and jumped, taking the bride and her long trailing veil over the cliff.

THE TURRIALBA AREA

The name Turrialba means "white tower" in archaic Spanish. As the number of visitors to Costa Rica continues to grow, this area—because of its great scenic beauty, attractions, and proximity to San José—has attracted increased attention.

Turrialba: Set in the base of the volcano of the same name 64 km away from San José, this agriculturally-based town of 28,000 sits at 2,050 ft. There's nothing much to pique the interest of a visitor here, but its proximity to the Río Reventazón has made it a major area for kayaking and white water rafting.

getting there: A bus runs hourly (7 AM–9 PM) from San José, departing from Av. Central, C. 13 for the under-two-hour trip. If you're coming by car, you can also come via San Isidro de Coronado and Rancho Redondo to Santa Cruz where you turn for Turrialba.

facilities and tours: Just outside of town, Balneario Las Americas (75 cents admission) has two large pools and a restaurant-bar. Located 200 yards from town to the W of the church next to a river, Parque La Dominica has swings, and basketball courts. For those wishing to tour the area, the COSANA travel agency (tel. 56–1513) operates tours here. La Calzada (tel. 51–3677, 56–0465) also offers tours to a local cheese factory, small ponds, and to a sugarcane plant. Hector Lezama at the Turrialtico (tel. 56–1111) will also arrange tours, including one to the top of Turrialba, but sufficient advance notice is required.

climbing Volcán Turrialba: From San José or Cartago one can go by bus to the village of Pacayas to reach the top of this semi-active 10,995-ft. volcano by horses or with a four-wheel drive. Another place to climb is from the village of Santa Cruz to the N. Although there's a 4WD road that winds up the mountain, it's too rough to ride up more than two-thirds of the 21 km to the top. To hike, proceed from Santa Cruz along the main road for three km where you'll find the Bar Canada. After turning R here, you'll find the sign marking the route after 600–800 feet. Here you'll turn R again and ascend. When you come to a fork (about every few km) take the trail going up; the other route usually goes to a farm. After about 12 km (7.5 mi.) of this, you'll come to a group of houses. Here, ascend via the R fork, and you'll reach a metal gate. After another km or so, you reach a fork where you go R and then go through a barbed wire gate (which can be rolled open). Pass by the cow barn and through another wire gate to its L. A few hundred yards thereafter is the last spot to obtain water enroute to the summit. The summit is another km or so up. There's a great camping area on top, and there are plenty of paths to explore on top.

accommodations: Inexpensively priced Hotel Wagelia (tel. 56-1566, 56-1596) is the most attractive. Their a/c rooms are in the moderate range. Also in town are the Central, Chamanga, Pensión Primavera, and the Interamericano (tel. 56-0142, $3.50 with shared bath). If you wish to be near Guayabo, stay at low-budget La Calzada (tel. 51-3677, 56-0465), named after the indigenous trail that passes through the property. Discounts are available here for YH members. To the S of town, seven km along the road to Limón, Turrialtico (tel. 56-1111, see description below under food) has two inexpensive rooms for rent with private bath; breakfast is included. A few km farther, Pochotel (tel. 56-0111) charges $20 for each of two, two-room cabinas with private bath. Naturalists and horse lovers might wish to stay in the Albergue de Montaña Rancho Naturalista (tel. 39-8036), up a dirt road from the village of Tuis to the SE. Laundry service and horse rental are included, and there is a three day minimum stay at $65 or $75 pp, pd. Write Apdo. 364, 1002 San José for more information.

food: About 10 km E of town, Pochotel offers Tico cuisine. They have a device which will bring your order up to the top of the observation tower. Located just four km from CATIE and two km from Pochotel, Restaurante Turrialtico offers spectacular views, coffee-root sculptures by famed primitivists Benjamin Paniagua and Victor Barahona, and traditional-style food cooked over wood stoves. Specializing in Jamaican-style fare, Restaurant Kingston is right outside town. Another good place to eat is at La Calzada on the way to Guayabo. **Posada de la Luna:** Located W of the church in Cervantes, halfway between Cartago and Turrialba, this restaurant is nearly as extraterrestrial as its name implies. Certainly, it is unique to this planet. Housed in an unassuming red and yellow concrete building and under a corrugated roof with peeling red paint, this informal restaurant is indubitably one of the nation's most spectacular museums. Among the collection, parts of which are housed in glass cabinets, are a sheathed sword inscribed with Arabic lettering, rusty irons, old smashed up radios, indigenous artifacts, a wooden Buddha, old newspapers (one headline reads "RENDICION TOTAL NAZI"), and a ceramic frog sitting in a brass chair. Packets of chile jalapeno are for sale. This is also one of the best places to try *típico* food: the *gallo pinto* and *tortilla de queso* here are legendary.

Monumento Nacional Guayabo: Located 19 km NE of Turrialba, this is the nation's most famous archaeological site. But it is more worth a visit for its natural surroundings and overall ambience than for its ruins. While similar sites are found in Ciudad Cutris in the San Carlos region and in the Barranca de San Miguel de San Ramón, only Guayabo has been placed under protection. There's a nature trail with two branches, one of which drops down to the river, and there are a variety of mammals and more than 80 types of orchids.

getting there: Get here by taking the Santa Teresita bus (daily at 10:30 and 1:30) which terminates at the beginning of a gravel road four km away. The bus returns from the crossroads at 12:45. You can also take a taxi from Turrialba or hitch. The archaeological site here is still under exploration and is open only on weekends and holidays from 8–4. You must go with a guide along a specified route.

history: The settlement here once housed as many as 10,000 and covered an estimated 37 acres. It is thought to have originated around 1,000 BC, thriving from 800 to 1300 AD, and declining thereafter. By around 1400 AD it was abandoned. The site's stone pedestals are thought to have been built between 800 and 1000 AD. Declared a national monument in 1973, it is the nation's only archaelogical park. In order to protect the surrounding premontane rainforest, the Guayabo River Canyon area was added in 1980; its 539 acres now protect the only extant primary forest in Cartago Province. Begun in Aug. 1989, a five-year restoration plan will increase the excavated area to 50 acres.

sights: The circular mounts (*monticulos*) here once supported large buildings. Some of the stones in the walkways (*calzadas*) are decorated with petroglyphs, and there's also a large boulder carved with representations of the crocodile and the jaguar, both indigenous deities. Although the meaning of the petroglyphs found at the site is unknown, it is commonly thought that they were carved to invoke supernatural protection. There's a system of aqueducts, and what may be the nation's oldest bridge: a broken black rock which crosses an aqueduct. There are great views to be had from the *mirador.*

white water rafting: One of the most popular activities for visitors to Costa Rica, even those who are not particularly athletically inclined, is rafting on the Río Reventazón, the "foaming" river. The Class I rapids on this river serve as an excellent introduction to rafting for the inexperienced, and rafting is one way to discover that a river has a life and personality all its own. Of the four companies rafting on the river, Costa Rica Expeditions (tel. 22–0333) is the longest established. Its owner-managers, Michael Kaye and Howard Solomon, first opened the river up for rafting in 1979. After a hotel pickup and a stop for a Costa Rican-style morning feed, you'll be bused through Turrialba to the river, where the rafts and equipment are assembled. You'll then be given safety instructions and perform a trial run before departure. Going down the river, you can expect to spin around backwards—one of the thrills! You'll pass *oropéndola* nests, giant ferns, hanging epiphytes, sloths in the treetops, and perhaps some agricultural workers; you may even spot a crocodile or toucan. There might be a place where you have to disembark and then reboard because of dangerous riptides, and you'll stop briefly for swimming. Lunch (stew, beans, rice, fruit juice, salad) is served in a tent off the river bank. After passing through some more rapids (and traversing a kayak endurance course), you'll come to the end of the run. The rubber rafts are hauled up and, after changing, you're on your way to a hotel where you'll watch the videotape of your trip. Then, it's back to San José. The other companies, Ríos Tropicales (tel. 33–6455) and Adventuras Naturales (tel. 25–3939), differ in small details such as lunch sites. All of the companies are reliable. Expect to pay around $65 for the day.

CATIE: Located four km E of Turrialba on the road to Limón, the Centro Agronomico Tropical de Investigacion y Enseñanza, a 27,500-acre agricultural research station, provides assistance to the small farmer. Established in the 1930s, it is one of the world's five major centers for tropical agricultural research. Supported with help of overseas governments, research here is devoted to producing high-yielding disease-resistant varieties of bananas, coffee, and cacao. Other research projects include studies on improving palms, plantains and on breeding livestock which will thrive on pasture alone without supplemental feed. New species are replicated in a tissue culture lab and packed for shipment worldwide. Tropical agricultural instructors from all over the world gather here for study. The world's largest collection of papers and books on tropical agriculture is here. There's also a collection of hundreds of species of palms. Visiting birdwatchers should be aware that, in addition to a lagoon, there's also a trail from behind the administration building to the Río Reventazón. If you wish to tour the grounds with an English-speaking guide, call 56-1149 three days ahead of time to arrange an appointment. A tour includes a visit to the seed lab and bank, the meat and dairy farm, orchids, coffee, cacao, and other research facilities. Organized groups are preferred. If you want to drop by, you can visit the nature trail on your own, but you will be denied access to the rest. Ask in town about buses.

PUERTO VIEJO DE LA SARAPIQUÍ

This wet but wonderfully scenic area is set on the slopes above the Caribbean coast to the N and NE of Braulio Carrillo Park and also bordering La Selva. Depending which of the two

routes you take getting here, you may pass *pejibaye* palm plantations, two of the nation's most beautiful waterfalls, banana
plantations, lush bamboo thickets, and some superb scenic
outlooks. Many activities are available in the area; one is to
kayak down the Río Puerto Viejo with Rancho Leona (tel. 71–
6312).

getting here: Buses depart thrice daily from C. 12, Av. 7/9.
There are two routes: Braulio Carrillo and Las Horquetas to
Puerto Viejo or through Varablanca and Chilamante to Puerto
Viejo. The latter (6:30 and noon departures) passes by Ca-
tarata La Paz and Braulio Carrillo. The other (4 PM), termi-
nating in La Virgen, passes by Horquetas, La Selva, Puerto
Viejo, and Chilamante. A San Carlos-Río Frio bus leaves at 6,
9, and 3.

Rara Avis: If you only have time to visit one private nature
preserve, this is the one to visit! Jan., Feb., and March are
busiest here. Established as a corporation in 1983, Rara Avis
S.A. comprises 1,500 acres and is the only place of its ilk in the
world. Biologist-entrepreneur Amos Bien's philosophy is that
development and conservation *can* be compatible and mutu-
ally reinforcing. His hope is to set an example which the local
people will follow. One way is through tourism: the reserve is
already the largest employer in Horquetas. Another is
through utilizing the rainforest commercially without destroy-
ing it. Future projects planned include the commercial production of tree ferns, wicker, and wood, all to be done in an
ecologically sustainable fashion. Amos is forming an organization called Eco Cadena Turistica which is planning to build a
60-room hotel next to Parque Nacional Braulio Carrillo and
hopes to construct similar lodges all over the country. It is set
2,000 ft. above the often-inclement Caribbean coast, so you
have a 75% chance of being rained on if you come for a short
visit. So don't plan your schedule too tightly. May is rainy and
is also "horsefly month;" Oct. is a good time to visit.

getting there: This is the fun part! When you reserve, Amos
will instruct you when and how to meet the tractor near Las
Horquetas; it pulls a green canvas-covered cart with seats. The

normal transit point is the "casa de Roberto Villalobos," tel. 76–4187, where the Rara Avis office is located. A "Jungle Train" truly worthy of the name, this infamous "tractor from Hell" takes you on a bumping and jarring four-hour ride, traversing only nine km. in the interim. Fording two rivers enroute, you pass slowly-moving panoramas of local life, past hill after rolling hill of sadly deforested terrain, most of it cut down by local farmers who eke out a living by using it for pasture. As an additional bonus, as you ride along you learn how clothes feel while they're in the dryer. Finally, you arrive at El Plástico, a former prison colony site. The name relates to the fact that prisoners slept on the ground outside under plastic tarps. The renovated lodge here formerly housed administrators. The area is surrounded by Volcanoes Barva, Turrialba, Irazú, and Cacho Negro, with the Caribbean coast also visible. Check out the framed portrait of the Patron Saint of the Jungle upstairs. El Plástico and the surrounding 1,400 acre area are owned by SelvaTica (tel. 53–0844). In the dry season, you will lunch here before proceeding; in the wet you'll likely continue on to the waterfall lodge where you'll dine and recuperate. The last stretch of the road is corrugated, ie. the mud has been covered with lines of planks, allowing for a smoother vehicular ride. But the track is suicide for horse hooves, so you'll have to walk (or is it slosh?) the remaining hour if you've come on horseback.

sights: The conception of the modest and innovative biologist Don Perry, the Automated Web for Canopy Exploration (AWCE) is a motor driven cable car that takes two researchers back and forth or up and down in the forest canopy. Before you are permitted on board, you'll have to virtually sign your life away, but you'll find that to be the scariest part of the trip. Engineered by John Williams, the system uses three steel cables which are strung between two trees on opposite sides of a ravine. Hydraulic winches run by a 10 hp motor move the platform either along the cables or up and down. In order to construct it, five men spent over two weeks fighting knee-deep mud. It runs high above the spectacular two-tiered Catarata

Rara Avis which has a swimming hole at its base. A bird-watcher's paradise, Rara Avis has had confirmed sightings of 335 species. Check out the hummingbird feeder as well as the area by the bridge. Other things to revel in include the spectacular collection of butterflies, the beautiful sunsets, the amazing night noises in the forest. You can see the lights of the banana plantations off in the distance on a clear evening.

practicalities: Albergue El Plástico charges $45 pp ($22.50 for student groups). There are four rooms with a total of 10 lower bunks and nine upper bunks, plus shared hot showers and flush toilets. The eight-room Waterfall Lodge can hold up to 32. Each room is equipped with a double bed, a single, and two fold-down bunks. There are hammocks for lounging outside and a reading area upstairs where the pressure lamp attracts an incredibly diverse flying etymology museum every evening. There is a two-night minimum stay. Although large groups may leave at any time, departures for small groups are scheduled every Tues., Fri., and Sunday. Aside from the meals, nothing else is available for sale so anything (including candy or any other snacks) that you might require should be brought with you. The beer, soft drink, and phone concessions belong to the cook. While Rara Avis has a large supply of rubber boots, essential for exploring the reserve, there is no guarantee that a pair will fit you, so you might consider bringing your own. For more information, write Apdo. 8105, 1000 San José or call 53-0844.

La Selva Biological Reserve: Deservedly or not, La Selva is second only to Monteverde as the nation's most famous private natural reserve. Located near the confluence of the Puerto Viejo and Sarapiquí Rivers, this 3,707-acre tract is owned and operated by the Organization for Tropical Studies (OTS), and its main function is to serve as a research station for visiting biologists. In the 1950s tropical biologist Dr. Leslie Holdridge began an experimental farm (*cacao, pejibaye,* and laurel) on the present-day site. In 1960, he sold the farm and the surrounding old growth to the OTS. There are a large number of lowland forest nature trails. On a walk, you might see anything from poison dart frogs to sloths to caimans. With over 100 species of mammals, 400 species of birds, thousands of species of insects, and 2,000 plant species, La Selva could never bore a naturalist. The site of a small field of *cacao* with a rich overstory of shade trees, the 8.7-acre Holridge Arboretum contains more than 240 species, more than two thirds of the native tree species at La Selva; its openness makes it easy to view the tree crowns.

practicalities: Reservations are essential. A day visit is $15. Three meals in the cafeteria and a night in the "rustic" quarters (bunkrooms with shared hotwater bathrooms) cost $70. The hefty fees help support ongoing research. Contact OTS (tel. 676-2050, Apdo. 676, 2050 San Pedro) about overnight stays. For day visits call La Selva directly at 71-6897. Ask about their bus that runs three times a week.

Selva Verde Lodge: Located in Chilamante, five min. W of Puerto Viejo, this attractively designed moderately priced lodge (tel. 71-6459) has a 480-acre forest reserve across the river. The lodge is popular with those who want a more comfortable experience than at Rara Avis. Prices, including meals and tips, range from $42 pp and up. Sarapiquí river trips and other excursions are offered. Write Costa Rican Lodges, Ltd., 3540 NW 13th St., Gainesville, FL 32609 or call (800) 451-7118 or, in FL, (800) 345-7111. You can also eat at El Rancho de Doña Rosa nearby or at Rancho Leona (tel. 71-6312) in La Virgen, 12 km SW of Puerto Viejo, which serves dishes such as eggplant parmesan. A tour company, they arrange kayaking and other trips and have a gift shop.

MUSA: On the R as you approach Puerto Viejo from Horquetas, this female-run cooperative sells local herbs. You can tour their farm and learn about natural remedies.

El Gavilán Lodge: Covering 432 acres, this private reserve opened in 1989. Nestled between the Sarapiquí and the Sucio rivers, it's set in a former cattle ranch, and also has a sister, Oro Verde Station: boat trips between the two are one of the attractions; others are German/Spanish cuisine and an outdoor Jacuzzi surrounded by nature. One-day excursions from San José, including a boat trip on the Sarapiquí or horseback riding, are also available as are river trips to Barra Colorado and white-water kayaking on the Sarapiquí. Write Apdo. 445-Zapote, 2010 San José or call 23–7479 or 53–6540.

THE NORTHWEST

Costa Rica's relatively arid NW is largely contained in the province of Guanacaste, an area quite distinct from the rest of the nation. Its culture is largely Mestizo with some Chorotega customs, such as the digging stick in agriculture and traditional forms of pottery. Another survivor is the *punto guanacasteco* which has become the national dance. Its name comes from the *guanacaste* (earpod) tree that offers shade on the pastures. In 1824, its inhabitants seceded from Nicaragua and elected to join Costa Rica. A sort of late 20th C Central American version of the Wild West, this is indisputably cattle country. And *boyeros,* tenders of oxen, as well as the *sabañeros,* the local cowboys with their ornately decorated saddles, are mythologized folklore figures. Commonly seen in Santa Cruz, Liberia, and Nicoya, bullfights are a confrontation in which the bull is not injured. Flat and dry, with ranches occupying large expanses of former rainforest, this province turns green after the rainy season commences. If you treasure solitude, May and June are really the months to visit Guanacaste. It *is* the rainy season, but it is *also* green, and, as the hotels are practically empty, you can stay in the ones of your choice.

Peninsula de Nicoya: The most popular piece of the province is the Nicoya Peninsula. There are literally dozens of beaches, many of which have seen little in the way of commercial exploitation. The down side is that there are few tourist amenities, the nicest beaches are the most difficult to get to, and most of the coastal villages get buses only once a day—once you miss them, they are gone. The up side is that you can

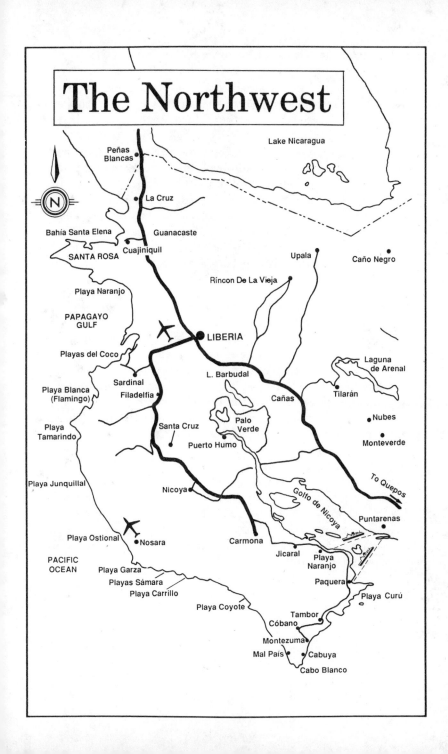

The Northwest

Lake Nicaragua

Peñas Blancas

La Cruz

Guanacaste

Bahía Santa Elena

SANTA ROSA

Cuajiniquil

Upala

Caño Negro

Ríncon De La Vieja

Playa Naranjo

PAPAGAYO GULF

LIBERIA

Playas del Coco

L. Barbudal

Laguna de Arenal

Sardinal

Filadelfia

Cañas

Tilarán

Playa Blanca (Flamingo)

Santa Cruz

Palo Verde

Nubes

Playa Tamarindo

Puerto Humo

Monteverde

Playa Junquillal

Nicoya

To Quepos

Golfo de Nicoya

Puntarenas

Playa Ostional

Nosara

Carmona

Jicaral

Playa Naranjo

PACIFIC OCEAN

Playa Garza

Playas Sámara

Playa Carrillo

Paquera

Playa Curú

Playa Coyote

Tambor

Cóbano

Montezuma

Mal País

Cabuya

Cabo Blanco

really have a place to yourself once you are there, and there are no hawkers, male prostitutes or any of the other problems that plague the beaches of other Third World nations in the Americas. If you find things a bit rough going, keep in mind that gradually roads are getting paved. So what may be a bumpy, dusty ride today, could be a nostalgic memory by your next visit. But the peninsula is not all beaches. There are also sugarcane, teak and pochote (rosewood) plantations; Nicoya is really village country. You can tell when you're in a really small town because there are *no* Chinese restaurants! There are a larger number of thatched-roof dwellings than you might see elsewhere, a reflection both of limited transportation and low income levels.

exploring: A two-lane road mostly paved leads from the Puntarenas ferry terminal through Liberia, and on to Santa Cruz, Nicoya, and Jicaral. There is plenty of bus transport along this route. This is one area where renting a car would definitely be an asset. You might wish to rent a car, tour around a few days and stay in different places; then settle down. One approach is to do a circle, proceeding up via Liberia, then heading to Santa Rosa or Guanacaste park, then over and back through Nicoya. If you pick Tamarindo, Nosara, or Samara, you may have the added advantage of flying back, thus avoiding a somewhat grueling bus ride. Another alternative would be to take the ferries from Playa Naranjo or (if you can get there) from Paquera. Despite the dust and the heat, Nicoya is a cycler's paradise as there are so few cars, and the surroundings are beautiful. Other regional activities include rafting down the slow-moving Corobicí, swimming, diving and sailing, horseback riding, and hiking.

RESERVA BIOLÓGICA DEL BOSQUE NUBOSO DE MONTEVERDE (MONTEVERDE BIOLOGICAL RESERVE)

If you haven't heard the name Monteverde before your arrival in Costa Rica, you certainly will have before long. Although Costa Rica has any number of cloud forests, Monteverde—despite its dusty, winding road—remains both the most accessible and the most developed. The combination of the Quaker colony, the reserve, and years of hype have transformed the area into a major tourist destination. An incredible 12,000 visitors entered the reserve during the first four months of 1990. Don't be under the illusion that Monteverde is a town. It isn't! Monteverde is a community of Quakers who have come here to live apart from the US "civilization." It is ironic that, in doing just that, and in seeking to preserve the cloud forest, they have attracted unwanted attention and loosed the devil of development upon themselves. Unless you have some particular fascination with Quaker-operated dairy farms, there really isn't much to see or do in Monteverde aside from visiting the reserve. And you should keep in mind that it rains a lot: have your umbrella in hand at all times. Although there is talk of opening more reserves, until that materializes, a day or two is sufficient unless you're a research biologist.

getting there: From C. 14, Av. 9, in San José a bus leaves at 2:30 PM on Tues. and Thurs., and at 6:30 AM on Sat.; there's no bus on Fri. A 6:30 AM bus also runs on Sun. during the high season. Call 61–2659 to check the schedule. A daily bus

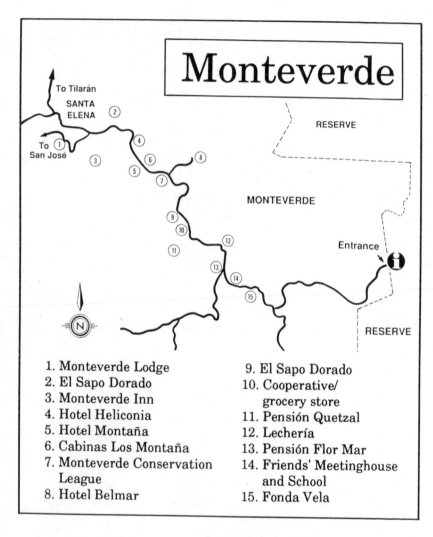

1. Monteverde Lodge
2. El Sapo Dorado
3. Monteverde Inn
4. Hotel Heliconia
5. Hotel Montaña
6. Cabinas Los Montaña
7. Monteverde Conservation
   League
8. Hotel Belmar

9. El Sapo Dorado
10. Cooperative/
    grocery store
11. Pensión Quetzal
12. Lechería
13. Pensión Flor Mar
14. Friends' Meetinghouse
    and School
15. Fonda Vela

(school bus type) operates at 2:15 PM from the bus shelter near
C. 2 in Puntarenas. To meet this bus from San José you must
leave by the 6:30 AM train or take a bus by 11 AM. Another
alternative is to bypass Puntarenas and take a bus from the
Coca Cola terminal heading towards Cañas, Liberia, or Peñas
Blancas. Depart no later than 11:30 AM and ask to be let off
at the Lagarto Junction (km post 149). The Santa Elena bus

passes here at about 3 PM. From here it's a two-hour climb. By car, take the Inter-American Highway (Rte. 1), to the junction at km 149, and then proceed another 32 km (20 mi.) along a dirt road; it may be impassable without a four-wheel drive during portions of the rainy season. Most hotels can arrange van transportation from San José.

services and shopping: Horseback rentals can be found at Meg's Riding Stable (tel. 61–0982) as well as other places; watch for signs. There are no public phones except at the taxi and telephone service up the hill. Check at your hotel to see if the rate is reasonable (one charges as much as 45 cents a minute!) and, if not, go up there or down to Santa Elena. The CASEM gift shop has local crafts and embroidered goods. While the goods may not enchant you that much, depending upon your taste, your purchase does support struggling local craftswomen. Open Mon. to Sat., 8–12, 1–5. There's also a watercolor art gallery and the Hummingbird Gallery, showing photographs, just before the reserve to the L. You may also wish to visit the workshop of musical instrument maker Paul Smith (tel. 61–2551, 44–6990)

orientation: A winding, deforested, and dusty road leads up to the village of Santa Elena past thoroughly deforested terrain. From the town there are two badly rutted roads that lead toward the reserve before merging. The N road passes by the clinic, and the S road passes by Costa Rican Expeditions' Monteverde Lodge. After the merger, the first landmark is El Sapo Dorado to the L. Up the hill, you pass the Heliconia, Monteverde Inn, Manakin, Cabinas Los Piñas, the Monteverde Conservation League, the road veering off to the L, with the gas station and nearby souvenir stand. This leads to Hotel Belmar, the El Bosque, the Co-op, Pensioń Quetzal, the Lechería, Pensioń Flor Mar, the Friend's Meetinghouse and School, the Fonda Vela, the taxi and telephone service, and then, onward and upward, past legendary nature photographers, the Fogdens', estate, to the reserve entrance. Straddling the low continental divide in the Cordillera de Tilarán at the junction of the provinces of Alajuela Guanacaste, and Puntarenas, the reserve ranges from 4,000 to 5,800 feet in elevation. Here, you are about to enter cloud forest country, one of the most luxurious found in all of the Americas. From May to Oct. it rains almost daily.

visiting the reserve: Stop in the visitor's center where you pay, ask your questions, and receive a detailed trail map of the reserve. Students pay $2.50, others $5; Costa Ricans pay around half that. Ask about daily and weekly passes. In addition to the entrance fee, tour groups are now required to pay a user's fee of $10 for each visitor they bring in. A limit of 100 visitors per day is now in force so get here reasonably early during tourist season (mid-Dec. through April) to avoid disappointment. Mysteriously, there are no food or drink facilities on the premises. Guided, four-hour nature walks ($15 including admission) are conducted every morning; proceeds go towards an Environmental Education Fund. Inside the reserve, the steps in part of the area are fashioned from logs covered with netting to prevent slippage. As you go farther out, the trails become less "civilized," and therefore less traveled. It's safe to refill your canteen at either of the two waterfalls.

suggested routing: This depends on your disposition and time requirements. You might go out on the Sendero Nubose, then go down the Sendero Brillante to Marker No. 28 where there's a view at the *ventana* (window) of rainforest stretching off into the distance. Then hike back up the Sendero Pantanoso and along the Sendero Río (with a stop at the gorgeous, two-tiered waterfall) and then back. Two side trails, the Sendero Bosque Eternal and the Sendero George Powell, connect the Sendero Río with the Chomongo.

flora and fauna: Vegetation is profuse and, despite the 300 species of orchids, very green. The 2,500 plant species include 200 kinds of ferns. Much of the canopy vegetation takes its nutrients directly from the mist and dust suffusing the air. The reserve is not all cloud forest: there are relatively dry areas, swamps, and dwarf trees. In addition to the endangered golden toad, there are a wealth of other reptiles and amphibians, 490 species of butterflies, and 100 species of mammals.

sighting a quetzal: If you really *want* to see one, you're

Golfito Airport

Shipwreck Hotel, Playa Cacao

Golfito

Manuel Antonio National Park

likely to be disappointed! One way to ensure sighting one is to visit in the wee morning hours, especially in their nesting months (March-June) when they are most conspicuous. Painted picture signs along the trail demarcate Quetzal Country. In addition to the quetzal, other birds to watch out for include the great green macaw, the ornate hawk-eagle, the bare-necked umbrella bird and the three-wattled bellbird as well as 50 varieties of hummingbirds.

history: Founded in 1951 by Quakers from Alabama seeking a better spot to live after some had been imprisoned for refusing the draft, the Monteverde farming community came in, purchased land, and struggled to establish itself. It discovered cheese which now provides both its principal income and that of the area's numerous Tico dairy farmers. Over the years the colony has grown, and some non-Quakers have settled here as well. The cloud forest reserve was initiated by George and Harriet Powell in March, 1972. Originally 6,200 acres of land were set aside as a reserve, and another 24,700 acres have been added.

Monteverde Conservation League: Attempting to prevent Monteverde from becoming a green, isolated island in a sea of deforestation, this organization hopes to expand the reserve by the end of the century to 30,000 acres. The offices are open weekdays 8:30–12:30, and you can traverse the Sendero de Bajo del Tigre, its private nature trail. The $1.25 admission includes a printed trail guide.

BEN: Already extending over 17,000 acres, El Bosque Eterno de los Niños (BEN, the Children's Rainforest), is perhaps the world's most singular rainforest conservation project, and it is the product of a single, farsighted individual. Teaching in Fagerveig, Sweden, Sharon Kinsman (originally from the State of Maine in the US) was showing slides about the cloud forest to her class when a student volunteered his pocket money to help save rainforest land. The class had soon accumulated funds sufficient to purchase 40 acres; students from the US, UK, and Germany also pitched in, and the preserve continues to grow. Fifty dollars buys an acre so you can earmark any collection and send it care of the Monteverde Conservation League, the Nature Conservancy, or the World Wildlife Fund. In return, you'll receive a letter showing how many acres you've saved.

accommodation: New hotels here are springing up faster than mushrooms after a spring shower, and many of them are quite attractive and tasteful. While you probably won't require reservations off season, they are mandatory during the dry season. The imaginative, moderately-priced Belmar (tel. 61–0011) rises like an Austrian chalet atop a hill. It has comfortable rooms with fine wood finishing and private baths with showers. Write Apdo. 10165, 1000 San José. Open late in 1990, expensive Monteverde Lodge (tel. 61–1157) is run by Costa Rica Expeditions. Inexpensive, Spanish-style Hotel Heliconia (tel. 61–0009) is one of the closest hotels to Santa Elena. Write Apdo. 10165, 1000 San José. About one km off the road to the R, inexpensive Pensión Monteverde Inn (tel. 61–2756) has good scenery. Cabinas Los Piños (61–0905) stand in front of moderately-priced Hotel de Montaña Monteverde whose cabins adjoin a farm and woods. Write Apdo. 70, San José or call (800) 327–4250 in the US. Pensión el Tucan is nearby. Well known, moderately-priced Pensión Quetzal (tel. 61–0955) is also popular. Write Apdo. 10165, 1000 San José. The least expensive place to stay in the reserve's vicinity (less than three km away) is the inexpensive Pensión Flor Mar (tel. 61–0909). Write Apdo. 10165, 1000 San José. Attractive, moderate Fonda Vela (61–2551) is nearest to the reserve. Although the area is damp and cold, you can camp here at moderate cost. Finally, El Sapo Dorado (tel. 61–2654) also has cabins.

food: All of the hotels have restaurants. In addition, the inexpensive El Bosque is open from 12 to 9 daily except Wed. Stella's Bakery has been incorporated in the small, overpriced food shop. If you have wheels, it's much better to buy provisions in Santa Elena. You can visit the Lechería or "Cheese Factory" (open Mon. through Sat. 7:30–12, 1–3:30; Sun. 7:30–12:30) where you can watch the manufacturing process as well as indulge in the nation's tastiest cheese.

Santa Elena: Situated on a ridge towering over the coastal plain this small mountain village is the closest town to Monteverde. With its small church and rusting buses, it takes on a special ambience when the fog rolls in. **practicalities:** All of the places here are low budget and spartan. The most popular place is Pensión Santa Elena. Eat at the El Iman across from the church. They have vegetarian *casados* for $1.50; they also have rooms upstairs, as well as the public telephone franchise. If you wish to stay in this area for a longer period contact Maximo Ramírez (tel. 61–2951) concerning homestays at a ranch 11 km away. You have to ride a horse or hike in; food and accommodation run around $5 pd. Aside from the evening mass at the church complete with guitar and singing, the only entertainment in town is the lively bar at the Taberna Valverde. Next to the entrance here, you might see a horse tethered up next to a sleek silver 4WD Suzuki jeep. Inside, songs ranging from a Spanish version of "My Tutu" to Joe Cocker's remake of "With a Little Help From My Friends" blare over loudspeakers. If you don't dance yourself, have fun just watching the locals work out. El Sapo Dorado is a bit further on up the steep hill and a bit upscale as well. If you're staying in Santa Elena and wish to visit the reserve, you can either walk uphill or take the bus early in the morning when it comes up to the top.

from Monteverde: There's no bus Mon. running from San José to Monteverde. A gravel road runs from Santa Elena to Tilarán. During the school year (Mar.-Nov.), a bus runs daily to Cabeceras (three hrs.) where you can connect to Tilarán. Ask at the Restaurant Iman (tel. 61–1255) about current schedules. The road down is the same one you came up on. With great views of the Gulf of Nicoya and the Nicoya Peninsula, it's a twisting and turning ride down; sit on the L for the best views. Buses to San José run on Tues. through Thurs. at 6:30 AM, on Fri. and Sun. at 3 PM. Runs increase during the dry season. When you wish to leave, you can flag down the bus anywhere from the Lechería on down. For schedules call 61–2659 or 61–1152. A bus runs to Puntarenas at 6 AM daily;

change for San José at the Lagarto junction. From the main highway here, buses run to the NW; the junction for Nicoya (via a ferry crossing of the Río Tempisque) is at km 168. Parque Nacional Barra Honda is enroute.

THE ARENAL REGION

This is an area which is just beginning to be explored by overseas visitors, the entirety of which has been proclaimed a forest reserve on paper but not in practice. It is surrounded by rolling pastures and feeding dairy cows. In the afternoon breezes blow across Lake Arenal—an artificial 82 sq. km (32 sq. mi.) lake, created by damming a river. Enlarged for the construction of a hydroelectric plant, the town of Nuevo Arenal was built by the ICE to resettle inhabitants of the original. The same holds true for Nueva Tronadora, on the other side between San Luis and Río Chaquita. Composed of 50–70% pastureland, the San Carlos area to the SE was developed after the 1963 eruption of Irazú left much of the Meseta Central covered with ash and unsuitable for dairying. Today, many of the farms here have been snatched up by expatriates.

getting here: This is one of the easiest areas to access from either San José or Liberia. You may traverse part of the N central plain, either by driving or riding a bus from Tilarán around Lake Arenal via Fortuna to Ciudad Quesada and returning via Zarcero and Sarchi to San José. Specifics are provided below.

Tilarán: Set high above Guanacaste plain. As you approach from a distance this small, virtually untouristed settlement appears as a white square set amidst rolling green pastureland. A combination of the indigenous words *tilawa* (of many waters) and *tlan* (the spot or the place), the town was a government-planned settlement constructed between 1909–12. It is clean, with a cool breeze that will really be a welcome relief if you're coming from the stifling Guanacaste plains. If you have the time to spare, it's a nice walk up to the cross on the hill overlooking town. A rodeo and livestock show is held here during April.

getting here: Take a bus here from C. 12, Av. 7/9 in San José. Another alternative is to approach via Ciudad Quesada, from Monteverde, or from Cañas.

practicalities: Everything is located on or very near the main square. The nicest low budget accommodation, Cabinas Mary charges $3 s, or $4 pp w/bath. Hotel Grecia charges $2.50 s, $5 db. Hotel Central charges $3–4 pp. Resembling a motel, Cabinas Naralit charges $6 s, $12 db. Probably the plushest accommodation in town, The Spot is $10 s, $20 db. Near the bus station, Cabinas El Sueño (tel. 69–5347) charges $6, $10 d, $3 add'l. Of the many restaurants, the most deluxe is the Catala in The Spot. The El Parque has good service and reasonable prices.

entertainment: For a drink, Maleko's Bar has the best atmosphere. Films are shown at the theater next to The Spot. Lots of heartthrobbin' tambourine beating and chanting at Iglesia Biblical Emanuel. Basketball hoops are in the main square, but you'll have to bring your own nets.

outlying accommodations: Located at the first corner of the lake you come to after leaving town, Mirador Los Lagos has a restaurant and cabinas. A few km. after the relatively affluent village of Arenal, with its gravel streets, is Albergue Arenal (tel. 69–5008, 82–7555). There is a great view of the lake from the lodge which charges YH members $7 pn with breakfast. After passing the Albergue, the rocky gravel road gives way to a paved road. Catering to fishermen (*guapote* heaven!) and naturalists alike, Arenal Lodge is almost at the end of the lake. The closest place to stay to the volcano is at the Arenal Volcano Observatory. Separated from the volcano by the chasm cut by the Río Agua Caliente, this macadamia plantation, owned by the wealthy Aspinwall family, was established as an official research station of the Smithsonian and the University of Costa Rica in 1987. Now open to guests, it offers home-cooked meals and five rooms with private bath and hot water. Good excursions from here include the macadamia farm, a hike up adjacent Cerro Chato with its green-colored crater lake, and across the hardened lava flows. For reservations phone Costa Rica Sun Tours (tel. 55–3518, 55–3418) or write Apdo. 1195, 1250 Escazú.

from Tilarán: On the way down to Cañas are immense ranches with names like "Los Angeles" containing green, almost totally deforested slopes filled with cattle munching their way to the slaughterhouse. Buses for here leave at 5, 6:30, 7:30, 10, 2:30, 3:30. From Cañas, you should change for Liberia. San José buses leave here at 7, 7:45, 2, and 4:55; for Tronadora at 11:30 and 4; for Cabecaras at 10 and 4; for Parcelas at 11:30 and 4; for Puntarenas at 6 and 1; for Libano (abandoned gold mines) at 11:30 and 4; for Guatuso at 12:30; for Arenal at 10, 4, and 10; and for San Carlos at 7 and 12:30. If you're driving to Monteverde, you can take a dirt road that goes via Quebrada Grande.

Tabacón: Named after a large-leaved plant cousin of tobacco, this is one of the world's great hotsprings, across a causeway and past a few km of lush scenery, Tabacón is about four km (2.5 mi.) beyond Lake Arenal. There's a counter-service bar and restaurant. Tables on a series of levels overlook a large swimming pool into which hot mineral water rushes down a chute. A curving water slide (children love it!) leads down to a circular, spoutless Jacuzzi. You can also bathe amidst rocks and steam in the river which runs under the bridge leading to the changing rooms. Admission is $1 adults, 50 cents for children. **getting there:** If you take a morning bus (2.5 hrs, $1.20) from Arenal, you can return in late afternoon. The road is bad, and there are likely to be encounters with cows and brahmin bulls blocking the road.

Volcán Arenal With its sheer, classically-shaped cone, this majestic 5,358-ft. active volcano occasionally rumbles, throwing up ash and rock. It is dangerous and definitely not recommended for climbers. One tourist died and another was severely burned in 1988 climbing its slopes. Arenal is best viewed from a distance at night, when the fiery bursts and shooting molten rocks are visible. Its last eruption, in 1968, eradicated the town of Pueblo Nuevo, killing 78.

La Fortuna: The town closest to Volcán Arenal, this settlement has some modest accommodation including low-budget Hotel La Central (tel. 47–9004), facing the park, and inexpensive Cabinas San Bosco (tel. 47–9050), 200 yards N of the gas station. Eat at El Jardin across the road which has a playground or at La Vaca Muca, three km. W and on the way to the volcano. To get here take the 5:45 AM San Carlos bus from San José or a bus from San Carlos at 6, 9, 1, 3, and 4:30. Two buses, which continue on to Tabacón, arrive at around 8 and 4.

Ciudad Quesada: Situated 48 km N of Naranjo and 95 km from San José, this town (pop. 27,000) is most commonly known as San Carlos because it's near the San Carlos Plains. To get here, take a *directo* (preferably) near-hourly bus (5AM–6PM) from Coca Cola. Another approach is to take the Tilarán-San Carlos bus at 12:30. A cooperative in the park's NW corner sells local arts and crafts. Stay at inexpensive Hotel La Central (tel. 46–0766, 46–0301) or low-budget Hotel El Retiro (tel. 46–0463) both of which are off of the park. Other, cheaper places include the Diana, Lily, Paris, Los Frenandos, Uglade, and La Terminal. Featuring a pool, two children's pools, restaurant, a small lake for fishing and boating, and a roller skating rink, Balneario San Carlos (tel. 46–0747) has inexpensive cabinas with refrigerators and hot water. To get here, follow the signs five blocks NW of the park. Beyond San Carlos, a road runs to Fortuna, in the vicinity of Volcán Arenal, then over the Tilarán range to Arenal Lake and down to the Pan American Highway at Cañas. The ruins of Cutris, a pre-Columbian city, are five km N of Venecia, and an hour's bus ride from San Carlos. From San Carlos, a Río Frio bus leaves at 6, 9, and 3. Buses for Fortuna leave at 6, 9, 1, and 4:30; and buses for Tilarán via Fortuna and Tabacón leave at 6 and 3.

Hotel de Montaña Magil: Located in the Guatuso hills of Guanacaste, the Magil Forest Lodge has rooms with bunk beds, writing desks, and private baths. Boat excursions to Caño Negro are also offered. To get here, take the road from Ciudad Quesada heading towards Florencia. Crossing the Río San Carlos, the road heads for Monterrey and then on to San Rafael de Guatuso. There one crosses the Río Frio on the rope bridge and heads on until Colonia Río Celeste. There is no public transport, and a four-wheel drive vehicle is recommended. Over 250 species of birds and animals such as sloths, tapirs, ocelots, and jaguars are found in the surrounding private preserve. For information contact PCI Tours, 8405 NW 53 St., Ste. A 108, Miami, FL 33166, tel. (305) 594-2149. Or contact Hotel de Montaña Magil (tel. 21-2825, 335991), Apdo. 3404-1000, San José.

El Tucáno Country Club: Set 8 km to the NE of Ciudad Quesada, at Agua Caliente de San Carlos, the large white gates of this expensive inn (tel. 46-1822) open onto immaculate grounds; the premises include saunas, thermal baths, three swimming pools, whirlpools, a small zoo, and a nearby miniature golf course. Packages are available. From here you can drive E 32 km (20 mi.) to Hwy. 9. To the NE you can head towards Puerto Viejo de la Sarapiquí while San José via Heredia is to the S.

Don Charlie's Ranch: About a half-hour from La Fortuna on the recently constructed road between San Ramón de Alajuela and San Carlos, this private nature reserve is after the town of La Tigra. There are cabinas, a children's pool, a small aviary, and creative cooking. Call Vesta Tours (28-9072) for information and reservations.

Zarcero: Famous for its dozens of boxwood hedges which stand in front of the cottage-style church. These are in the shape of animals (bull, rabbit, and an elephant), dancers, ox-carts, an airplane, and a helicopter. The bus (about 2.5 hrs.) leaves from the corner of C. 16 and Av. 3 near Coca Cola daily at 9:15 or you can take any of the hourly San Carlos buses from Coca Cola. Check in the Soda Los Amigos, to the S of the park, for the bus schedules. If you're driving, get off at the Naranjo-Ciudad Quesada exit. If you're in the mood for Italian food, try Restaurant La Montaña just before the town. Roadside stores in the town's vicinity sell good jams and excellent cheeses.

Cañas: At km 188, this farming center marks the turnoff to Tilarán and Lake Arsenal. To get here take one of five buses daily from C. 16, Av. 1/3, San José. Base yourself here for the Palo Verde National Park. Stay at Cabinas Corobicí (US$4 pp), six blocks E from the highway. Other alternatives here include the Cañas, El Corral, Guillén, and Luz.

Finca La Pacifica: This inexpensive Swiss-owned and managed 3,300 acre "centro ecológico" (tel. 69–0050), is located off the E side of the highway six km (four mi.) N of Cañas. Named for the lady who designed the Costa Rican flag, this private reserve has labeled trees, over 225 species of birds, and a pool. All of the hardwood cabinas are equipped with fans and private baths; some also have hot water and kitchens. Many of the photos in Dan Jantzen's classic *Costa Rican Natural History* were taken of captive animals here. Besides the forest reserve, which comprises one third of the area, visitors may tour the farm and the reforestation project. In addition to the reserve's restaurant, Rincón Corobicí is right on the river of the same name, just after the entrance. Write Apdo. 8, 5700 Cañas, Guanacaste.

Reserva Biológica Lomas Barbudal: Meaning "bearded hills," the origin of this reserve's name is obscure. This area was put under protection in 1986, partially because of its value as a watershed; as one might expect there are a number of natural springs. It also serves as a refuge for migrating birds including egrets, herons, and grebes, and 201 species of birds have been identified thus far. There are also over 250 species of solitary bees—which live alone rather than in hives. It also has a number of the extremely rare cannonball trees (*balas de cañón*) whose dangling pungent fruits are hard spherical capsules the size of bowling balls and can number up to 300 per tree. The largest of the 175 tree species present, the sandbox tree lures scarlet macaws from nearby Palo Verde National Park to feed on its fruit. Camping is permitted, and there's a refreshment stand and a swimming hole.

getting there: About three hrs. by car from San José, this biological reserve has its station 15 km (9 mi.) SE of the town of Bagaces, six km (four mi.) from the km 221 marker on the Inter-American Highway; it's just half an hour from Liberia. Four-wheel-drive vehicles are recommended during the rainy season.

practicalities: The Centro Patrimonial de Lomas Barbudal, a visitor and community center, offers information as well as lodging for volunteers. A 9 km trail leads from the northernmost section of the Río Cabuyo to the cannonball valley at the middle SE section of the reserve. Other trails lead to the two small oak forests at the N end of the reserve. Bagaces is an attractive place to base yourself while visiting the reserve. Very basic cabins are available for rent.

LIBERIA

The provincial capital of Guanacaste, Liberia (14,800 pop.) is also its major town. It is clean and attractive with streets shaded by flamboyant trees and more bicycles than cars. There are no street signs so you have to ask directions. The separation from Nicaragua, which was announced in 1814 and finally confirmed by an 1820 plebescite, is celebrated on July 25. Although most areas can be reached by bus, you'll want to have a car if you plan on taking day trips.

getting there: Buses leave from C. 14, A. 1/3 in San José daily at 7, 9, 11:30 and at 1, 4, 6, 8 for the four-hour trip. There are also buses from Av. 3, C. 18/20.

by air: An important new development, the Aeropuerto Llano Grande opened in 1990. It is largely intended to service charter flights.

sights: There's not a lot to do in Liberia except walk around, and many of the houses do have a colonial flavor. The town square features an avant garde Swiss-chalet-shaped church with a large broadcasting antenna. Grackles flock in the trees here at dusk, and a band plays on occasion in the evenings. Located in a very verdant and quiet neighborhood, La Agonía, a white church with a small park in front, dates from the era when the region was still part of Nicaragua. It's the perfect destination for a late afternoon stroll. Also find the recently opened Museo de Liberia and the Museo de Sabañero. If you're heading up for Santa Rosa, you might wish to visit the ecological museum, located in the old customs house once used to check incoming cattle, where volunteers from the UCR are working in conjunction with the NPS to create an ecological museum which will cover the area's life and culture as well as include a plant nursery. It's at Agua Buena, near the turnoff from the Inter-American for Santa Cecilia.

accommodation: Hotel Nuevo Boyeros (tel. 66–0722, 66–0157) has friendly management, comfortable a/c rooms with double beds and cold water showers, two pools surrounded by palm trees, and an outdoor lounge as well as a large dining room. Write Apdo. 85, Liberia, Guanacaste. Inexpensive Hotel El Bramadero (tel. 66–0203, 66–0371), which features a/c or fans, pool, and restaurant, is right at the crossroads across from the Nuevo Boyeros. Write Apdo. 70, Liberia. Located 2.5 blocks to the R from Farmacía Lux in the town's center, inexpensive Hotel La Siesta (tel. 66–0678) has a pool and is quiet. Hotel El Sitio (tel. 66–1211) is on the road towards Nicoya and has a/c and two pools. Write Apdo. 471, 1000 San José. Expensive but well maintained and comfortable Hotel Las Espuelas (tel. 66–0144) has a/c, pool, restaurant, and gift shop. It's about two km before the town on the R as you approach from San José. Write Apdo. 88, Liberia. Nearby La Ronda (tel. 66–0417) is inexpensive and has a pool. You'll need reservations for all of the above during the dry season. The best low-budget

Liberia

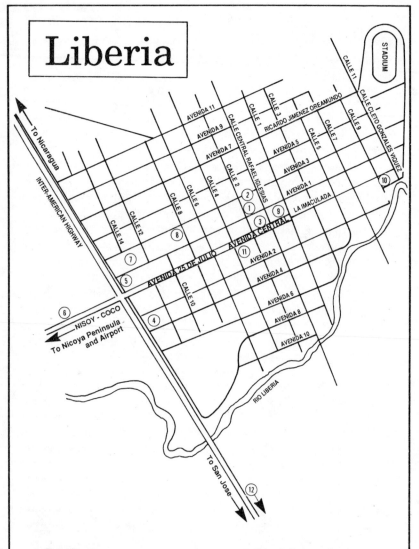

1. Bus Station
2. Central Market
3. Parque Central
4. Hotel Boyeros
5. Hotel El Bramadero
   (Guanacaste Tours,
   Adventure Rent A Car)
6. Restaurante Pokopi/Disco Kuru

7. Hotel Oriental
8. Post Office
9. Cathedral
10. La Agonía
11. Pharmacy
12. To Hotel Las Espuelas

place to stay is probably Hotel Oriental ($4 s, $5 db) which has an inexpensive restaurant in which you might meet a father and daughter cycling on a tandem from Managua to Limón or find a ventriloquist with a loquacious dummy. It's just around the corner from El Bramadero. Other low-budget places include Hotel Costihijo, and Pensión Margarita.

food: Fabrica de Café near the market sells coffee and spices such as *canela* (cinnamon), *nuez moscada* (nutmeg), and *rojo vegetal* (paprika). Panadería Alfa (5AM–9PM) is good for breakfast. Panadería y Repostería Montevidio is just down from the church. There's an excellent *licorera* (liquor store) near the market in Centro Commercial El Bambu. An attractive place to dine is the Jardin de Azucar which has a wide selection and counter service. Two of the numerous Chinese restaurants near the market are Hit Wa and Chop Suey. Others are grouped together in back of the church. Soda La Rueda and Rancho Guayami are pleasant places to eat down the street from the Nuevo Boyeros which has 24-hour service; the expensive but popular Gran China is across from the Boyeros as is Relax-Comidas Rapidas. Located in the Casa de la Cultura, the Museo de Liberia serves *comidas tipicas* on Sat. and Sunday from 10 AM. Restaurante Pokopi is along the road to Santa Cruz.

services and entertainment: There's no branch of the ICT here as yet. With offices in El Bramadero, Adventura Rent A Car (tel. 66–2349) offers car rentals. With offices in the same hotel, Guanacaste Tours (tel. 66–0306), one of the nation's best tour companies, offers tours to the Tamarindo Wildlife Refuge, Santa Rosa, Palo Verde, rodeos and bullfights, and to three Nicoya beaches. Write Apdo. 55, 5000 Liberia. Libreria Arco has great postcards. There's a movie theater and Salon Riabeli has live music on occasion. The trendiest place in town is undoubtedly the Disco Kuru next to the Restaurante Pokopi along the road to Santa Cruz.

events: The *fiestas civicas de canton* are held in the first week in Feb. except during an election year when they are in mid-March. Three events—the Annexation of Guanacaste, Día de

San Santiago, and the *feria ganadera*—are celebrated simultaneously on July 25. Held every July 25, the Anniversary of the Annexation of Guanacaste Province commemorates the province's secession from Nicaragua. The fiesta features folk dancing, marimba bands, horse parades, bullfights, rodeos, cattle shows, and local culinary specialties. The *Semana Cultural* takes place during the first week of Sept. On Dec. 24, the *pasada del niño* (children's parade) takes place.

from Liberia: This is the transport hub of the NW. Buses leave for San José at 4:30, 6, and 7:30, and at 2, 4, and 6. Buses for El Coco beach leave at 5:30, 12:30, and 4:30. Buses depart for Playa Hermosa and Playa Panamá at 11:30, and 5:30; for La Cruz and Peñas Blancas (Santa Rosa and the Nicaraguan border) at 9 and noon and, passing through from San José headed to the same destination, at noon and 5. For Filadelfia, Santa Cruz, and Nicoya buses depart at 5, 6, 7, 8, 8:30, 9, 9:30, 10, 11, noon, 1, 2, 3, 4, 5, 6, 7, and 8:30.

Las Imágenes Biological Station: Located N of Liberia between the Interamerican and Rincón de la Vieja, this 2,470-acre ranch features a working water wheel, batallions of butterflies, birds, and deer. Horseback trips to Rincón de la Vieja and neighboring San Antonio Cattle Ranch are offered. Transportation can be arranged through the Hotel Las Espuelas (tel. 66-0144, 25-3987). Room and board is $50 pp, pd. Write Hotel las Espuelas, Apdo. 88, Liberia, Guanacaste.

PARQUE NACIONAL RINCÓN DE LA VIEJA

One of five active volcanoes in the Guanacaste range, Volcán Rincón de la Vieja, NE of Liberia, rises to 6,216 ft. The mother of 32 small rivers and streams and 16 water-collecting gorges, it is surrounded by a national park which preserves 34,799 acres of terrain including tropical dry forests, bubbling mud pots, steaming vents in the earth, hotsprings, and a whole host of wildlife.

flora and fauna: Found in groves, twisted and aromatic copel clusias delineate the border between the tropical intermediate forest and the volcano's summit. Owing to the presence of four life zones within the park, wildlife is very diverse. There are peccaries, coatis, tapirs, sloths, jaguars, white-faced, spider, and howler monkeys, as well as over 200 species of birds. One of the most eclectic inhabitants is a type of cicada that croaks just like a frog.

history: Its name probably derives from the old lady who once lived there. The region was first explored by German Karl von Seebach in 1864–65. The main crater's last active period was in 1966 when it erupted violently, inundating grazing land on the S slope. Eruptions continued into the next year. It erupted again in 1966–67 and in July 1970.

getting there: There is no public transportation to the park. You must either hitch, hire a taxi, or drive in your own (preferably 4WD) vehicle. The main route to the park (25 km N of town) leaves through Liberia's Barrio Victoria, and it may be possible to get a ride here with the park vehicle; contact the park service in advance. Another route extends off of Guadeloupe, eight km (five mi.) N of Liberia on the Inter-American Highway. It passes through Currubandé and the Guachipelín Hacienda where you can stay at the Albergue or the nearby hotel.

sights: Volcanic ground activity here is paralleled only by places in the Minhasa area of Sulawesi in Indonesia, Java's Bleduk Kuwu, and in some of Japan's national parks. Twelve km (7.5 mi.) from the park headquarters, Las Pailas (the large pans) cover 123 acres. In separate sections semi-enclosed by brush are boiling mud pots, ventholes leaking sulfurous steam, and mud leaping wildly from pits, surrounded by vege-

Rincón de la Vieja
National Park

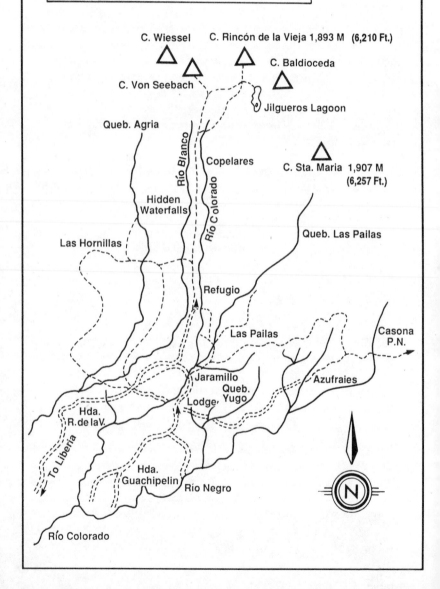

C. Wiessel
C. Rincón de la Vieja 1,893 M (6,210 Ft.)

C. Von Seebach
C. Baldioceda

Jilgueros Lagoon

Queb. Agria

Río Blanco

Copelares

Río Colorado

C. Sta. Maria 1,907 M (6,257 Ft.)

Hidden Waterfalls

Queb. Las Pailas

Las Hornillas

Refugio

Las Pailas

Casona P.N.

Jaramillo

Azufraies

Queb. Yugo

Lodge

Hda. R. de la V.

To Liberia

Hda. Guachipelin

Rio Negro

Río Colorado

N

tation spotted with white mud. At the seven bubbling grey mudholes called Sala de Belleza (Beauty Salon), you may dip in a finger, let the mud cool off a bit, and apply it to your face as a mud pack. Surrounded by wild cherry, Las Hornillas (the kitchen stoves), a group of sulfurous fumaroles, are found on the devastated SW slope. Thermal springs of 42° C (108° F) three km (two mi.) from headquarters, the outdoor hot springs of Loz Azufrales are surrounded by groves of encino trees. Composed of four falls, three of which are more than 230 ft. high, the hidden waterfalls are located on the SW slope of the volcano and have a bathing hole at their base. Set SE of the active crater, the whale-shaped, 15-acre Laguna Jilgueros (Linnet Bird Lagoon) has a small island; quetzals, tapirs, and linnet songbirds inhabit the area.

climbing the volcano: It's about 35 km (22 mi.) to the top and back, which can be done in one day on horseback. Las Espuelas, the park post beyond the mudpots, is the best place to base yourself for a climb. As the routes are not clearly marked and it's easy to become disoriented when fog descends, you may wish to hire a guide. There are two routes, high and low. The high route goes directly to the summit while the low one passes by the hot springs. From the hot springs a meandering cattle path leads to the summit; when in doubt, steer R. This path leads through private property (ask permission) to Las Pailas. From here you climb to Las Espuelas where you should fill your canteens. Camping places are at the tree line; you might wish to stop for the night if it's overcast. It takes a good two hours to the crater's edge and back; be sure to watch the weather because you can easily get lost in the mist. If it's clear you'll find the trip to have been well worthwhile: the summit commands a view that can stretch as far as Lake Nicaragua, taking in the Nica peaks of Concepción and Madera and the Peninsula de Nicoya to the W. **other trails:** The Sendero Bosque Encantado—with a small waterfall, mosses, ferns, and orchids—lives up to its name "enchanted forest."

accommodations: The park's adobe headquarters building has beds for $1; bring a sleeping bag or other warm bedding. Meals are about $7, and horses are rented for $7 ph. Call the park's radio contact number (tel. 69–5598) in advance to make arrangements. Also inquire if transportation is available. Another alternative within the park is to camp, and this is the best way to see wildlife. You can camp by the hot springs or, if you wish to see tapirs and possibly quetzals, by the lagoon; the best months for this are Mar. and April. You may also be able to stay in the old administration building: contact the NPS concerning the current situation. Otherwise you may stay at Albergue Rincón de la Vieja (tel. 66–0473, 53–8431), a small but comfortable 42-bed lodge and cabin run by born-again environmentalist Alvaro Wiessel Baldioceda on his Hacienda Guachipelín. Set in the middle of the estate, you'll meet Alvaro's four cats, three dogs, and toucan. A water-powered turbine provides power. From the lodge, all parts of the park are accessible by horse or on foot. In addition to the prices listed here (with YH member prices in parentheses), Alvaro has a number of packages available. Horses (1–10 hrs. with guide) cost $36/day ($15/day); guide alone is $10/pp, pd ($5/pp. pd); beds are $15 ($8) each; meals are $10 ($6); and RT transport from Liberia is $35 for up to six. Scheduled for opening in Sept. 1991, his 60-room Hotel de Montaña will offer 40 doubles and 20 two-room suites along with two pools and a hot spa. For more information write Apdo. 114, Liberia.

PARQUE NACIONAL SANTA ROSA

Located off the Inter-American Highway some 37 km (23 mi.) N of Liberia, the nation's oldest national park, Santa Rosa was ironically first established to preserve a battlefield. It was here that Costa Ricans battled with William Walker, successfully fending off the attack (see "History" section under Introduction). Featuring dry tropical forests and white sand beaches, the park has two entrances off of the Inter-American Highway.

getting there: Take a La Cruz bus from Liberia. Although there is no door-to-door service, buses to will drop you eight km from the entrance. Take bus to Peñas Blancas from San José (5 and 7:45, C. 16, Av. 3, tel. 55–932) or a La Cruz (not Santa Cruz) bus from Liberia at 5:30, 9:30, or 2 and ask to be dropped at the "entrada a Santa Rosa." From the entrance, you can either walk or hitch a ride (easy during the dry season) for the remaining 7.2 km (4.5 mi.). Another alternative is Geotur, Guanacaste Tours, and Jungle Trails (tel. 55–3486), all of which have tours.

practicalities: The official camping facilities are excellent. As there are fig trees for shade and no mosquitoes, you could sleep outside during the dry season. The *comedor* will provide meals if you order in advance. As tapirs often both bathe and defecate in the same water, it's advisable to carry your own.

flora and fauna: Vegetation varies from pastureland to cactus, from calabash forest to mangrove swamps by the coast. Fauna ranges from green iguanas and ctenosaurs, to sloths, tapirs, and opossums as well as 15 species of bats and 253 species of birds. Some 3,410 species of butterflies and moths are among the 10,000 or so insect varieties. Extraordinarily large populations of crabs live near the coast. The best time and place to see animals is at dawn or dusk during the dry season at the watering holes scattered through the park when the park's residents arrive to drink. Even during the wet season, when the animals have no need to congregate at waterholes, wildlife abounds here. Despite the year's heaviest rainfall, a Sept. visit is a good time to see leatherbacks laying eggs.

sights, beaches, and hiking: You can go as close as you like and as far afield as 20 km (12.4 mi.); try to plan your walks before 8 or after 4. Historic hacienda house Casa Casona (open daily, 8–4) contains a reconstruction of the Battle of Rivas. Its contents include period furniture, farm tools and other accessories. They also have displays of rifles and swords as well as a natural history exhibit. There are also stone corrals which date back more than 300 years. Sendero Indio Desnudo runs in back of the house; animals abound along the trail. In the dry season, wait for their arrival by the water hole near the three rocks with petroglyphs. Over two acres in area, Platanar, a natural lake, is four km N of the Casa Casona. A number of fossils can be found five km upriver from the spot where the road crosses the Río Nisperal. An indigenous rubbish heap with potsherds galore is near the Casa Argelia. The navigable Argelia estuary's birds range from roseate, white, green, and great blue herons to the Mexican tiger bittern. **to the beaches:** This is ideally done over two or three days. You walk along a four-wheel-drive track, ford a stream, and come to a sign marked "La Cuesta," where you descend 2.5 km to the sea, passing a viewpoint called the "Cañon del Tigre." At 66 ft. in elevation, there is a crossroads: the R hand path, El Estero, leads to a picnic area about four km away. The L hand one, La Playa, extends to a Playa Naranjo via a small river (fill your canteens), a salt marsh abounding with waterfowl, and Casa Argelia, a rangers' home and camping area. Despite a population of sandflies and mosquitoes, this six km (four mi.) beach, where leatherbacks nest in Sept., is a splendid place to be. Laguna el Limbo, at its S end, is another area for birdwatching. Isla Peña Bruja, a gigantic rocky refuge for seabirds, lies just offshore. This "witch rock" is legendary in the surfing universe as the spot with "the perfect wave." Continuing to the S, the beach changes to rocky bluffs. To the N, there's an estuary. Crossing it, you follow the trail back inland to the Estero Real picnic area. About four km and two or three hours away, a steep, winding path leads to isolated Nancite beach which is two km long. During the first 3.5 months of 1971, an estimated 288,000 Pacific ridley turtles arrived to nest here. A small stream provides water for camping, but a permit is required.

history: Nationalized in 1966, the area surrounding the historic battle of Rivas was declared a national park. Originally a second and non-contiguous portion of the park, the Murciélago Addition, established in 1979 added 24,700 acres expropriated from ousted Nicaraguan dictator Antonio Somoza, the remainder of the "state within a state" he had built in Guanacaste. In 1987 the Arias administration added the land separating the two parts making the park a total of 122,352 acres. Included in the addition was another historical site: the airstrip used by the CIA to supply the contras.

Sector Murciélago: This addition to the park, comprising some 24,710 acres, is spectacularly scenic. Enter via Cuajinquil, located near Junquillal Recreation Area where there's a locally owned and controlled restaurant. Down a dirt road from there is isolated Playa Junquillal. The ranger station has swimming holes and a camping area. Swim at Playa Blanca on the peninsula's tip. Many of the coves formed by the irregular coastline are excellent for camping.

Parque Nacional Guanacaste: Comprising 210,000 acres, from mangrove swamps at the edge of Santa Elena to cloud forests on the slopes of Volcán Cacao, this park was established in 1989 to protect the migratory paths and animals. The 150,000-acre central area is where biologist Daniel Jantzen hopes to restore the dwindling tropical dry forest.

practicalities: Set amidst cloud forests, Mengo Biological Station has spartan dormitories for $5 pp plus $13 pd for food. Drive from Potrerillos on the Inter-American, then seven km on a dirt road to Quebrada Grande and on another 10 km beyond; it's about an hour by foot or horseback from there. Paths from the station lead to the summit of Volcán Cacao and to Maritza (three hrs. on foot). Also accessible by a four-wheel-drive vehicle road, Maritza ($20 pp, pd for room and board) sits at the base of Volcán Orosí. Featuring around 80 petroglyphs amidst pasture, Llano de los Indios is less than two hours away. To get here drive 15 km/ one hour on a dirt road beginning opposite the Cuajinquil turnoff. You'll have to open and close six barbed wire gates enroute. Located on the Atlantic watershed, splendidly scenic Pitilla Biological Station has spartan dormitories for $5 pp and $13 pd for food; you must have a four-wheel-drive. To get here turn R at a guard station about five min. N of the Cuajinquil turnoff and then go 25 km (15 mi.) on a paved road to Santa Cecelia, then nine km on a dirt road to Esperanza and the station. For information on the park call the Guanacaste Regional Conservation Unit (tel. 69–5598).

Los Inocentes: Another nature preserve molded from a cattle farm, this hacienda is a frequent stopover for tour groups. In addition to horse riding and nature watching on the estate, day trips can be arranged. Room and board in the remodeled hacienda house is about $50 pp, pd. To get here, turn R at a security post five min. N of the Cuajunquil turnoff where the sign reads "Upala" and "Santa Ana;" follow the road for 14.5 km until you see the "Los Inocentes" sign. By bus, disembark at La Cruz and take a taxi; ask if a pickup is possible here when making reservations. Call 39–5484 or write Apdo. 1370, 3000 Heredia.

Isla de Boñanos: Sitting five km (three mi.) offshore from Puerto Soley, SW of La Cruz, this 37-acre reserve protects nesting seabirds: brown pelicans, American oysterbirds, and magnificent frigatebirds. There are no facilities here, and visits are prohibited, but you can observe from offshore.

Refugio Nacional de Fauna Silvestre Caño Negro: Located 124 km (77 mi.) N of Ciudad Quesada and 36 km E of Upala, this 24,633-acre tract is one of the most inaccessible of the nation's wildlife refuges and thus one of the least touristed. A lake covers 1,977 acres, and you need a boat to explore here. Endangered species include crocodiles, ocelots, cougars, and tapirs. Among the ample birdlife is the nation's largest colony of neotropic olivaceous cormorants. Camping is permitted, and there is also limited, low-cost lodging, with boat and horse rentals available. Contact the reserve via the San José radio number (tel. 33–4070) or call 46–1301, the area's public phone. A bus runs daily from Upala. To get there take a direct bus from Av. 5, C. 14 at 2:45. In Upala you can stay in the inexpensive Hotel Rigo, Pensión Isabela, or the Pensión Buena Vista.

THE BEACHES

This is really Guanacaste's claim to fame. Because of the higher comparable airfares, the coast's beaches are not exactly Acapulco. In fact, there are few facilities, and most are difficult to reach. But they are well worth visiting.

Playas del Coco: Although this term refers to all of the beaches in the area, it's commonly used for this particular beach, the major Tico tourist center on Nicoya's coast. Although the place is pleasant enough, there's not much here. Despite its name, there are few palm trees. Off-season and weekdays, it's a very peaceful place. The beach is dramatically set on an extensive horseshoe-shaped bay dotted with gigantic boulders, sailboats, and fishing boats.

accommodations: Most of the accommodation is fairly basic and inexpensive, in keeping with the budgets of the Tico clientele. The Hotel Luna Tica (67–0127) has rooms for $5s, $10d. Similarly priced, the Hotel Anexo Luna Tica is nearby. Lower-priced Cabinas El Coco are directly on the beach. Better to stay at than to eat at, the Casino de Playas has rooms for $5s, $10d, $13 tr, and $15.50 quad. One km from the village, Flor de Itabo (tel. 67–0292, 67–0011) is the classiest joint in the area with a/c and pool. Write Apdo. 32, Playa del Coco. On the road way out of town just past the junction for Hermosa, Cabinas Costa Alegre (tel. 57–1039) has an enormous thatched pavillion restaurant situated next to two adjoining pools. About 2.5 km to the E of Playa del Coco is luxurious Hotel Ocotal (tel. 67–0230) which overlooks a great beach covered with tidal pools. Diving and dive packages (tel. 24–0033) are available. Write Apdo. 1013, 10002, San José or call 800–327–5662 in the US. Right beyond it, Bahía Pez Vela (tel. 21–1586) has cabinas and a small black sand beach.

food: Some of the least expensive and possibly the best places to eat are Soda Teresita and Jardín Tropical. With a friendly and hospitable German expatriate owner, the latter features spaghetti for $1. Across from the tree-lined Guanacaste soccer field is a supermarket.

entertainment: There are a number of discos here. Try the Discoteque Cocomar.

getting there: Bus leaves Liberia at 8 AM, returning from Coco at 3. On the way you pass by the town of Sardinal, a town where the major industry is beef not sardines and where three different styles of commodes (take your pick) stand in a store window across from the *parque*. One bus per day leaves for El Coco from C. 12, Av. 9, San José at 10 AM.

Playa Hermosa: This is much quieter, virtually deserted curved beach just N of Playa del Coco. Several km long, this handsome beach lives up to its name. There are a couple of restaurants and a lady selling coral here; that's about it. Good swimming and water sports. Near the N end, Aqua Sport rents out equipment and runs dives out to the Islas Murciélago. A bus runs from Liberia twice daily. **practicalities:** Surrounded by gardens, inexpensive Cabinas Playa Hermosa (tel. 67–0136) is right on the beach. Write Apdo. 112, Liberia. Overlooking the beach, Hotel Condovac la Costa is the most remote and fully equipped resort imaginable. Non-guests are prohibited from entry, and the only Ticos you'll meet here will be your servants. It's the perfect spot for those who are ignorant about Costa Rica and wish to remain so. If money is no object and your idea of travel is isolated escape this is the place. Call 21–8949 or 33–1862 or write Apdo. 55, Playa González Viquez.

Playa Panamá: Named after the tree, this sweeping, panoramic and very deserted beach looks out onto the Gulf of Papagayo. Get here soon before the planned extensive development materializes. Bars and *pulperías* are at the S end; the best option here is to camp to the N. Playa Nagascola across the bay is an Indian archaeological site; hire a fishing boat to take you across. The Fiesta de Virgen del Mar is held here July 8. Buses depart for Liberia at 6 and 4.

getting here: To get here from Playas del Coco, continue S on 21 to an intersection on the other side of Filadelfia and take the road that heads SW. Or take any bus and get off at Comunidad (also known as Bar Tamarindo) at the intersection of the Liberia-Nicoya road. From there take any bus and get off at Belén, where buses pass at approximately 10:30 and 2:30 for Playas Brasilito and Potrero. Just after the town plaza, a road leads to Huacas where you go R., then R again after about 200 yards to reach Brasilito, Flamingo, Potrero, and Pan de Azúcar. SANSA flies on Mon., Wed. and Fri.

Brasilito: N from Tamarindo across from the lagoon and river mouth, this settlement has a grey sand beach, fishermen, small stores, basic cabinas, and good camping. Luxurious condominium hotel Hacienda Las Palmas (tel. 31–4343) is up on the hill just outside of town. It offers a/c, pool, restaurant, and cable TV. Inexpensive Mi Posada (tel. 68–0953) has basic, clean rooms with private baths. Two buses per day from Santa Cruz run here. Go along the beach half an hour to reach Conchal, a sheltered white sand beach with a huge shell mound. There are no facilities; if you wish to camp here, get water from the local ranch hands.

Playa Flamingo: Just five min. N of Brasilito, this development's real name is Punta Plata. There's no town here and very little shade. The huge, luxurious Flamingo Beach Hotel and Presidential Suites (te. 39–1584), offer facilities including condos with maid and laundry service, car rental, water equipment rentals, pools, boutiques, gourmet restaurants, sportsfishing, private airstrip and marina. Aside from the gourmet hotspots, you can eat at Marie's Restaurant and the Marina Trading Post. A Tralapa bus departs San José daily at 10:30 (C. 20, Av. 3) to begin the six-hour haul.

Playa Portrero: Around the bay from Flamingo and six km from Brasilito, this beach's mainstay is the luxurious Bahía Flamingo Beach Resort (tel. 68–0967). It's spacious with restaurant, pool, and kitchen; rentals include water sports craft, bicycles, and horses. *Norteamericano* video flicks are the rage at night. At the nearby estuary you can see wildlife, and a camping charge of $7 pd., pp allows full use of their facilities. Located three km before the village, Cabinas Cristina (tel. 68–0997) offers three inexpensive units with cooking facilities and refrigerator. A bed and breakfast, Sunset House Inn (tel. 68–0933) overlooks the coast, 2.5 km from Bahía Flamingo.

Playa Pan de Azúcar: Located 15 km (nine mi.) past the turnoff at Huacas, this beach, claimed by the hoteliers to be most beautiful in the nation, provides the scenic backdrop for moderately-priced Hotel Sugar Beach (tel. 68–0959). Facilities include a/c and charter boat rental. The bus runs only as far as Potrero.

Playa Grande: Formally known as Refugio de Fauna Silvestre Tamarindo (Tamarindo National Wildlife Refuge) this 230-ft. wide beach is a nesting site for leatherback turtles from Nov. to Jan. when as many as 200 of these bulky *baulas* may nest; it's also a popular surfing spot. The offshore groves of protected mangroves, which include all five species and occupy the majority of the 1,236-acre reserve, can best be seen by boat. Rent one in Tamarindo. To get here, proceed straight ahead on the road from Huacas in lieu of turning R for Brasilito. There are no buses.

Playa Tamarindo: This small village is developing a resort atmosphere. The area is famous for deep-sea fishing, especially for sailfish and marlin. Playa Grande, across the bay, has been transformed into a wildlife refuge (see above). The prosperity exuded by the resorts here contrasts sharply with the impoverishment of the surrounding countryside. To get to the surrounding beaches, take buses from Villa Real, three km away.

getting there: This resort is 13 km (eight mi.) S of Huacas and is easily reached by public bus year round from San José; it's about an hour from Liberia by car. An Empress Alfaro bus (tel. 22–2750) leaves at 3:30 PM from C. 14, Av. 5 and a Tralapa bus (tel. 21–7202) leaves at 4PM from Av. 3, C. 20. Buses depart Santa Cruz for Tamarindo daily at 10 AM and 3PM. Sansa flies Mon., Wed., and Fri., a flight which continues on to Playa Samara. Most hotels have airport pickup.

accommodation and food: Canadian retirees Al and June run a hotel where you can stay for $10 d in the company of dogs, cats, parrots, and a monkey. There's a TV and use of the kitchen is included. Also ask about their rental apartment. The gate is just S off the beach from Bahía Flamingo. Charging $12 d and $27 for four, Cabinas Pozo Azúl (tel. 68–0147) has fans, hotplates and refrigerators. Fan-equipped Cabinas Zully Mar (tel. 26–4732) charges $12 s and $16 d. Low-budget Pensión Doly ($6 s, $10 db) offers spartan but clean accommodations. Expensive Hotel Tamarindo Diria (tel. 68–0652) offers a/c, tennis, pool, satellite TV, and a restaurant. Write Apdo. 4211, 1000 San José. Fiesta del Mar, a restaurant run by ex-Peace Corp volunteer Denise, features great food, bike rental, pay phone, and other services. On Fri. Bahía Flamingo has a fish special for $1.50. Another place to try is Johan's Belgian Bakery, open 6–5:30.

from Tamarindo: Buses depart for San José at 5:30 and 7AM. For Junquillal, head S 18 km to the crossing "27 de Abril," then turn R onto an unpaved road and proceed 12 km through Paraíso, then turn L.

Playa Junquillal: Another wide, nearly deserted beach and surfing hotspot. Tralapa (tel. 21–7202) runs a direct bus daily at 2 PM. Other buses run from Santa Cruz. You can also take the Tamarindo flight (see above).

practicalities: An exclusive, nature-oriented resort, luxurious Villa Serena (tel. 68–0737) features fans, pool, sauna, tennis, horseback riding, and an extensive videocassette collection. Write Apdo. 17, Santa Cruz, Guanacaste. Moderately-priced Hotel Autumalal (tel. 68–0506) has restaurant, fans, tennis courts, pools, and horses. Least expensive is Hotel Playa Junquillal; they charge campers $4/night for the use of their facilities.

from Junquillal: The direct bus to San José departs at 5 AM. It's possible to continue down the coast all the way to Playa Carrillo, but a 4WD is recommended.

Playa Nosara: The name of this seaside village derives from the river which, in turn, is named after an Indian. The daughter of a chief, Nosara married a young warrior named Curime from another tribe. Despite his outsider status, he was appointed guardian of some gold statues. After another tribe attacked, Nosara slashed her wrists to prevent their capture, and the blood springing from her wrists generated the river. Many retired foreigners live in this area, the peninsula's center of expatriate life. Wildlife abounds—owing both to the nature reserve and a moratorium on hunting that stretches back nearly two decades. Surfers flock to Playa Guiones and to the mouth of the Río Nosara; snorkelers will want to plunge down into the reefs off of Playa Guiones.

accommodations and food: Campers should stay near the restaurant on the Playa Pelada which will supply water. Next to the gas station in the village, low-budget Cabinas Chorotega (tel. 68–0836) supplies fans; baths are shared. Moderately-priced Hotel Playa Nosara (tel. 68–0495) offers a pool, restaurant, and spectacular views of both beaches. Serving soups and sandwiches, the Gilded Iguana (tel. 68–0749) rents moderately-priced, furnished efficiency apartments. The Condominio de las Flores (tel. 68–0696) has two-bedroom, two-bath apartments. For information on weekly or monthly home rentals which include maid service and utilities, call 68–0747. The most popular eating spot with resident expats is La Lechuza, about two km from the beaches towards the village.

Parque Nacional de Fauna Silvestre Ostional: Established to protect this vital nesting site for ridley, leatherback, and green turtles, this 9,692-acre reserve also contains stretches of forest inhabited by coatis, monkeys, kinkajous, and other wildlife. As many as 120,000 ridleys arrive during four- to eight-day stretches between July and Dec.; these are separated by two-week to one-month intervals. In exchange for patrolling the nests, locals here have been granted limited rights to harvest the eggs of the first arrivals. When you visit, report to the turtle cooperative at the beach's upper end. Although there are tours, there are no buses coming here. A bus runs here daily from Santa Cruz at noon during the dry season, it can be approached by road either from Santa Cruz through Marbella (dry season through July or later) or you can drive through a river (dry season only) N from Nosara.

Bahía Garza: With thatched huts and cool sea breezes, expensive Villaggio la Guaria Morada (tel. 68–0784, 33–2476) here offers diving, sportfishing, horseback riding, a restaurant, and a disco. Write Apdo. 860, 1007 C. Colon, San José.

Playa Sámara: With a long grey beach which widens at low tide, this fishing and farming settlement is popular with windurfers and swimmers.; it has more facilities than the average village. To get to adjacent Playa Cangreja, you can walk through the river or ride around the airstrip.

getting here: Empress Alfaro (22–2750, 23–8227, 23–8361) runs direct, six-hour buses daily at noon from Av. 5, C. 14/16. The bus schedule to and from Nicoya varies according to the season. If you're driving from Nosara, you'll have to ford a small river; it's about a 1.5-hour drive direct from Nicoya. SANSA flies on Mon., Wed., and Fri.

accommodation and food: Campers should stay at El Acuario, 100 yards S of the soccer field; a campsite (shower and toilets) is $1. There are a number of hospedajes and cabinas here, of which the most attractive is Hospedaje Yuri. Expensive Hotel Las Brisas del Pacifico (tel. 68–0876, 55–2380) has outstanding German cuisine, fans, pool, Jacuzzi, horseback riding, and watersports equipment. German is also spoken. Write Apdo. 490, 3000 Heredia.

Playa Carrillo: Some five min. by car from Samara, this white sand beach has waters becalmed by the offshore reef. There are spartan, inexpensive cabinas here. Specializing in fishing, the luxury-class Guanamar (tel. 34–1518) offers fans, restaurant, pool, and water excursions including diving. Write Apdo. 1373, 1000 San José. From Carrillo, the road to Hojancha is bad, but it's paved from there to Mansión. If you're traveling S towards Playas Coyote and Caletas, you must ford the Río Ora at high tide.

SANTA CRUZ

Surrounded by hills, this small, very attractive, somnolent town (pop. 15,000) has the ruins of a bell tower from an old church and more greenery than you'll find in all of San José. The brown-colored, traditional Chorotega-style pottery commonly seen here comes from Guaitil, a craft center near Santa Bárbara, 10 km to the E. A bus runs there about every half-hour between 7 and 5.

getting there: Tralapa buses (tel. 21–7202) leave for Santa Cruz from Av. 3, C. 18/20, at 7:30, 2,4, and 5:30. Also try the Alfaro Co. on C. 16, Av., 3/5.

practicalities: Stay at either inexpensive hotels Diriá (tel. 68–0080) or Sharatoga (tel. 68–0011) both of which offer a/c and swimming pools. There are also some low-budget places. Coopetortilla, a former airport hangar converted to restaurant stands three blocks S of the church on the main square. For nightlife check out thatched-roof Salon Palenque Diriá.

festivals and events: The celebration held every Jan. 15 in honor of the Black Christ of Esquipulas includes folk dancing, bullfights, and marimba music. Held every July 25, the Anniversary of the Annexation of Guanacaste Province commemorates the province's secession from Nicaragua. Featured are folk dancing, marimba bands, horse parades, bullfights, rodeos, cattle shows, and local culinary specialties.

from Santa Cruz: A Tamarindo-bound bus departs at 3:30. At 10:15 and 3:30 buses leave for Paraíso, four km from Playa Junquillal. Buses for San José are 4:30, 6:30, 8:30, and 1:30. Call Telephone Tralapala (tel. 21–7202) to confirm schedules. The bus for Tamarindo leaves at 3:30 from the bus stop two blocks W and one block N of the church. For Paraíso (four km from Playa Junquillal) buses leave at 10:15 and 2:30. Another alternative is to hire a taxi to take you out to the beaches.

Nicoya: Located 78 km (48 mi.) from Liberia, this is the last stop in a slow-moving but beautiful bus ride. Named after an indigenous chieftain, this pleasant place (pop. 10,000) is the peninsula's major town—one which makes a good base for exploring the area. Its chief feature is the white colonial Iglesia San Blas which also functions as a religious art museum.

practicalities: Set down the street and across from Coretel, Hotel Ali charges $2.50 pp. Chinese restaurants are grouped around the very verdant main square. Hotel Elegante charges $5.50 d. Next door, airy Pensión Venecia charges 275 s, 450 d. Stop and have a fruit drink along the main square. Slightly upscale, a/c Hotel Jenny (tel. 68-5050) charges $10 s, $13 d. Set at the edge of town, Hotel Curime (tel. 68-5238) has 20 noisily a/c cabins with refrigerator, TV, and separate living area. Write Apdo. 51, Nicoya. Also try inexpensive Los Tinajas (tel. 68-5081). A large number of Chinese restaurants border the square.

Fiesta de la Yeguita: In this event, held on Dec. 12, solemn-faced villagers carry the image of the Virgin of Guadalupe through the streets. To the accompaniment of flute and drums, two dancers, one of whom carries a doll, pass through *La Yeguita*, "the little mare," a hoop with a horse's face. Other festivities include bullfights, fireworks, and band concerts; traditional foods made from corn are dispensed.

from Nicoya: The bus station is at the edge of town. Buses depart for San José at 4:30, 7:30, 9, 12, 2:30, and 4:20. For Liberia buses depart half-hourly or hourly from 4:30 to 7; Playa Naranjo buses leave at 5:15 and 1; Mansíon at 9:30, 11:30, 2:30, 430; Nosara at 1; Sámara at 3; Quebrada Honda at 10 and 3; Cupal at 10 and 3; Belén at 6:30, 12, and 4; La Virginia at 12 and 4; Quirmán at 6 and 12. Juan Diaz at 10 and 2. Playa Parmona at 9:30, 12, and 1. Hojancha at 11:30 and 4:30; Pozo de Agua, Puerto Humo (Palo Verde), and Rosario at 2; and Moracia and Corralillo at 10:45 and 3.

PARQUE NACIONAL BARRA HONDA (BARRA HONDA NATIONAL PARK)

Extending from 50 to 600 ft. into the bowels of the earth, the series of caverns found here are Barra Honda's main attraction. Located 14 km (nine mi.) from Nicoya, water and hiking trails are the only facilities found at this 5,671-acre park. The caverns may be visited only in the company of a ranger guide. The abundance of animals living inside the caves include bats, rats, birds, and sightless salamanders and fish.

getting there: Get here via the Nicoya-Santa Ana bus and the Quebrada Honda bus which passes within one km of the entrance. If driving from San José, take the Tempisque Ferry (if functioning) and then go through Quebrada Honda and Tres Esquinas to get to the park. From Liberia, take Rte. 21 S and turn N just before Mansión. The nearly flat, white peak can be climbed from the NW side. Atop the 1,886-ft. summit, you encounter large numbers of holes in some places as well as reverberating echos. Bordered by whimsically-shaped rock formations, the view from the S edge is extraordinary. A six-km trail also leads to a waterfall graced with formations of calcium carbonate.

history: Because visitors had taken the smell of bat excrement emanating from Pozo Hediondo for sulfur and the whirring of bat wings for volcanic activity, Barra Honda had been mistakenly thought to be a volcano. At the behest of the NPS, the Cave Research Foundation of the US surveyed the caves in Dec. 1973. The results show that these caves date from the Paleocene epoch, some 70 million years ago.

caves: One of the most explored caves with the most numerous and striking formations, La Terciopelo (Fer-de-Lance) is

Playa Espadilla Sur, Manuel Antonio National Park

180 ft. deep. One formation in this cave, known as the organ, produces different musical tones when struck. With a total depth of 590 ft., La Trampa (The Trap) has the steepest dropoff at 171 ft. Containing the largest caverns, it has one whose interior is composed of eye-dazzling pure white calcite. El Perico (The Parakeet) is 69 ft. deep. Home to millions of buzzing bats, Pozo Hediondo (Fetid Pit) sinks to 361 ft., and the Sima Ramón Canela (Ramón Canela Pothole) is 115 ft. deep. Los Seis (The Six) decends for 656 ft. Human remains have been found in Nicoa cave. Santa Ana has small grottos containing intricate and delicate rock formations. There also are amazing collections of stalactites and stalagmites inside. Unusual formations found in the caves include grapes, curtains, fried eggs, pure white chalk flowers and needles.

practicalities: If you wish to go down in the caves, make arrangements a week in advance; no visits are allowed during the rainy season or during Holy Week. While there's no water on the mesa, there is a designated camping site near Terciopelo. Another good spot is in the forest which has streams, but it's 1.5 hours away, and is difficult to find.

PARQUE NACIONAL PALO VERDE (PALO VERDE NATIONAL PARK)

At the head of the Gulf of Nicoya in the "V" formed by the merger of the Río Tempisque with the Bebedero, this park is set amidst limestone hills. Most of the park either floods or turns to swamp during the rainy season with the exception of the limestone outcrops to the N. Although there's a nature trail along a dike, the birds assemble on the riverbanks during the dry season; a boat would be the ideal way to explore. Named after the famous biologist, Refugio de Vida Dr. Rafael Lucas Rodriguez makes up the adjoining jigsaw puzzle piece of this reserve. While this park-and-reserve combo may seem an integral whole to the visitor, confusingly, slightly different rules and regulations apply to the wildlife refuge and to the park (see below).

flora and fauna: Hundreds of different species of waterfowl either migrate here or reside permanently; among these are the rare jabiru stork and all manner of ducks, spoonbills, and herons. At park headquarters you can see the scarlet macaw in a tree pining away for his lost mate (one of the reasons macaws are endangered is that they mate for life). At the waterholes one can observe armadillos, deer, peccaries, howler monkeys, and coatis.

history: The park was originally the S end of an enormous ranch, extending from the Río Tempisque to the slopes of Volcán Miravelles, established by David Russell Stewart in 1923. It was commonly known as Finca Wilson after Stewart's pseudonym. At that time the Organization of Tropical Studies (OTS) chose Palo Verde as the dry forest site for a comparative ecosystem study, a relationship which has continued to this day. The government expropriated the property for ITCO agricultural project in 1975, and the Palo Verde National Wildlife Refuge was created in 1977.

getting there and practicalities: From San José take the 7:30 AM bus (C. 14, Av. 1/3) to Cañas where you transfer to the 11 AM Bebedero bus from the market. From Bebedero you can either hike three hours to the park passing by 15 km (nine mi.) of rice plantations on rough roads, take a taxi or, if you've called ahead by radio (tel. 33-5473), rangers might be able to pick you up. A final alternative instead of staying in the park is to stay in Cañas and drive out daily. Although the ranger's bunkroom is available by reservation, you'll need to bring your own mosquito net. You can also camp at park headquarters.

tours: Guanacaste Tours (tel. 66–0306) operates a fine tour here. After hotel pickup early in the morning, you are speeded to the dock in an a/c bus where you board a boat for the park. Along the river, startled birds fly up as you approach, monkeys roam the trees, crocodiles scurry into the water—leaving a muddy groove in their wake—and sloths may appear. After a picnic lunch ashore, you walk to the administration building. Along the way you might see families of iguanas, and birds. A corral at the center of the administrative area occasionally holds bands of steer who exhibit behavioral patterns reminiscent of some sexually-deprived prison inmates. After hiking around the area, you return to the boat and are treated to a spin past the Isla de Pájaros ("Island of Birds"), which is populated by cormorants, cattle egrets, ibis, and herons.

Refugio de Vida Silvestre Palo Verde: Also known as the Rafael Lucas Rodriguez Caballero Wildlife Reserve, this refuge occupies the N portion of the reserve, containing a variety of habitats ranging from marsh and lagoons to dry forest, evergreen groves, and pasture. Inhabitants include deer, peccaries, white-faced monkeys, waterfowl, and crocodiles. In addition to wildlife, from its trails you can see the adjacent Río Tempisque and Isla de Pájaros, as well as the Tempisque floodplains.

practicalities: At Puerto Humo, across the river from the refuge, there's a makeshift dock with a marooned boat. A pig wanders about in the mud foraging for food. Nearby are ducks, chicken, squatting longhorn steers, and cud-chewing cattle. Ask around about renting a boat here. A bus runs here from Nicoya. Keep in mind that this route is better attempted during the dry season. The other entrance to the refuge is 32 km to the L from the gas station in Bagaces, to the N of Cañas. You may be able to stay at the OTS facility in the reserve if it's not chock-a-block with researchers. They charge $35 pd for room and board. Contact them before your arrival: tel. 676–2050, Apdo. 676, 2050 San Pedro. For more information regarding this reserve and the necessary permit, contact the Departamento de Vida Silvestre, Ministry of Agriculture (tel. 33-8112, C. / 19, Av. Central/2).

Tempisque Ferry: This ferry (20 min.) crosses every hour from 7-6 daily. In recent years, there have been problems with this service. The old ferry, badly in need of replacement, stopped operating in 1990. Unfortunately, the new $500,000 ferry, contracted during the regime of His Excellency Oscar Arias, has too much draft for the shallow route and is incompatible with either of the ferry piers. Check with the ICT to see if the dilemma has been resolved by the time of your visit.

THE SOUTHERN NICOYA PENINSULA

This area is so difficult to reach from the N that it's really almost a separate region; administratively, it's considered part of Puntarenas rather than Guanacaste. Infrequent buses run from Nicoya to Naranjo, but from there to Paquera, you will need your own vehicle. Two ferries, to Naranjo and to Paquera, ply the waters from Puntarenas. Another dead-end route is to take a bus from Jicaral to Playa Coyote a deserted beach with few facilities. This is true horse and cattle country—an area which has a large number of thatched roof homes, where you can watch the monkeys scamper through the trees lining the roadside, and where you can walk miles without seeing a passing vehicle—just as well considering the dust on the roads. This area is slated for development in a big way.

Playa Naranjo: There is no beach and only a small settlement here. But there are a few places to stay in the area. On the edge of town towards Nicoya, the inexpensive Hotel de

Paso (tel. 61-2610) has a/c and fans, pool, and a restaurant. With a shuttle bus that meets the ferry, moderately-priced Hotel Oasis del Pacifico (tel. 61-1555) has fans, restaurants, pool, and some rooms with hot water. Write Apdo. 200, 5400 Puntarenas. For less than $3, you can use their pool, beach, and shower facilities for the day. On the bluff overlooking Bahía Gigante, on the way to Paquera, moderate-expensive Hotel Bahía Gigante (tel. 61-2442), has nature trails, pier, fans, restaurant, horseback riding, and fishing. Write Apdo. 1866, San José.

Paquera: Staying in this town might be an alternative to staying overnight in Puntarenas and catching the 6 AM ferry. However, the ferry terminal is five km from town, and you'll have to squeeze yourself on because the ferry is always packed by the time it passes by. With only two short streets which intersect at right angles, there's not much to do, except perhaps shop for a machete or a saddle in the general store or shoot pool in the bar. Pensión Bengala has small rooms with fans and shared bath for $2.50 pp. The main disadvantage is that they're next to the pool hall. More expensive cabins $6 s or d. More attractive Cabinas "Ginana" (tel. 611444 x 119) are down the road. Their garden restaurant has the most pleasant environment. Salon Bar Indico's posters include Rambo, Bruce Lee, Marilyn Monroe, Judas Priest, Madonna and a chimpanzee soccer star. There are also two other large *salons* as well as another bar.

Refugio Nacional de Vida Silvestre Curú: With three sand beaches, and a wide variety of flora and fauna, this small reserve seems larger than its 85 acres. It is off the main highway between Paquera and Cóbano and you can also visit by boat. Cabins may be available if they are not occupied by researchers. Even if you're only visiting for a day, you should call Doña Julieta at 61-2392 or 61-6392.

Playa Tambor: On the S coast of Nicoya Peninsula, Playa Tambor is a calm black sand beach. Many *norteamericano* retirees have settled in this area. The Cóbano-bound bus goes here from the Paquera ferry terminal. With its own private airstrip, moderately priced Hotel Hacienda La Tambor (tel. 25-9811, 61-2980) offers a restaurant, fans, swimming pools, croquet, birdwatching, horseback riding. Write Apdo. 398, 2050 San Pedro de Montes de Oca. In the village of Tambor on the S rim of Bahía Ballena, Hotel Dos Logartos charges $9s, $12 d for a room with private bath. Eat here or at Christina's. Past Tambor's, the Tango Mar Surf and Saddle Club (tel. 23-1864, 61-2798) has a pool, restaurant, satellite TV, tennis, and fishing or diving gear. Write Apdo. 3877, 1000 San José.

Playa Montezuma: The most popular spot in the region for visitors, this remote area contains some of the nation's finest beaches. With one exception, there's no separate phone, so you must dial 611-1122 (the operator in Cóbano) and ask for the proper extension.

getting there: A ferry (one hour, $1) leaves from Puntarenas to Paquera at 6 and 3:30. A small, packed bus leaves from the ferry landing to Cóbano. At times the two-hour journey may seem so sluggishly interminable that you'll think you're on a slow boat to China. All that's missing are the sails, seas, and salty breeze. From Cóbano you can take a communal taxi, from $1-5 depending upon the number of passengers.

accommodation: The most expensive place to stay also has the most unusual design. Located on the beach about a 15 min. walk from town, Lenny and Patricia have a beautifully designed, hand-crafted cabin overlooking the beach with a refrigerator, stove, sink, toilet, miniature fan, and an exterior cold water shower. A similar two-bedroom cabin is nearby. They charge $40 pd during the dry season and $20 pd during the wet. Weekly rentals are $250 ($150 during the wet). They also have large dome tents available at a cheaper rate. Contact them at El Saño Banana (x272). Proceeding downscale, a/c Hotel Moctezuma Pacifica (x200), located next to the church past Parque Infantil, charges $13 s or d. Past the waterfall to the L, Villa Esmeralda (x262), priced at $6 s and $10 d, has shared bath and fans. They also have a cabina that rents for $20/day. Farthest out of town, Cabinas Karen is undoubtedly the best place to stay. Set back from the beach on her private 170-acre tract of land, it's very basic but reasonable ($3 pp) and beautiful. To stay here contact incredibly sweet-natured Karen, a Danish expatriate who, together with her late husband Olof, was instrumental in establishing the Cabo Blanco reserve. Her house, in which she also has two rooms for rent, is right at the village's entrance. Ask Doña Marta Rodríguez in the house next to Karen's about renting rooms in the Casa Blanca as well as in two other houses. The two lowest-budget places are Pensión Arenas ($2.50 s, $5 d) and Hotel Lucy (x 273, $3.50 s, $5 d). Hotel Montezuma (x 258) charges $3.50 w/o bath, $4.50 w/bath; $7 d. Cabinas Mar y Cielo (x 261) charges $7 s, $14 d for its rooms which include fan and private bath. A final place in town to try is Hotel Chico (tel. 61–2472). Restaurante El Ancla de Oro, well past town on the road to Cabo Blanco, offers inexpensive cabinas or camping.

food: Food here is comparatively expensive, partially because almost everything is brought in, and partially because the locals have found that tourists will pay that much. During the peak season and early in July, a number of small restaurants service Ticos and charge moderate prices. But the rest of the year the least expensive is the small porch-top place to the R way up the hill after the waterfall on the way to Cabo Blanco. El Saño Banana offers vegetarian food; dinners are $4 a feed. That includes admission ($1 otherwise) to the laserdisc cinema, which shows flicks around three nights per week. Marisquería y Soda La Cascada is just to the R of the entrance to the waterfall. A vegetable truck arrives once a week. Finally, the *pulpería* is legendary for overcharging foreigners. They also have a small restaurant so ask before you eat.

sights: The premier attractions of the area are its beaches. From the village, the main ones are all the way to the NE— one after another. Exceptional among the exceptional, Playa Grande appears to stretch on forever. There are two waterfalls. The first is a seemingly interminable walk to the NE past beach after beach. It falls into a cove inaccessible at high tide. The second is off to the R after the bridge on the way to Cabo Blanco to the S. After a short path, you reach the river which you follow along as best you can until the falls come into view.

At their base is a swimming hole. Don't climb this waterfall; an American visitor fell to his death in Jan. 1990.

from Montezuma: It's possible to walk or to ride horses even as far as the Cabo Blanco Biological Reserve which is undoubtedly the best side excursion. A taxi ($10 pp, RT) marked "Cabo Blanco" also makes the trip; the driver will wait for you to return. Unless you have your own vehicle, getting out of Montezuma can be every bit as exhausting as getting in. To meet the morning ferry, take a taxi ($1-5, depending upon the number of people) at 4:30 to Cóbano where you meet the bus at 5 and reach the pier in plenty of time for the 8 AM ferry. Another alternative is to charter a group taxi at 6 all the way to the ferry; this allows you both to sleep later and to enjoy a more comfortable ride. Yes, this is a "democracy," but you'll still have to produce your passport before you can buy a ticket ($1). From the dock in Puntarenas, it's a 10 min. walk to the bus stop.

Reserva Natural Absoluta de Cabo Blanco: One of the most isolated parts of the nation set aside for nature, this 2,896-acre peninsula is chock-a-block with numerous species of evergreen and other trees and wildlife. It is open 8-4. You need either a horse, a four-wheel-drive, or a taxi to get here. No camping is allowed.

flora and fauna: In addition to the large variety of trees, there are innumerable animals ranging from monkeys and anteaters to cougars and jaguars, as well as a great variety of birds. Frogs and toads congregate around a pond in the center of the reserve. A number of small caves also house bats. Tidepools abound at Balsita and Pais beaches: here you can find crabs, starfish, mollusks, and sea cucumbers. Leaving their caves to lay eggs, crabs mass on the beaches from March to June.

history: This "white cape" has been known since the days of the *conquistadores*. Although the reserve was established in 1963, it is the only stretch of wilderness in the nation that had been preserved intact before the creation of the NPS in 1970.

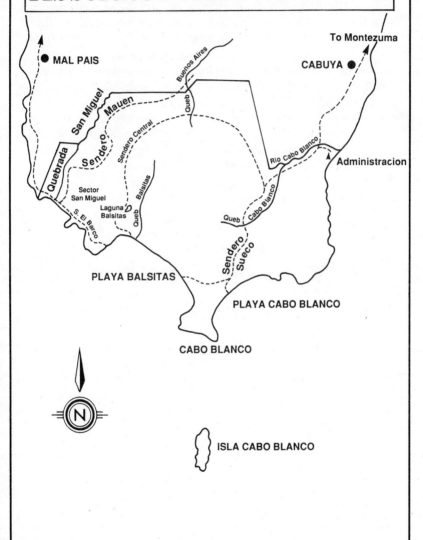

Cabo Blanco Absolute Nature Reserve

This protection was due to the farsighted vision of Olof Wessberg, a Swedish expatriate, who raised the money to save the area; a plaque near the museum memorializes him.

sights: Covered with thousands of seabirds, Cabo Blanco island is around two km from the reserve's S tip. A rocky mound with almost sheer walls, it measures about 1,604 by 259 ft. If you have a boat, it's possible to land on the island and climb to the top by the abandoned lighthouse. At the reserve's tip, the great mass of rocks which gives the reserve its name is 20 million years old. There are magnificent views of the sea and diving birds from the paths which run along the water. On the W side, Playa Balsita is one of the nation's few totally undeveloped beaches. Unfortunately, the sand fleas here make life miserable. Playa Cabo Blanco is on the other side and is linked by a trail. Both are about three hours RT from the ranger station. Ask there if the tidal levels will allow you to return via the beach.

PUNTARENAS TO PANAMA

One of the nation's last frontiers, this area is one of the least explored by visitors. Most head S from Puntarenas to Manuel Antonio and skip the rest. There are the botanical gardens of San Vito, the national parks of Chirripo and Corcovado, and La Amistad, and the surfing hot spot of Pavones to name only a few.

exploring: If you use SANSA, you can fly to Quepos, Palmar Norte, Coto 47, and Golfito. Planes also fly into the Osa Peninsula. Buses run to San Vito and as far S as the Panamanian border. The Inter-American is the best road.

PUNTARENAS

The Pacific coast equivalent of Limón, Puntarenas (pop. 39,000) is a major port town, one which has little to offer the visitor but does serve as a transit point to the Gulf of Nicoya and Nicoya peninsula. Near the major port of Caldera, which nowadays handles the shipping business, the town remains the business center of the western region. On an extended sandspit which gives it its name, the town has universally been described in disparaging terms. While Limón has a funky kind of charm, Puntarenas has largely only filthy funk. Nevertheless, it's not nearly as bad as its detractors make it out to be. Among the pluses are an attractive yacht club and port headquarters as well as a very friendly populace. And, as it is only four blocks wide for most of its length, it's never far from the sea.

getting there: Buses leave from C. 12, Av. 9 in San José every hour from 6 to 6 for the two-hour trip. Trains (four hrs.) leave for Puntarenas from the Ferrocarril Pacifica station (tel. 26–0011, C. 2, Av. 20) at 7 and 3; the Paso Ancho bus runs from the square to the station. Constructed between 1897 and 1910, this railway ran parallel to the old cart road and was electrified in 1926–30. The views and local color make this an unforgettable trip.

history: Founded during the 18th C, Puntarenas was opened to foreign ships in 1814, but few arrived until 1846 when the completion of the cart road opened the coffee export trade. Unattractive because it lacked a natural harbor, proper wharves and customs sheds were constructed only in the 1870s. After its linkage to San José by rail in 1910, it became *the* paramount Pacific lowlands port and commercial center. It suffered considerable damage during the March 1990 quake.

sights: Except for the church, there's not much to see, only the seaside atmosphere to savor. Take a walk along the Paseo de los Turistas, a tree-lined walkway adjoining the beaches. Cruise ships dock at Caldera to the S. **swimming:** Reported by the Ministry of Health to be polluted, the beach here isn't the greatest. To get to the best nearby beach, Playa Doña Ana, take the Mata Limón bus. **Refugio Silvestre Peñas Blancas:** Located NE of the city off the Inter-American Highway, this forest reserve is the most proximate plot of nature. Established to protect valuable watersheds, there are no facilities in this 5,930-acre reserve, but there are a few trails along the Río Jabonal which cuts through its center. Rising from 1,970 to 4,600 ft., its wildlife includes monkeys, racoons, pacas, kinkajous, oppossums, and 70 species of birds.

accommodations: A wide selection is available. However, it can be difficult to find a room on weekends. On the road from San José, moderately-priced and highly attractive Hotel Porto Bello (tel. 61–1322, 61–2122) has a/c, pools, and a restaurant. Write Apdo. 108, 5400 Puntarenas. In the same area and somewhat less expensive, Hotel Colonial (tel. 61–0271) as a/c, pools, tennis, marina, and parking. Write Apdo. 368, 5400 Puntarenas. Another place to stay in the vicinity, the moderately-priced Costa Rica Yacht Club (tel. 23–4224, 61–0874) has a pool. One block N of the microwave tower, inexpensive Hotel Cayuga (tel. 61–0344) is clean and modern with a/c. Write Apdo. 306, 5400 Puntarenas. On the Paseo de los Turistas (Av. 4), inexpensive Hotel Las Hamacas (tel. 61–0398) is the least enchanting of the centrally located hotels. Another inexpensive a/c hotel in the vicinity of the downtown bus stop is the Cayuga (tel. 61–0344). Even cheaper, the a/c Ayi Con is near the market. Near the tip of the peninsula is Hotel Las Brisas (tel. 61–2120), an inexpensive hotel with seaward-facing rooms. Moderately priced Hotel Tioga (tel. 61–0271), located downtown, features a/c, pool, restaurant, and beach umbrellas. One of the most decent inexpensive hotels is Hotel Imperial (tel. 61–0579) facing the water near C. Central. **San Isidro area:** About eight km to the E, Cabinas San Isidro has special rates ($5 pp) for YH members; reserve through the San José YH (tel. 24–4085). Moderately-priced Cabinas los Chalets (tel. 63–0150) here, which feature a pool, are perhaps the plushest. Other inexpensive cabina compounds are in the near vicinity.

food: Open air diners line the beach. Although the area yields a lot of shrimp, most are exported making it expensive locally. Try the Hotel Cayuga downtown or the Hotel Las Brisas near the terminal for Nicoya. The Mandarin is good for Chinese food. You may also eat at any of the town's many inexpensive sodas or in the central market.

tours: The yacht *Calypso* offers day tours stopping at a secluded beach (see "Islas de Tortuga" below) in the Gulf of Nicoya. It brings passengers from San José and departs from the yacht harbor. Taximar, a charter service, takes individuals or groups out to fish or for a cruise.

festivals and events: Beginning on the Sat. nearest July 16, Puntarenas Carnival, the Fiesta of the Virgin of the Sea, commences with a regatta featuring beautifully decorated fishing boats and yachts. The carnival which follows has parades, concerts, dances, sports event, fireworks, and the crowning of the queen.

from Puntarenas: This is the aquatic jumping-off point for Nicoya. For Playa Naranjo, a large vehicular ferryboat (tel. 61–1069) leaves at 7 and 4 daily with additional trips at 11 on Thurs., Sat., and Sun. The launch to Paquera on Nicoya Peninsula leaves from behind the market twice daily except Sun. at 6 and 3 and is met on the other side by a bus to Cóbano. There's also an additional car ferry which departs three times daily for Naranjo; it's met by a bus to Nicoya and Santa Cruz. **by bus:** When returning to San José, even a day or two after a holiday, buses can be crowded, and you may be forced into a lengthy wait in the sun. Buses leave from C. 2, Av. 4, one block E (towards the mainland) from the main square. Other buses leave from the seaside shelter opposite the bus station for San José. These include the Santa Elena bus (near Monteverde) at 2:15, and the Quepos bus at 4 and 2:30; the Barranca bus leaves from the market. **by train:** San José-bound trains depart at 6 and 4 from the terminal three blocks E of the bus station for San José.

THE OFFSHORE ISLANDS

Islas de Tortuga: One of these islands in the Gulf of Nicoya is privately owned and rented out for day use by charter companies. With its own beach and coconut glade, this is the subject of a popular picture-perfect shot: a couple entering a classically beautiful palm grove with a deserted beach to their rear. It is a popular destination for excursions and three or four boats may arrive here almost simultaneously, which can make this private paradise a bit cramped. Of the tour companies operating excursions out here, Calypso Island Tours (tel. 33–3617) is the longest and best established. On their boat, to the accompanying refrains of an elderly marimba player, you cruise past beautifully landscaped islands through the Gulf of Nicoya and on to the Pacific. Food and fruit are served on the way. You are bussed to the embarcation point from San José or you may board in Puntarenas. Buffet lunch (loads of vegetables, beans, *corvina,* and *tortillas*) is served at tables covered with white tablecloths in a shady grove on the beach. The other lines differ mainly in details. Bay Island (tel. 31–2898) has an air conditioned boat with tinted windows, while the *Fantasia* (tel. 55–0791) is geared towards the smaller budget. A catamaran may also be running.

Isla San Lucas: From behind the market on Sun. AM at 9 (arrive early), a boat runs to the prison colony on San Lucas Island where inmates sell crafts. Bring toothpaste, razors, cigarettes, and other such items for trading. Single women can expect to be singled out for attention. You can also spend time out at the beach which faces the polluted bay. The boat returns around 1 or 2.

the biological preserves: One of the nation's most beautiful scenic regions, the Gulf of Nicoya is sprinkled with an array of beautiful glistening, gemlike islands. Rescued from development, the islands of Guayabo and the two Negritos were protected in 1973 and Los Pájaros followed in 1976. Taken together, they cover 363 acres, all featuring thorny *huiscoyol* palms and huge populations of birds. Really just an enormous, almost inaccessible 17-acre rock, Guayabo has over 200 nesting brown pelicans, the largest such colony found in Costa Rica; frigatebirds and brown boobies abound as well. Some 16.5 km (11 mi.) S from Puntarenas, the twin Negritos (198 acres in total area) are separated by the Montagné channel. Both are difficult to get to. Set 13 km (eight mi.) NW of Puntarenas, nine-acre Pájaros shelters a variety of nesting seabird species including the easily-terrorized pelican.

FROM PUNTARENAS HEADING SOUTH

One of the nation's newest roads, the *costanera* runs to the S passing Playa Doña Ana, Mata Limón, Caldera, Playa Táracoles, Playa Herradura, Carara Biological Reserve, Playa Jacó, Esterillos, Quepos, and down to Playa Dominical before cutting inland to San Isidro de General. Between Puntarenas and down the coast to Jacó and beyond there are a number of good surfing beaches.

Doña Ana recreation area: This sheltered beach, along with neighboring Boca Barranca, is popular with surfers. Stay at inexpensive Hotel Río Mar (tel. 63–0158).

Mata Limón: One of the nation's original beach resorts, set on an estuary across from Caldera. Split in half by a river which is crossed by a wooden footbridge with one plank missing, it has two separate entrances along the highway. The train stop is in the N part where there are two older hotels. The S and main part has several cabinas and the Costa El Sol restaurant (tel. 67–4008) where owner Ringo Lastro serves as a one-man tourist information office and booking agent. Check out the wildlife—everything from crocodiles to scarlet macaws—in the mangrove swamps upstream. It may be possible to charter or rent a boat to take you around. Hotel Viña del Mar, Villas Fanny, and Villas America offer basic accommodation. Also try Cabinas Las Santas (tel. 41–0510, 41–0013) which has cooking facilities.

Reserva Biologica Carara: Set near the mouth of the Río Grande de Táracoles and by the Río Turrubales, both of which partially form the park's N boundary, beautiful Carara Biological Reserve preserves what remains of the central Pacific coast's once abundant forests. There are a number of access roads, making for easy hiking, and a trail near the ranger station leads to riverside hot springs. Camping is prohibited.

getting there: Buses between Jacó and San José pass by the entrance. Be sure to ask the driver to let you off. You can also take the Hotel Irazú shuttle which runs to Jacó to the S. The best times to visit are early morning and late afternoon. If you make radio contact (tel. 33–5473, NPS) in advance, a guard may be available to show you around. As Carara is 110 km (68 mi.) from San José, you may wish to base yourself at more proximate Jacó. One really good way to go for the novice is with Geotur (tel. 34–1867). Serge Volio and his group of trained biologists conduct professional tours. You are guided around portions of the reserve in the morning, lunch and relax in Jacó during the hot early afternoon, and then return briefly before going back to San José. The tour leader also packs a scope which enables you to view wildlife much closer than you would be able to otherwise.

flora and fauna: Most of the area's original forest cover and the surrounding ecosystems remain intact. Set in a transition zone between the dry N Pacific and the more humid S, Carara has 61 plant species, six species of palms, and a number of portly trees including the ceiba. Meaning "river of crocodiles" in the Huetar language, presumably after the denizens in the Tarcoles, Carara has a wealth of species, many of which fled from the surrounding terrain after their abode had been transformed into palm oil plantations and become laden with toxic waste. Hummingbirds, toucans, and scarlet macaws number among the avian all stars. Its small lake is almost entirely covered by water hyacinths and other aquatic plants.

history: The reserve's land was originally part of La Coyolar, a 44,478-acre estate founded by Fernando Castro Cervantes.

After his death in 1970, the hacienda was controlled by a foreign corporation until it was expropriated by the government in 1977 as part of an agrarian project for settling landless farmers. The next year 11,600 acres were peeled off to form the reserve.

Playa Herradura: Set three km from the highway, this sheltered black sand beach is the site of one of the most ambitious development projects in Costa Rican history. Hotel Playa Herradura is to have features such as an elaborate water slide, casino, disco, and convention facilities for 350. The Canadian Department of External Affairs has requested the extradition of Kenneth Ford, the entrepreneur behind the project, who is wanted there on charges relating to a $1.5 billion fraud. However, there is no extradition treaty between Canada and Costa Rica. The complex is still scheduled for opening in 1992. Meanwhile, a private campsite, inexpensive cabinas, and a cattle ranch operate here.

Táracoles: An undeveloped fishing village one km from the highway. Set 200 yards from the center, Hotel El Parque charges $8 per room for one to four persons.

Playa Jacó: Largely popularized by the efforts of the Hotel Irazú which opened its Jacó Beach Hotel here, this small settlement has been transformed into a resort village catering to charter tourists. It has one of the nation's famous surfing beaches—one with dangerous rip currents. Only capable swimmers should enter its waters. (If you are caught, don't try to fight a rip current: just swim parallel until you are freed from its grip and then return to shore.) If you're not a surfer, you won't find the rock-laden beach to be particularly attractive and may prefer to hang out by your hotel's pool. The ICT has built a complex near the beach with parking, showers, and lockers. For information on the area, contact the Jacó Chamber of Commerce (tel. 64–3003).

getting there: Buses (tel. 64–3074, 41–5980) leave Coca Cola at 7:30 and 3:30 for the 3.5-hour trip; they're packed on weekends. All buses to and from Quepos also pass by. You can also take the much more expensive Hotel Irazú shuttle (tel. 32–4811) which saves at least an hour and is more comfortable. Buses from Puntarenas depart at 1:30 from near the train station.

accommodation: Next to the main bus stop, Cabinas Antonio (tel. 64–3043) is clean and has fans. On the beach 100 yards from the bus terminal, inexpensive Hotel El Jardín (tel. 64–3050) has a fine restaurant and includes breakfast in its rates. Cousin of the Irazú, expensive Hotel Jacó Beach (tel. 32–5627, 64–3064) has a restaurant, swimming pool, and rents surfboards. It offers a discount for surfers who bring their boards with them. Renting three bedrooms by the week, luxurious Chalets Tangerí (tel. 42–0977) have kitchens and adult and children's pools. Moderately priced Villas Miramar (tel. 64–3003) offers pools, gardens, and kitchens. Cabinas Zabamar (tel. 64–1374) has a pool and refrigerator in the rooms. On the beach, moderately-priced Hotel Cocal (tel. 64–3067) has pools. Attractive and of relatively recent construction, moderately-priced Las Gaviotas (tel. 64–3092) has a pool and rooms with kitchenettes and patios. Inexpensive but dark Cabinas Doña Alice (tel. 25–7132, 64–3165) is between the beach and the Red Cross. Featuring a pool and kitchens, Apartamentos El Mar (tel. 25–7132, 64–3165) are safe and secure. With kitchens as well as a small pool in front of each unit, moderately-priced Cabinas Casas de Playa Mar Sol (tel. 64–3008) are ideal for families. With kitchenettes, a/c, pool, and TV, Hotel Jacofiesta (tel. 64–3147) is one of the best around. Moderate Hotel Club Maraparaíso (tel. 64–3025) has fans, Jacuzzi, pools, and more expensive units with kitchens. Also offering camping ($1 pn), inexpensive Cabinas Madrigal (tel. 64–3230) is somewhat deteriorated. Other places to camp include Tropical Camping and another site near the Maraparaíso.

food: Good places to eat include Cabinas Doña Alice, El Jardín, and Pollo Asado Borinquen. El Bosque is good for breakfast.

from Jacó: Buses run to San José at 5 and 3. Inquire about buses arriving from Quepos to San José or ones running to

Quepos or Puntarenas. It's about a two-hour drive from San José: take the Atenas turnoff on the Puntarenas road. From Puntarenas, it's about an hour on a good road.

QUEPOS AND MANUEL ANTONIO

Sometimes you'll hear it called Quepos, at other times Manuel Antonio. While Quepos refers to the town (8,000 pop.) just before the resort area begins, Manuel Antonio refers to Parque Nacional Manuel Antonio, the national park, as well as the surrounding resort area. There are three major beaches. Two of these, Espadilla del Sur and Playa Manuel Antonio, are more sheltered and offer safer swimming. Taken together, all three measure 1.5 km.

getting there: Buses leave for Quepos from the W end of Coca Cola at 7, 10, 2, and 4. Buses go on to Manuel Antonio from here. Direct buses for Manuel Antonio leave from Coca Cola at 6, 12, and 6. If you're having luggage placed in the baggage compartment, keep an eye out: things have been stolen. Buses from Puntarenas leave at 4:30 and 1:30. SANSA flies daily except Sun. During the tourist season, Sportsfishing Costa Rica (38-2729, 38-2726, 37-5400) runs charter flights to Quepos daily for around $40 pp.

getting around: It's a great area to walk around in, but the roads are very steep. Buses ply regularly back and forth between the terminal in Quepos and the park entrance. Many hotels have shuttle services. The developed portion of the park itself is quite small.

history: This area was first explored by Juan Vásquez de Coronado who found the Quepoa, a subtribe of the Borucas, in

Manuel Antonio

QUEPOS

Playa La Macha

Doctor's Beach
Biesanz Beach

Punta Quepos

Playa La Macha

Rio Naranjo

Manuel
Antonio
National
Park

Playa Espadilla

Islas
Gemelas

Playa
Espadilla
Sur

PACIFIC
OCEAN

Entrance

Administration

Punta Catedral

Isla Olocuita

Playa
Manuel Antonio

Puerto
Escondido

Punta Serrucho

Isla Mogote

1. Cabinas Pedro Miguel
2. Hotel Plinio
3. Bahías
4. Hotel El Lirio
5. Restaurant Barba Roja
6. Hotel Divisamar
7. Hotel La Mariposa

8. Makonda by the Sea
9. Hotel Byblos
10. Hotel Karahe
11. Hotel Arboleda
12. Mar y Sombra
13. Hotel Vela Bar/
 Albergue Costa Linda

residence when he arrived in 1563. These native Americans were largely wiped out in succeeding years from disease, intertribal warfare, and the theft of their lands by the Spaniards. Built by United Fruit in the 1930s, Quepos, like Golfito, was originally laid out as a company town, established to service nearby plantations. As production of African palm oil supplanted bananas during the 1950s after Panama disease had destroyed the banana crop, Quepos became the only town in the country to actually suffer a population *decline* during the last half of the 20th C. The name "Manuel Antonio" for the area to the S, came from a now-vanished memorial plaque to a Spaniard who died during a skirmish with a group of Quepoa. As with Cahuita and (in part) with Tortuguero, Manuel Antonio, the smallest national park, was established for preservation of the offshore marine life which the development of tourism facilities would have finished off. Around a half-century ago, before the government gave it away, it was public land. After an American purchased the area in 1968 and erected iron gates to prevent access by outsiders, the townspeople responded by demolishing them. The municipal government ruled that, as the road was public, barriers could not be erected. Tiring of the problem, he sold the property to a Frenchman in May of 1972 who, in turn, erected concrete barriers to prevent cars from passing. After journalist Miguel Salguero suggested that the park be nationalized, the local community enthusiastically rallied around the cause. The fact that the new owner was working on plans for a resort clinched the matter. The land was expropriated from the owner, and the 1,685-acre park was established in Nov. 1972. It was increased by more than 988 acres in 1980.

sights and hiking: Next to town is an astonishingly wide beach. At low tide you might see a local practicing his karate moves or some expatriate American jocks hauling surfboards out of their 4WDs. It's advisable to avoid swimming at this beach which has been found to be contaminated. Up the hill is the old banana plantation residence compound which now services the palm oil trade. A town within a town, this private estate is pretty amazing. It even has its own cliffside swimming pool complex, perched above the sea, with thatched huts.

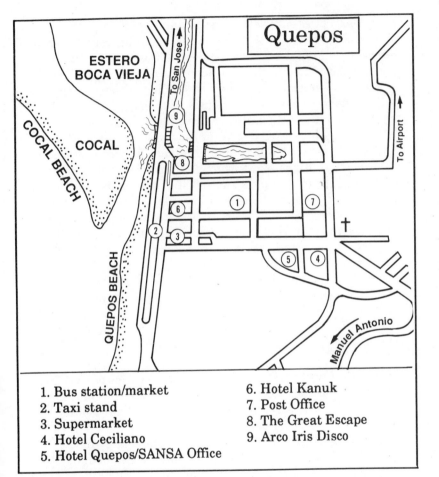

1. Bus station/market
2. Taxi stand
3. Supermarket
4. Hotel Ceciliano
5. Hotel Quepos/SANSA Office
6. Hotel Kanuk
7. Post Office
8. The Great Escape
9. Arco Iris Disco

The area's fishing operation is just across the bridge on the way out of town. Up the hill in Manuel Antonio, a trail leads down to the beach from the Mariposa; continue along the road, turn L by the house just across from the Biesanz cabinas, and then follow the trail down. Another trail goes to the R down to nearly deserted Playa Biesanz which offers good snorkeling.

visiting the park: You must walk through an inlet (or *wade* during the rainy season, when the water may reach waist-level or higher) to get to the entrance. It is open 8–4 and you pay here before proceeding. The first beach, Espadilla del Sur, has a spread of *manzanillo* (machineel) trees. This northernmost beach, curved and rather steep, has large, boulder-like isles just offshore. The next path leads to Cathedral Hill, a detour which offers great views of the surrounding seascape including the 12 offshore cays which are part of the park. An enormous rocky promontory separates the two beaches. It was once an island; over the course of tens of thousands of years, sand deposits have connected it to the mainland—a formation known as a *tambalo*. Right across the way, Playa Manuel Antonio is the best place to stop for a swim. The most beautiful beach, it is calmer with a gentle slope; at low tide, it has a shallow pool on its W side filled with hundreds of multicolored fish. From here, a steep path leads to a *mirador* with a great view. If you proceed ahead across another promotory, past the turnoff for the administrative building, you come to the park's third beach, Puerto Escondido ("Hidden Harbor"). The beach practically disappears during low tide. From here a very deteriorated trail leads across Punta Serrucho to Playita de Boca de Naranjo. **note:** Watch your valuables closely while on these beaches.

flora and fauna: There are at least 138 species of trees here including the *vaco o lechoso* (milk tree) which, when tapped, produces a milky sap that was once an important dietary staple. The nation's only dangerous tree, the *manzanillo* lines the beaches. (See "forbidden fruit" under "Plant Life" in the "Introduction"). A small red mangrove swamp lies behind Espadilla Sur. All told there are 99 mammals (including 59 bats) and some 353 species of birds. The park is one of the best places around to see agoutis, rodents which appear to be a cross between a rabbit and a guinea pig with the mannerisms of a squirrel. During the early morning and late afternoon hours, you can see wildlife as diverse as capuchin, squirrel, or white-faced monkeys, and three-toed sloths. As you proceed along the paths in the park you'll be sure to notice the most ubiquitous wildlife: scores of black-shelled land crabs who smoothly duck into their homes on your approach. With their orange eyes and Chinese-eggplant purple claws, they look like the end product of a hyper-imaginative toddler turned loose with his first set of Crayolas. If cornered, these crustaceans will raise an open claw in defense.

accommodation: Since this is a major tourist area, things tend to be pretty pricey. Proceeding up the hill from Quepos, inexpensive Cabinas Pedro Miguel (tel. 77–0035), one km out, has a pool and a *tipico* restaurant that operates in season. Across the road, Hotel Plinio (tel. 77–0035), whose rates include bed and breakfast, is inexpensive. Surrounded by a private nature reserve, Cabinas el Salto (tel. 77–0130) offers pool, horseback riding, and a bar and restaurant. Write Apdo. 119, Quepos. Expensive Hotel El Lirio (tel. 77–0403) has fans and hot water; breakfast served. Write Apdo. 123, Quepos. Farther up, expensive Hotel Divisamar (tel. 77–0371) has hot water, a/c or fans, restaurant (high season only), and pool. Write Apdo. 82, Quepos. Down the road from the Mariposa, anthropologists and real estate magnates the Biesanzes offer two beautiful cabinas with caretaker; a funicular leads up to them. For information contact agent Robert Benton in Ecazú (tel. 28–9373). Luxury-priced Albergue Turistico El Byblos (tel. 77–0411) has a/c cabins for up to three and pool, restaurant, and hot water. Write Apdo. 15, Quepos. Featuring a garden, fans, refrigerators, and hot plates, El Colibrí (tel. 77–0432) accepts only children over the age of 10. Write Apdo. 94, Quepos. Located off of a dirt road, moderate La Quinta (tel. 77–0434) has rooms with or without kitchenette. Write Apdo. 76, Quepos. Arboleda Beach and Mountain Hotel (tel. 77–0414) has beachfront cabins with bath, fan, and terrace on its 19-acre grounds; surfboard and catamaran rentals are available. Write Apdo. 55, Quepos. Moderate-expensive Apartamentos Costa Verde and Condominios Verde (tel. 23–7946, 77–0584) have kitchens. With a pool and cabins, expensive Karahé (tel. 77–0170) has a restaurant, fans, and refrigerators. Write Apdo. 100, 6350 Quepos. Contact Anita Myketuk (tel. 77–0345) at the Buena Nota near the Karahé Hotel concerning the house she has to rent. Near the Mar y Sombra and right on

Playa Espadilla, Cabinas Ramirez (tel. 77–0510) charges $9 for its fan-equipped cabinas which hold up to four. Equipped with kitchenette and fans, Cabinas Espadilla (tel. 77–0416) charges $14s, $18d. Write Apdo. 30, Heredia. Cabinas Los Almendros (tel. 77–0225) features fans and restaurant; it charges $27 for up to three. Billed as a "youth hostel," low-budget and spartan Costa Linda (tel. 77–0304) has cooking facilities. Vela Bar (tel. 77–0413) has inexpensive and expensive cabinas to its rear; some have balconies, a/c, and kitchens. The Grano de Oro (tel. 77–0578) also has low-budget rooms next to its restaurant. Inexpensive Cabinas Los Almendros (tel 77–0225) are on the L at the road's end. Back on the main road, Hotel Manuel Antonio (tel. 77–0290), with fans and restaurant, charges $16d. Low-budget Cabinas Manuel Antonio (tel. 77–0212, 77–0255) is popular and right on the beach. Because of sustained environmental damage, camping is no longer permitted inside the park, but you can camp on Playa Espadilla. If you're interested in an extended stay, ask around about renting a house.

luxury accommodation: Perched on a hillside with a classic postcard view of Punta Cathedral off in the distance, the Mariposa (tel. 77–0355, 77–0456) is renowned throughout the land for its view and atmosphere. The Spanish-colonial-style hotel centers around its terrace restaurant. A lower level holds a swimming pool and bar. Below in a semicircle are five two-story white houses. Each has two rooms with two beds. Taking a bath in your room here is like bathing in a small garden. The hotel strikes a happy medium between elegant politeness and warm informality. It's named after the butterflies that continued to visit even after the structure was completed. While you're on the premises be sure to check out the early Quepos "weatherstone." Their van offers free shuttle service to and from the SANSA flight as well as to and from the park. Call (800)223–6510, US; (800)268–0424, Canada; or write Apdo. 4, Quepos. The only local place even close to the Mariposa in reputation is the newly opened Makonda By the Sea. For info call 77–0442.

Quepos accommodation: Although you'll be closer to the beaches if you stay up the hill in Manuel Antonio, many visitors prefer Quepos in order to experience its small town flavor. It's generally less expensive for food, better value for lodging, and has a great disco, the Arco Iris. One of the best places to stay is Hotel Ceciliano (tel. 77–0192). Run by friendly, hospitable, and lively Señora Ceciliano, who lives together with her family in the new ultramodern white house next door, this hotel has clean rooms with fans and private bath ($7pp) and other rooms with shared bath ($5pp). Be sure to get a room away from the TV set, and bargain for the large dorm rooms if you come with a group. Just nearby, inexpensive Hotel Quepos (tel. 77–0274) is quite good. Low-budget accommodations ($2.50–$4pp) include Hotel Majestic, Hotel Mar y Luna, Hotel El Malinche (tel. 77–0093), Hotel Ramus (tel. 77–0245), and the Viña del Mar. Apartotel El Coral (a/c) is just around the corner from Hotel Linda Vista. Right at the beginning of the road to Manuel Antonio just past the road sign are Cabinas Grylor (tel. 77–0501) and Cabinas Delcia (tel. 77–0306). The moderate-expensive a/c Hotel Kanuk (tel. 77–0379) is the priciest place in town.

food: The most famous place to eat is the Mariposa where continental breakfast (including coffee, cheese, rolls, and *gallo pinto*) is laid out from 7:30 to 10 daily and a fixed menu dinner, featuring their unique, French-influenced cuisine, is served from 7:30 PM. Call for reservations. They also have *a la carte* food available during the day. Hotel Plinio is renowned for its Italian food and homemade bread. El Byblos rivals the Mariposa for French cuisine. Bahías offers 46 different varieties of cocktails and seafood dishes. Serving US-style food, the Barba Roja bar (opposite the Divisamar) is expensive but popular. Mar y Sombra, set where the road from Quepos meets the beach, is the most reasonably priced of the beachside restaurants; the Del Mar Bar is nearby. The Arboleda has the El Cangrejo snack bar and the Mallorca restaurant. Vela Bar offers vegetarian and seafood specialties.

fishing and tours: An enthusiastic and environmentally conscious expert on local flora and fauna, Leodan Godinez conducts walking tours through private property and then into the park. Starting at dawn, the best time to see local wildlife, he'll pick you up at your hotel and take you along—pointing out animals you might not otherwise see and showing you medicinal herbs, trees, and plants. There's a stop for coffee at the park entrance. On the hike—which is tailored to suit your age, physical condition, and interests—you might see sloths, monkeys, and agoutis. The price is $15 pp ($20 with hotel pickup), and you can make reservations through the Mariposa (tel. 77–0355, 77–0456). For fishing charters, contact Costa Rican Dreams (tel. 77–0592; 39–3387 in San José). Or write Apdo. 79, 4005 San Antonio de Belén, Heredia.

Quepos food: Just across from the bridge heading out of town, Mirador Bahía Azul has moderately-priced seafood. There are any number of other moderately-priced places to eat. The most popular with foreign visitors is The Great Escape. Others include Cafe Triangular, La Torre de Pizza, and a number of places across the bridge. The best dining values are in and around the bus terminal in Quepos.

events: The three-day Fiesta del Mar, Festival of the Sea, takes place around the end of Jan.

vicinity of Quepos: Playa Isla Dama, five km from town, features the Tortuga, a floating bar. Set 14 km (nine mi.) E of Quepos, Isla Cristine (tel. 26–6698 in San José), an island in the Río Naranjo, has very inexpensive camping and reasonable food.

from Quepos: Buses return from Quepos at 5, 8, 2, and 4. Direct buses depart Manuel Antonio at 6, 12, and 5. Buy advance tickets at the bus terminal office which generally closes for lunch between 11 and 1. If you take the San Isidro-bound bus (daily at 5 and 1:30, five hours), you pass through extensive palm oil plantations on the way to Dominical. The ride really gives you a feel for the immense size and range of the industry, the workers and their lifestyle, and the characteristic plantation-style architecture. Bridges on the way bear the imprint of the US Corps of Engineers.

HEADING SOUTH FROM QUEPOS

Naturalistica S.A.: A private nature reserve featuring a 750-acre hacienda with rainforest, lowland forest, pasture, *cacao* plantations and fruit orchards, mangroves, a beach, and an estuary. A variety of tours are available, and accommodation is in the works. Call 71–1903 for information and reservations (24-hour advance notice).

Playa Dominical: Located in a spectacular natural area, this seaside village, 30 km (19 mi.) S of Quepos and 36 km (22 mi.) W of San Isidro, offers basic accommodations. The beach here is beautiful, but rip tides can make it deadly. **practicalities:** About one km S of town are the dilapidated inexpensive Cabinas Costa Brava. Slightly higher priced but very high quality Hotel-Cabinas Punta Dominical (tel. 25–5328) has good food and horse rentals. Priced at $20d, they have four hardwood cabins with private bath and fans. Trips to Isla del Caña can be arranged here. Write Apdo. 196, 8000 San Isidro de General 1200. Less expensive are Cabinas Abavacú which have kitchenettes. Write Apdo. 364, San Isidro de General. There's also other basic accommodation in the village. Eat at Salon el Coco, Rancho Memo, or palm-thatched Soda Laura. **getting there:** Other than the buses from Quepos already mentioned, you can take a Uvita-bound bus from San Isidro at 3 or Quepos-bound buses at 7 or 1:30. Memo's Restaurant (tel. 71–0866) in Dominical has the bus schedules.

Parque Nacional Marina Ballena Uvita: Located to the S of Dominical, this is the nation's newest (and only offshore) reserve. Facilities are limited. Contact the ICT for further information.

GOLFITO

Laid out as a company town, hot and humid Golfito was established to service nearby plantations. After disease and strikes led United Fruit to flee from the Limón area in 1938, the company set up shop in Golfito, literally constructing the town. Approximately 15,000 migrated, and the town bustled with vitality. Prolonged strikes, among other factors, led to the area's abandonment in 1985. The copper sulfides left as residues of pesticides employed by banana cultivation have rendered the soil unsuitable for cultivating anything other than African palms which do not require much labor. While the establishment of the duty free zone has brought about some improvement, it threatens to ruin the languid, seedy atmosphere which gives the town its appeal. With new hotels and restaurants springing up like mushrooms, the area may never be the same again. On weekends, the town now becomes a circus with 28 buses and up to 250 cars besieging the Pueblo Civil. Here people line up for hours at the municipalidad where they receive the chit that entitles them entrance to the Zona Libre. Topping this all off, the area is in the midst of a property boom. Still the town has a truly majestic backdrop, and locals calculate time not in terms of hours but in low and high tide.

getting there: It takes seven hours by bus over the Talamanca mountain range on the Inter-American Highway. Buses (tel. 21–4214) leave from San José (C. 4, Av. 18) at 6:30 and 11. You can also take any Zona Sur bus to Río Claro where you can intercept one of the frequent buses from Villa Neilly. SANSA also flies daily.

sights: There really isn't much to do around the town of Golfito itself. One yachtie pundit tells the story of two decked-to-the-heels *gringas* who walked into Las Gaviotas at Playa Tortugas and asked where the beach was! The honest truth is the nearest beach is two hours away and named after a mosquito. Getting sloshed is more popular than getting splashed: the main pastime in Golfito is sipping beer and bullshitting.

The town is full of characters, including a number of aging retired military expats, and it's a joy to have a drink here. For teetotallers there's not much else to do except take a walk through the Pueblo Civil and on down to the Zona Americana—which now has been retitled the Zona Libre after the duty free zone. Or you can hike up the hill to the facility-free, wet and very wild, wildlife reserve: Refugio de Fauna Silvestre Golfito. This 3,235-acre reserve safeguards the area's water supply. All four types of monkeys reside here as do margays, jaguarundis, agoutis, pacas, and anteaters.

Zona Libre: Costa Rica's answer to the pyramids, this last conception of the Arias Administration opened in April 1990. Created in order to spur business in economically moribund Golfito, the complex has excited enormous controversy—becoming the subject of innumerable banner headlines in the national press. Because San José businesses (mainly the Av. Central crowd) have felt the competitive crunch, they are pushing to have the "duty free" zone's duties pushed upwards from the current 60%, a move which would undoubtedly tranform the complex into another governmental white elephant or, in this case, given the scale of the project, a white mastodon. The original plan was to have visitors spend 72 hours. Since the computerized enforcement mechanisms were not ready, and there were too few hotel rooms to make minimum stays enforceable, the limit was initially waived and will be applied in incremental stages as hotel capacity increases.

accommodations: Because there are only 80 or so hotel rooms, it is impossible to get a room if you arrive on weekends when the consumers converge on the town. While there is no luxury here, the best place to stay is Las Gaviotas (tel. 75–0062) which doubles as a yacht club. The very large, comfortable rooms have a/c and hot water. One low-budget place is Hotel Golfito; get the two rooms which face the water. The Delfina (tel. 75–0043) charges $2.50 pp with shared bath; more expensive rooms have a/c. El Puente (tel. 75–0034) is higher priced but a/c. The Costa Rica Surf has windowless rooms for $4. The low-budget Pensión Familiar is well down the road towards the pier.

food: There are a number of good places to dine within the compact Pueblo Civil. One of the best places is at Louis Brene's Pequeño Restaurant which has large portions, long hours, and good prices. A survivor of the jungles of LA, Louis speaks wonderful English. Other places to try include the Costa Rica Surf, the expensive French-owned Samoa, and Chinese El Uno near the dock.

entertainment: Town really gets lively only on weekends. The Samoa has a disco with live entertainment at times; another disco is the Palanque, and the Club Latino is down the road.

getting around: Buses run from Las Gaviotas through to the duty free port and airport. Shared taxis are 50 cents a ride. Water taxis run to outlying destinations.

from Golfito: San José buses leave from near the ferry terminal. SANSA flights (tel. 75-0303) depart from the airfield. If they tell you the flight is full, it's well worthwhile to show up; two seats are always held until the last minute for passengers coming from Puerto Jiménez, and chances are that you'll get on. For Puerto Jinénez, the gateway to Corcovado, you can take the ferry next to El Uno, or fly for $7.50 pp.

VICINITY OF GOLFITO

Playa Cacao: This is the ultimate in offbeat. Boisterous one-legged Captain Tom arrived nearly four decades ago aboard his aging converted sub chaser. At that time both he and the boat were in "a state of emergency." The remains of his boat can be seen nearby and, by comparison, the Captain is in just dandy shape. He'll happily show you his visitor books and talk about how he bought the land for $30 as well as the adven-

Food vendor

Waterway to Tortuguero

Train to Limón

tures he's been through since then. He'll tell you how his house was destroyed by an earthquake in 1983, and you may read and sign his visitor books. Since this is the closest swimmable area to Golfito, it's popular with locals who come to eat the Captain's legendary "jungleburgers." Retired devout American Legionaire Dwight Haskins has a bar here as well. The adventurous may want to stay in the Captain's Shipwreck Hotel ($7 pp). In this salvaged ship, Tom has installed four doubles and a single. There's little privacy, you must share the Captain's toilet facilities and wash in the "jungle shower" (a creek), but there are cooking facilities and you can fish off one side of the boat without getting wet in the rain! A generator operates from 4 to 8 PM daily. To get here, you must take a water taxi (about 20 min.), or in the dry season brave the "road" that was built in 1968.

Zancudo: Aptly named after the mosquito, this large beach is $30 RT by water taxi. Otherwise, you can take the bus to Ciudad Neilly and then a bus at 1 PM to the beach. Basic, inexpensive accommodation is available at the Sol de Mar or at Roy's.

Pavones: A legendary surfing spot, and that is the only reason to go here. Water taxis cost $60 RT or you can take the daily bus at 2 PM. Very basic accommodation and food are available.

Tiskita Lodge: The brainchild of owner Peter Aspinwall, this private 400-acre farm has an extensive 37-acre fruit tree orchard with over 100 varieties of fruit—from guava to durian to starfruit and guanabana—available. And of course the presence of these fruit trees insures superb birdwatching in the area, as well as luring animals from the surrounding primary forest. It's necessary to fly or charter a taxi to get here. It's an expensive place to visit; packages are available. Write Costa Rica Sun Tours, Apdo. 1195, 1250 Escazú (tel. 55–3418 or 55–3518).

Golfito Sailfish Rancho: Operated by the same owners as Parismina Tarpon Rancho and with similar policies. Write

Downtown Limón

PO Box 290190, San Antonio, TX 78280 or call (800)531–7332 or (512)492–5517.

Las Cruces (Wilson Botanical Gardens): Founded by Robert and Catherine Wilson in 1963 with the intention of establishing a world-class collection of tropical plants as a Noah's Ark-style seed bank, this beautifully landscaped garden preserve is maintained by the Organization for Tropical Studies. Here are 30 acres of gardens bordered by 358 acres of forest reserve including extensive trails (five main and six secondary) and, with over 1,000 *genera* of plants from some 200 families, one of the world's finest collections of bromeliads and other tropical flora—including orchids, ferns, heliconias, marantas, and over 100 species of palms. In 1983, UNESCO designated the gardens, along with the adjacent reserve, as part of the Amistad Biosphere Reserve which borders the national park of the same name. There's also an organic vegetable garden which uses regenerative and sustainable methods of growing vegetables.

getting here: Take the San Vito bus from San José (six hrs.) and then another bus or taxi for the last six km. By car, take the Inter-American S past Buenos Aires to the San Vito road marker. From Golfito, you take the Ciudad Neilly bus or drive there, turning N on Rte. 16 to Agua Buena.

practicalities: Day visits ($15, free on Sun.) include lunch in the price. For day visit reservations or for information on group tours call 77–3278 or write: Robert and Catherine Wilson Botanical Garden, Apdo. 73, 77–3278 San Vito de Jaba. For reservations to stay in the dormitory ($40 pp, pd room and board), contact the OTS (tel. 36–6696), Apdo. 676, 2050 San Pedro.

San Vito de Java: This town (pop. 37,000) was settled by Italian immigrants and originally dependent on coffee growing. Located in the fertile Cotos Brus Valley, early settlers hoped that this town would be on the Pan-American Highway, thus providing access to plantations in Costa Rica and Panama where there was demand for fresh fruit, vegetables, and dairy products. Stay in inexpensive Cabinas Las Mirlas (tel. 77–3054), low-budget Hotel Pitier (tel. 77–3006), or El Ceibo (tel. 77–3025).

getting there: Direct buses (tel. 23–4975) leave at 7 and 2 from Av. 18, C. 13 near Plaza Víquez in San José. Numerous buses also run from San Isidro and Golfito; the US-built road from San Vito to Ciudad Neilly was constructed in 1945 because of its strategic proximity to the Panama Canal.

OSA AND PARQUE NACIONAL CORCOVADO

Owing to its isolation, biological diversity, and its large tracts of old growth forest and other undisturbed nature, this peninsula is one of Costa Rica's most important natural areas. In the heart of the SW's Golfo Dulce region, it has extensive stretches of mangroves to the N, a large forested plateau on its W flank, and a huge lagoon in the center which is nearly surrounded by mountains. In addition there are estuaries, wetlands, rocky headlands, rivers, waterfalls, and beaches. Its lowland forest, the area's largest, is the last bastion of indigenous plants and animals in the nation's SW. Surrounded by jolillo palms, 2,471-acre Laguna Corcovado, a herbaceous freshwater marsh in the lowlands' center, provides a home for waterfowl, reptiles, and amphibians.

getting there: There are a number of ways to enter both the peninsula and the park, and the way you choose will depend upon your time, finances, and energy. **Golfito–Rincon–Corcovado:** Only a madman would take this route, but you'll

want to know about it. Inquire in Golfito concerning boats to
the small settlement of Rincon. If you can get one, it's a 12-
hour trip from there to Rancho Quemado and about three additional hours to the Río Drake where you can swim and relax.
From there the next town is Drake, and then its another 90
min. to Agujitas. If you can't then get a ride with a boat to the
park station of San Pedrillo (one hr.), you must walk another
20 km (12 mi.). In all of these towns, only the most basic provisions, along with a small selection of fruits, is available. It
takes 2.5 hrs. down the beach to Llorona. From here there are
two trails: one goes to a waterfall and another (2–3 hrs.) goes
to a shelter near Laguna Corcovado. Another alternative is to
walk along the beach four hrs. to Sirena. You must wade
through three sandfly-infested rivers (Llorona, Corcovado, and
Sirena) that can be crossed only at high tide and, as there's no
shade, the sun beats down unmercifully. Be sure to check tide
tables before departing! You must put your pack on your head,
cross the river naked, all the while scratching sand fleas and
watching out for the small sharks that reside at river cross-
ings. **Golfito–Puerto Jiménez–Corcovado:** From Golfito take
the daily noon boat (1.5 hrs.) to Puerto Jiménez. (There's also a
bus from Ciudad Neilly at 7 and 3 which you can intercept on
the Inter-American). Stay at inexpensive a/c Cabinas Man-
glares or at less expensive Cabinas Marcelina, Brisas del Mar,
and Pensión Quintero among other places. A morning bus (at
5:30) and trucks (one hr.) run regularly to the small village of
La Palma. From Sirena it's about three hrs. to the NE entrance at Los Patos and then another four to six hrs. by trail to
Sirena. From there, you can proceed to Playa Madrigal (four
hrs.) and then camp at La Leona where it's an eight-hr. hike
back down to Puerto Jiménez. Every Mon. and Sat. a four-
wheel-drive taxi runs from Puerto Jiménez S along the coast
to Carata near La Leona. Taxis can also be chartered through
the park office. **by plane:** Aeronaves de Costa Rica (tel. 21-
4214) offers charter planes that will fly you in to Sirena from
Golfito or San José. **other routes:** Other alternatives are to
fly in, entering at Drake's Bay or Marenco Biological Station
on the N side of Osa Peninsula. Jungle Trails (tel. 55-3486)
also offers tours.

preparations: It's better if you can bring your own food as you'll be less of a burden for the park personnel. While a tent is not mandatory, a mosquito net and spray-on insect repellent are. It's too hot and humid for rain gear, but an umbrella is another must as are rubber boots. Be warned that the chiggers and sand fleas are ferocious so take appropriate precautions! Be aware that all of the roads become impassable after a rain; 4WD vehicles here often use snow chains. If you're planning to fly into the park, you must call the ranger station in advance (78-5036) and inform them of your arrival and length of stay. Its headquarters are now in Puerto Jiménez.

history: The idea of turning Corcovado into a national park was put forward in 1970. However, factors such as the area's remoteness, the creation of other new parks, and the lack of finances in the NPS prevented its realization. As the decade wore on, more and more families began to settle in the peninsula, hunters were decimating the wildlife (in one instance shooting an entire herd of peccaries just for amusement) and one lumber company, which owned a major section of the future park at that time, cemented a logging partnership agreement with some Japanese companies. The original 88,956-acre park was created in Oct. 1975; 19,113 acres consisting of rugged highlands in the peninsula's center, were added in 1980 making a total of 108,069 acres.

flora and fauna: Eight different habitats have been identified, and the park has the nation's greatest wealth and variety of wildlife and the richest biological zones; there are 13 major ecosystems within the park. Forests here are the prototypical rainforest: a multitude of species, and tall trees with spectacular buttresses and large woody lianas. In each of the 13 distinct habitats, there are innumerable species. Areas of high foliage density, such as the Llorana Plateau, contain over 100 tree species per acre. In places, canopy height reaches 180–262 ft., the highest trees in the nation. The park's largest tree is a silk cotton located near the center of the coast. With a large number of endemic species, the park is also fauna rich. In an area only half the size of Yosemite National Park, there are

285 species of birds (more than in the US and Canada combined), 139 species of mammals, 16 species of freshwater fish, and 116 reptiles and amphibians. It may be the last remaining Costa Rican habitat of the severely endangered harpy eagle. Corcovado offers a visual feast of wildlife. Among the other endangered species residing here are squirrel monkeys, jaguars, and scarlet macaws.

two leggers: Former inhabitants of the park, the *oreros* (gold panners), once resided in the river, ekeing out a living. After environmentalists protested that silt generated from their panning was filling up the lagoon, they were legislated out of existence, but were promised recompense. When this was not forthcoming, they arrived en masse in San José and camped out in the parks until payment was made. Panning continues today on the park's outskirts, and, despite the destruction it causes, the government has taken no action against it. Another conflict is between squatters, who see the park's lands as the last frontier. Fundación Neotrópica is attempting to deal with this threat through its BOSCOSA project which attempts to find positive, productive, and ecologically sustainable solutions to this dilemma.

Sirena and vicinity: Stay either in the attic of the ranger station or pitch a tent down below it. Expect to pay $3 per meal. Be prepared to meet some of the local inhabitants: giant cockroaches, chiggers, and ferocious, insatiable mosquitos. Horses can be hired here, meals are available, and there are laundry facilities. Although much of the land around the station is secondary growth, there's a path running through old growth to the Río Claro. Since it's ringed by swamps, Laguna Corcovado is accessible only by boat. There's one path, marked "Quebrada Camaronero," that heads towards it.

Marenco Biological Station: Remote and roadless, this is one of the nation's foremost privately-established reserves, originally established to provide a base for biological researchers exloring the wonders of the peninsula. Covering 1,250 acres, its bamboo and wood bungalows are on a hill and have a capacity of 40. A "rainforest trail" runs behind the dining hall. It leads to the Río Claro and then along the Beach Trail and back to the main facilities. Optional tours include day visits to Corcovado, Isla de Caño, and the Río Claro. The way to get here is by chartered plane or by land and boat. Packages are available. Call 21–1594 or write Apdo. 4025, 1000 San José. Their offices are upstairs at Edificio Cristal, Av. 1, Ca 1/3.

Drake's Bay Wilderness Camp: About 10 minutes N of Marenco by boat, this lodge offers a number of guided tours. Charter flights and packages are available. Call 71–2436 or 20–2121 or write Apdo. 98, 8150 Palmar Norte, Osa.

Reserva Biológica Isla de Caño: Located 20 km (12 mi.) off the coast, this 480-acre park rises 296 ft. above sea level. Most of the 740-acre island is covered by virgin forests, and it is thought that the island was an indigenous cemetery and, later, a pirate hideaway. Some go so far as to claim that it was the inspiration for Robert Louis Stevenson's Treasure Island. Although the tombs have been looted, perfectly fashioned stone spheres remind you of their presence. Its central plateau floods during the rainy season. Nearly transparent water surrounds the high cliffs and miniature (100 yards or so) beaches. In 1973, the island was rented out to a foreign firm which intended to start tourist development, The planned wharves and marinas would have devastated the surrounding coral reefs, the largest colony on the Pacific coast. In 1976, this island was declared part of Corcovado National Park, and it gained independent status in 1978. The only large animals are feral pigs.

Río Sierpe Lodge: A deep sea and tidal basin fishing lodge located in the NE section of the peninsula. Scuba and snorkeling day trips to Isla de Caño can be arranged as can two-day RT cruises to Isla del Coco. Contact Apdo. 6635, 1000 San José or call 22–2297.

getting there: Unless you have your own boat, a tour or charter is the only way.

Parque Nacional Isla del Coco: Blessed with abundant springs and waterfalls, this steep and rocky island of volcanic

origin can be accessed only at Chatham and Wafer bays. By
the small stream at smaller, Rocky Chatham—named after an
18th C. expeditionary ship—there are a number of rocks inscribed with the names of arriving mariners. Wafer, a few km
to the W, is named after a 17th C actor, physician, and writer
who kept company with pirates. Located about 500 km (311
mi.) off the Pacific coast, the island covers 24 sq. km. (9.3 sq.
mi.). As one might guess, it was named because of the abundance of its coconuts. In reality, however, coconuts are few and
far between with most of the palms belonging to the species
Rooseveltia franklinia (named after FDR who visited the island four times). The trees appear to be coconut palms when
viewed from a distance. The island gets 276 in. of rainfall per
year; its highest point is 2,080-ft. Cerro Iglesias. Be careful
while visiting here. A tourist mysteriously disappeared in 1989.

getting there: The Okeanos Aggressor (tel. 800–348–2628,
504–385–2416, PO Drawer K, Morgan City, LA 70381) and
Ríos Tropicales (tel. 33–6455, Apdo. 472, 1200 Pavas) both
have very expensive trips.

history: Legendary Portuguese pirate Bénito Bonito and
Captain James Thomson and his crew, who made off with the
Peruvian valuables they had contracted to escort, are among
those who are alleged to have buried treasure here. Historical
happenstance gave Costa Rica sovereignty over the island
when Costa Rica rescued 13 seamen shipwrecked here after a
Chilean frigate capsized in 1832. The flag was raised over the
island in 1869, and German treasure hunter Augusto Gissler
spent 18 years from 1889 searching for treasure unsuccess-
fully on the island under cover of a governmental "agricultural" contract.

flora and fauna: Although there are not many animals here,
those present are not afraid of man since they have been given
no reason to be. Birds include the frigatebird, the white tern,
the masked and red-footed boobies, green and blue herons, per-
egrine falcons, and many others. Three of the seven land birds
are unique, including the Coco Island finch, closely related to
the species found on the Galapagos. The other two are the

cuckoo and Ridgeway's papamoscas. Aside from two small lizards, reptiles and amphibians are entirely absent. Because mammals were absent when the finely-tuned ecosystem evolved, feral pigs and cats wreak havoc. In their search for roots and grubs, pigs dig up the ground, causing trees to topple and soil to erode. The same type of devastation is wrought by the smaller numbers of goats and deer. Cats prey on birds and lizards; their only virtue is that they keep down the population of rats, another imported species with no natural enemies. Many cultivated plants have also gone wild here, including coffee and the guava—which threatens to supplant some of the native plant species.

San Isidro de General: Located 137 km (85 mi.) from San José and founded in 1897, this town (pop. 32,000) has grown up since the opening of the Pan American Highway. This very pleasant town has the ambience of the frontier. You can see *campesino* cowboys strutting their stuff down the main street. Built on slopes surrounding a flat central area, the town is ridiculously compact. Note the prosperity of the town center: almost every home is nice and shelters a car. San Isidro is a good place to prepare for a trip to Chirripó or to use as a base; the beaches at Dominical are just 35 km (22 mi.) away.

sights and entertainment: For information about the area, contact Chamber of Commerce President Luis Quesada (tel. 71–2525) at the Hotel Chirripó. Its main square features what surely has to be one of the nation's least architecturally endearing churches—a pink and white concrete structure whose bells appear to be undergoing an epileptic fit each time they ring! Inside, the church isn't much better. Up by the front to the R of the altar are slots for *caritas* (offerings to San Isidro, Jesus Crucifado, etc.), and the small room behind contains a mysterious white box covered by a white veil: it represents the body of the crucified Christ. Visit the cultural complex here, inaugurated in 1990, which features a 400-seat theater, museum, exhibit hall, and workshops for artisans and fine artists. Born out of the need to protect the surrounding water supply, Centro Biológico Las Quebradas is the area's newest project. Call 71–0532 for information or write FUDEBIOL at Apdo.

44, 8000 Quebradas, Pérez Zeledón. A beautiful waterfall is a few km past Brujo on the R. It's also possible to tour the Pindeco pineapple processing plant in Buenos Aires to the S. There isn't much to do in the town itself—unless you catch one of the mobile discos coming through. One place that you will want to check out is the wonderful rollerskate disco to the N side of the park; the best view is upstairs.

getting there: If you're going to Golfito by bus either from San José or from Quepos, you'll probably want to break your journey here. It's also the perfect place to base yourself for a trip to Chirripó. On the way you pass over Cerro de la Muerte, the highest spot on the Pan American Highway. Watch on the L for the ruins of a shelter; it's possible to see both coasts from here when it's clear. During the next 45 km (28 mi.), the road drops down from 10,938 ft. to 2,303 ft. From San José, buses leave hourly from three bus companies (tel. 23–3577, 22–2422, 23–686) along C. 16, Av. 1/3. Get advance tickets on weekends and holidays.

accommodation: The best deal around is the Hotel Astoria, under the "Derby" Restaurante Pepe Timba neon sign on the square. The rooms with private bath ($3.50 pp) are the best value. Try to get one of the six rooms in the area to the rear of the reception desk. Offering rooms with shared bath at $6s and $10d, Hotel Chirripó (tel. 71–2525) is right beside the park and across the way. Inexpensive Hotel Ameneli (tel. 71–0352) is also right in town; be sure to get a room which is not facing the Inter-American. Low-budget Hotel Igazú is one block from the square. Inexpensive and clean a/c Hotel de Sur (tel. 71–0233), five km (three mi.) S of town, offers a restaurant, pool, gardens, tennis court and other sports facilities. Write Apdo. 4, 8000 San Isidro de General. A ranch nearby that is open to the public, Genesis II (tel. 51–1577, lv. message) charges $550/week including meals.

food: A good place to eat lunch or dinner is the Marisquería Marea Baja which is near the main square. Also try the Bar Chirripó and El Tenedor.

festivals and events: The town's *fiesta civicas* is held from the end of Jan. to the beginning of Feb. Activities include a cattle show, agricultural and industrial fair, bullfights, and orchid exhibition. On May 15, the Día del Boyero ("Day of the Oxcart Driver") is celebrated with activities including parades featuring brightly colored oxcarts and the blessing of animals and crops by the local priest.

PARQUE NACIONAL CHIRRIPÓ (CHIRRIPÓ NATIONAL PARK)

Made into a park in 1975, this 105,000-acre park includes 12,530-ft. Cerro Chirripó, the nation's highest point, as well as two other peaks over 12,500 ft. The area is famed for its *páramo*—a high, tundra-like zone which often frosts over, though it never snows here. A hiker's paradise, it's best explored during a two- or three-day hike using mountain shelters.

getting there and practicalities: Take a bus from San Isidro de General at 5 AM and 2 PM (be sure to take the bus to San Gerardo de Rivas). It's a beautiful two-hour ride up to San Gerardo. Here you check in at the ranger station where it's possible to camp. There's a steep shortcut up to the park from here which can cut an hour from your time (see below). If you're planning to make it up to the mountain hut in one day (a rough trip with an altitude gain of 6,900 ft.), it's better to stay put for the day. In town you may be able to sleep on the floor of the Salon Comunal or rent a room at the low-budget Soda and Cabinas Chirripó. During the rainy season, it rains

Chirripó National Park

C. URAN
3865M

C. WEYL

R. Chirripo Atlantico

VALLE DE
LAS
MORRENAS   C. SEGUNDO

C. LAGUNAS
3749M

N

R. Chirripo Pacifico

Lagos Chirripo

C. CHIRRIPO
3820M

C. TRUNCADO
3865M

C. PIRAMIDE
3807M

P. NORESTE
3744M

C. VENTISQUEROS
3812M

LAGUNA DITKEBI

VALLE DE
LOS
CONEJOS

C. PARAMO
3699M

P. SURESTE

C. TERBI
3760M

CRESTONES

BASE
CRESTONES

CAVE

R. Talari

SENDERO
A LA SABANA
DE LOS LEONES

R. Terbi

To San Gerardo

daily, generally in the afternoon, so you'll have to get an early
start. There are three mountain huts where you can stay.
tours: Jungle Trails (tel. 55-3486) offers tours, and Costa
Rica Expeditions (tel. 22-0333) can custom tailor a tour for
you. **preparations:** Warm clothes and sleeping bag are neces-

sities here as temperatures often drop to freezing. Also bring binoculars, rain gear, a compass, and at least one one-liter water container per person. Two basic maps are provided at the station; if you plan to go off the beaten track at all, you should have purchased a map in San José. Don't count on the rangers to be well informed about the park.

flora, fauna, and topography: The lakes at the peak were formed by glaciation more than 25,000 years ago during the Pleistocene Era. Situated at 10,170 ft., the Sabana de los Leones (Savanna of the Lions) is so named because "lions" (pumas) and cougars are frequently spotted here. Surrounded by a cloud forest the "savanna" itself is treeless, covered instead with six different types of *páramo* (cold region) vegetation, including a species of dwarf bamboo. Surrounded by rocky peaks and mountain passes, sandy Valle de los Conejos (Rabbit Valley), from which all the rabbits beat a hasty retreat during the 1976 fire, is covered with dwarf bamboo. Cerro Crestón borders it on the SE, and its pinnacles rise towards the N and W. Lakes are found at the base of the Moraine (Valle de los Morrelas) and Lake (Valle de Lagos) Valleys. These crystal-clear cold lakes, which measure up to half an acre, are popular bathing spots with tapirs, and all the animals—from large cats to brocket deer and rabbits—arrive to drink their fill on occasion. There are 73 species of birds; variety diminishes as the altitude climbs. The quetzal is very abundant. Another feature of the higher cloud forest, the jilguero (black faced solitaire) cries out from the treetops. The edge of the *páramo* region is found at 10,826 ft. and above. The often-thick, stunted vegetation rarely tops 12 feet. The most common tree is the evergreen oak.

entering the park: The best way is via the "Thermometre" shortcut. From the ranger station turn L and walk through the village. Going R at the first fork, descend and cross a bridge, then continue on to another river and bridge; get water here. After a few houses, you'll see a sign marked "Entrada al Potrero." Walk through the pasture. Keeping about 1–200 yards away from the forest on your R, head up until you come to a wired enclosure with a gate on the R. Enter and head R, following a path which ends suddenly; then follow the ridge on your L up to a wire fence crossed by a set of stone steps. The shortcut has ended, putting you on the main trail which follows the ridge, Fila Cemeterio de Maquina. The park boundary is one or two hours farther, and the first camping spot (Llano Bonita: a flat, grassy area) is two or three hours after that. Signs are placed every two km along the way. To get water follow the trail another 20–30 min. to find a fork on the L marked "Agua Potable 200 m." There's a rough shelter here (not a place you would choose to sleep in) and a steep path behind it takes you down to a small stream. Continuing through a once burned out area (La Cuesta del Angel) for another three to four hours, you enter Monte Sin Fé and then reach a small stream with a large cave *(refugio natural)* to the L, about 1.5 hrs. from the huts below. Next you must climb La Cuesta de los Arrependitos where the trail circumnavigates the side of a mountain. The first proper shelters are another hour or so away; you'll pass a "Valle de Leones" sign about 20 min. beforehand and the shelters lie in the valley below the sharp peaks of Los Crestones. The yellow one is the best shelter. Depending upon your physical condition, it will have taken you eight to 16 hrs. to reach the first hut and ranger station.

mountain climbing: Chirripó is not as difficult to climb as it appears. On a clear day, it's possible to see the Valle de General, parts of the Atlantic and Pacific coasts, the Turrialba and Irazú volcanoes, and several other peaks. Continue on to the second hut and follow the sign; it's about an hour to the base of Chirripó Grande and then another half-hour to the top; the Lago San Juan is on the way. Start before dawn from the second hut to get the best views. There's also a trail from here to Cerro Terbí (12,352 ft.), a peak which, unlike Chirripó, can be seen from the first hut. From the top of this peak, you can see well down into Panama. The Crestones, a series of steep, needle-like rock pinnacles are nearby; they can also be reached from the first hut in about an hour. From the first hut, there's a rough trail down to Sabana Chirripó, a large, light-brown colored marsh. From the top of Cerro Terbí, it's possible to continue on to Pico Sureste (12,247 ft.), Pico Noreste (12,283 ft.), and Cerro Pirámide (12,490 ft.). Other peaks that may be climbed include Cerro Páramo (12,136 ft.) and Cerro Ventisqueros (12,506 ft.), Cerro Uran (10,935 ft.), Loma Larga (12,254 ft.), Cerro Truncado (12,680 ft.), and Cerro Lagunas (12,300 ft.).

Parque Internacional de la Amistad: Take the bus from San José to San Vito and then on to Las Mellizas. This enormous 479,199-acre "friendship" park straddles the upper slopes of the Talamancas, and may someday mesh with a promised twin park in adjoining Panama. The nation's newest park, its incorporation more than doubled the size of the park system. No facilities or services are available and there are very few trails.

flora and fauna: The park has rain forest, cloud forest, and *páramo* with resident populations of jaguars, tapirs, and pumas. The 400-odd bird species include quetzals and harpy eagles. Elevation within the park ranges from 650 to 11,644 ft.

getting there and around: There are few trails and all are unmarked. Contact the NPS regarding the possibilities of hiring a guide and horse. If you have a car, this would be a good day trip from San Vito or San Isidro. Contact Costa Rican Expeditions regarding custom tailored tours.

practicalities: Camping is permitted near entrances at Las Mellizas, Aguas Calientes, and at Helechales. Easiest to access, Las Mellizas is best for hiking. To get here take a San Vito-La Lucha bus (9:30 departure) and walk six km, or drive all the way. Trout fishing is possible here with a permit, and the cooks at Las Mellizas farm may be able to feed you. Horses and guides can also be hired here.

Rey Currё: At this village, there's an Indian craft cooperative, Fiesta de los Diablos. The sole remaining such festival, it takes place every Feb. in this village in the SW Talamancas, between Paso Real and Palmar Norte. In an allegorical recreation of the struggle between the *Diablitos* (the local Boruca Indians) and a bull (representing the Spaniards), masked *Diablitos* pursue the bull, which is made of burlap topped with a carved wooden head. Local crafts, corn liquor *(chicha)*, and *tamales* are for sale.

Boruca: This Indian village is 18 km (11 mi.) off the Inter-American Highway. During the school year, a bus leaves for here from Buenos Aires at 1:30. If you walk in, get off at the *entrada* about half an hour by bus after Buenos Aires, and take the two hour, eight km path which branches off the main road. Held on Dec. 8, the local version of Fiesta de los Negritos features wildly costumed dancers in blackface. It is held in honor of its patron saint, the Virgin of the Immaculate Conception. Participants dance to flute and drum accompaniment in time to the *sarocla*, a frame with a horse's head.

THE CARIBBEAN COAST

Covering almost 20% of the nation's land mass and with over 170,000 inhabitants, this is the nation's banana frontier—an area carved out for that purpose. Although today less than 25% of the population is African-American, you'll still hear the distinctive dialect of their colorful local English all along this coast. A common greeting is "Whoppen" (What's happening) and "all right" or "OK" is substituted for *adiós*. Fortunately for the visitor, its touristic potential remains virtually untapped with miles of palm-tree-lined beaches along the coast.

exploring: Anytime is a good time to visit this area, but the best months for the beaches to the S are Sept. and Oct. The best possible introduction to this region is to ride the train to Limón. There's really only one main road: it runs across to Limón and then down the coast to Sixaola.

LIMÓN

The first town to be successfully established in the nation's tropical lowlands, hot and humid Limón (pop. 65,000) was originally founded with the intention of rivaling Puntarenas as a coffee shipping port. Instead, it came to be devoted mainly to banana export.

Founded in the 1880s in an unpopulated swampy area facing the Atlantic 168 km (104 mi.) from San José, Limón grew to 7,000 by 1927. In its golden age, it rivaled San José as a commercial center where North Americans, Jamaicans, Cubans, Panamaneans, Britons, Germans, and Chinese lived and traded. The nation's very first "company" town, Limón fell victim to its own slavish dependence on the banana. Limón never recovered after the industry's early slump, despite the banana's reemergence in the 1950s. Today, Limón is a small, sweaty town with atmosphere galore.

getting there: From the Atlantic Station (Av. 3, C. 21) Costa Rica's most famous train ride—to Limón (7–8 hrs.) on the Caribbean coast—used to depart at 10 AM daily. The train stopped a total of 54 times, at places as diversely named as San Antonio, Florida, Boston, Buffalo, and 9 Millas. Known as the "Jungle Train," it was suspended in early 1991. You can still take the bus to Limón. It leaves hourly at the terminal directly across from the train station (Av. 3 near Parque Nacional). Buy tickets in advance if traveling on a weekend or holiday. **by car:** Open since 1987, the Guápiles Highway, a toll road, has shortened driving time from San José to 165 km (102 mi.) or 2¼ hrs. A tunnel runs under Barva and through Braulio Carrillo to Guápiles and then on to Limón.

sights: There's not much to see in Limón proper. Other than the bars, the best place to hang out is the park. Ask any sloth! Mainly preoccupied with the fine arts of sleeping and tummy scratching, they occasionally descend to defecate or sip water from the fountains. Across from the park is the cream-colored, stuccoed Alcaldía (city hall). Containing historical material relevant to the area, the Ethnohistorical Museum is theoretically open Tues.–Sat. 10–5. Also here, situated on Av. 2, C. ¾, the market is a lively place to visit. Off the town's coast is the small island of Uvita where Columbus anchored during his first voyage. The Asociación China has a Chinese shrine inside along with a map showing Chinese routes of emigration

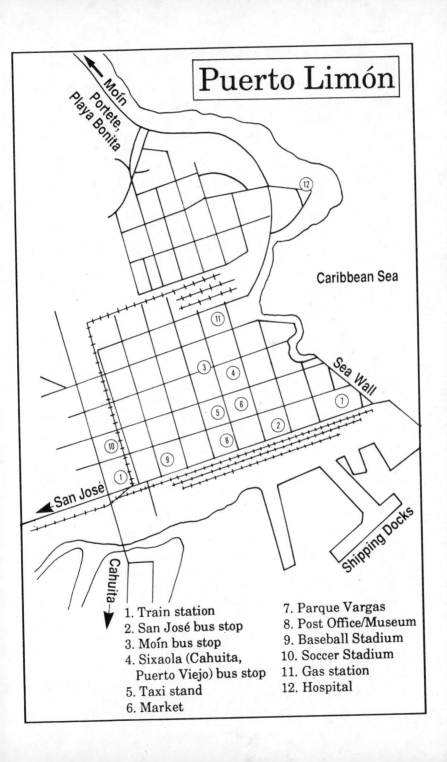

Puerto Limón

Moín
Portete,
Playa Bonita

Caribbean Sea

Sea Wall

San José

Shipping Docks

Cahuita

1. Train station
2. San José bus stop
3. Moín bus stop
4. Sixaola (Cahuita, Puerto Viejo) bus stop
5. Taxi stand
6. Market
7. Parque Vargas
8. Post Office/Museum
9. Baseball Stadium
10. Soccer Stadium
11. Gas station
12. Hospital

all over the world. Vicious mahjong games—alive with the lyrically loud snap of slammed pieces—take place here at night. **nearby beaches:** Four km N of town, there's a small beach at Playa Bonita (safe swimming *only* on the N end) and a rocky overlook, where local fishermen ply their trade, at Portete where you can watch lobster traps being prepared. It's possible to buy fish and lobster from these fishermen. Note the dugout canoes here which are stored under a bamboo-fashioned stand along the shore. Two bar-restaurants are here. The 31-acre Parque Cariari, set between Bonita and Portete, has paths with toucans, parrots, sloths, iguanas, basilisks, and innumerable butterflies. A place to avoid swimming is at Playa Cieneguita, located just S of town, which is reported to be the most polluted in the nation.

getting around: Limón is laid out similarly to San José except that there is no segregation of odd and even streets, there are no street signs, and no locals seem to understand the numbering system. Distances are usually given in terms of how many meters it is from the market, park, or small radio station. One positive feature amidst all of this confusion is that many residents speak English—or at least Jamaicatalk English. The main street is Av. 2 ("Market Street") which extends E from the train station to Vargas Park near the waterfront. Av. 3, 4, and on up, run parallel and to the N. Calle 1 runs N–S along Vargas Park. The higher numbered *calles* run along parallel to the W. To get to Moín, take a public bus which runs past Portete enroute. Taxis wait at the S side of the *mercado* from the wee hours of the morning on.

accommodations: As it's so hot, you'll probably want to have a room with a fan. Spartan and inexpensive Hotel Acón (tel. 58–1010) has a/c, disco, and a communal TV; it's centrally located. Write Apdo. 528, Limón. Aged but still charming, inexpensive Hotel Park (tel. 58–0476) is at Av. 3, C. 1/2. Around the same price are the Internacional (tel. 58–0434) at C. 3, Av. 5, and a/c Hotel Miami (tel. 58–0490) at Av. 2, C. 4/5. Write Apdo. 2800, 7300, Limón. The more deluxe hotels are all near Portete to the N. Located a few km to the N, inexpensive Hotel Las Olas (tel. 58–1414) has fans or a/c, swimming pools, restaurant, satellite TV, and sauna. Write Apdo. 701, Limón.

Near Playa Bonita with restaurant, pool, and zoo, Hotel Matama (tel. 53–6528, 58–1123) charges $20s and $25d for its a/c rooms. Featuring round thatched bungalows with a/c, restaurant, car rental, and pools, there is also expensive Hotel Maribú Caribe (tel. 58–4543, 58–4010). Write Apdo. 623, 7300 Limón or call 34–0193 in San José. Located 22 km (14 mi.) to the S of Limón, inexpensive and basic Club Campeste Cahuita (tel. 58–2861) has swimming pools and restaurants. Camping ($3) is permitted across the road, and rooms are only available to nonmembers during slack times.

low-budget accommodation: Try around the market (Av. 2, C. 3/4) for the cheapest accommodation, most of which is also noisy. Places include the Hotel Lincoln (tel. 58–0074, Av. 5, C. 2/3, Pensión Los Angeles (Av. 7, C. 6/7), Pensión Costa Rica (1.5 blocks E of the Parque Vargas), Pensión El Sauce, Paraíso (C. 5, Av. 5/6), Pensión Dorita (Av. 4, C. 3/4), the Balmoral, the Fung, the Linda Vista, and the Caballo Blanco.

food: Shrimp and lobster are slightly less expensive around here. Try the a/c dining room of the Hotel Acón or, two km to the N, Hotel Las Olas. For Chinese food try the Cien Kung, across from the Texaco station or the Palacio Encantador. Inside the Internacional (C.3, Av.5) is the Turkeski. La Fuente is at C. 3, Av. 3/4. Also try the American Bar (C. 1, Av. 2 opposite Vargas Park) which features seafood and beef. Market food (Av. 2, C. 3/4) is the cheapest around. The Soda Gemini nearby has a good buffet and cakes. Rasa's serves international food. Also try the Apollo Once, around the corner from the Baptist Church. Part of the *supermercado,* Soda Mares features fine fruit drinks. Heading along the seawall up to Moín, you first come to the seafood-oriented Arrecife, then Springfield which serves typical local food for about $5/meal. Next is the Manchester, the deluxe El Zapote, and then the Soda Encato. Ranchita Westphalia, enroute to Cahuita, specializes in US President George Bush's favorite snack: fresh *chicharrones.*

entertainment: Hookers and sailors frequent some of the bars. Opening onto the street, the American Bar (C. 1, Av. 2 opposite Vargas Park) is a live wire. The Mark 15 disco is across from the Anglican Church. Also try the Springfield on the N outskirts or visit the Johnny Dixon Bar at Playa Bonita. The Atlantic Cinema shows films for 90 cents.

events and festivals: On Oct. 12, Columbus Day is the highlight, with calypso and reggae, parades, dancing in the streets. The celebration centers around the market where there's gambling and food stalls. The Limón area celebrates May Day with cricket matches, picnics, quadrille dances, and domino matches.

from Limón: The bus to Playa Bonita, Portete, and Moín leaves hourly from C. 4, Av. 4 in front of Radio Casino in Limón. Since there's no bus station, tickets are sold at the bus stops. Buses leave here, running S through Cahuita and Puerto Viejo to Bribri and Sixaola bordering Panama. Buy tickets the day before to ensure getting on and arrive early to secure a seat.

RESERVA BIOLÓGICA HITOY CERERE (HITOY CERERE BIOLOGICAL RESERVE)

The name of this isolated 22,620-acre reserve stems from the Indian names of two rivers in the area. *Hitoy* means "woolly" in the sense of mossy or covered with slimy vegetation, and *cerere* means clear waters. Set between the heavily cultivated Estrella and Telirre river valleys, its rugged topography rescued the area from development. Its steep peaks, which include Bobócara (2,618 ft.) and Bitácara (3,363 ft.) have served to isolate it even from the three surrounding Indian settlements.

flora and fauna: Rising to heights of 100 ft. or more, the lofty trees include the wild cashew, the Santa María, balsa, and the calyptrogyne or "dovetail" tree. There are also a large number of medicinal plants and trees within the reserve. More than 118 in. of rain fall annually, and the average temperature is between 22.5° and 25°C (72.5° and 77°F). Wildlife found here include three species of opossum, pizotes, sloths, anteaters, agoutis, pacas, raccoons, margays, kinkajous, otters, jaguars, tapirs, white-faced and howler monkeys, as well as 115 species of birds.

practicalities: Accessible by four-wheel-drive vehicles or you can get taxi service from Finca 16 in the Estrella Valley Standard Fruit Co. Banana Plantation. This, in turn, can be reached by the Valle de la Estrella bus from Limón. By car, head W from Penhurst. In order to reserve meals and lodging in the reserve, call 33–5473 about a week beforehand. Camping is permitted. While there are no formal trails, you can follow the ones used by the rangers and the Indians who live around the reserve's perimeter.

PARQUE NACIONAL TORTUGUERO (TORTUGUERO NATIONAL PARK)

The area known as Tortuguero, "region of turtles," is on the NE side of the country above Limón. One of the nation's most

popular parks, its waterways provide some of the best places to
see wildlife. It is a tropical wet forest life zone, and the average
annual rainfall here exceeds 197 in. While June and July are
among the rainiest months, Aug. and Sept. have the least
rainfall.

flora and fauna: Despite rampant deforestation in the surrounding area, Tortuguero remains an area that fulfills one's
expectation of what a tropical jungle should be. The coconuts
found here are introduced relics of the days that plantations
flourished in the area. Seagrapes dominate the coastal dunes.
Of the 16 endangered mammals in Costa Rica, 13 are found in
or near the park. One of them is the rarely-sighted manatee.
Three of the four species of sea turtles, the crocodile, and the
cayman are also found. The more than 300 species of birds
include green and scarlet macaws, the Central American
curassow, and the yellowtailed oriole. Considered to be a living
fossil because it resembles similar species which lived during
the upper Cretaceaous period 90 million years ago, the gar
(*Attratosteus tropicus*) has a body covered with bony or plaque-
like scales. Ranging in length between four and seven ft., it
has a long, narrow snout supporting strong jaws with
crocodile-like teeth. Often it lies motionless, as if suspended in
the water.

orientation: Commonly known as Los Canales, 160 km (99
mi.) of inland waterways flow up the NE coast to Tortuguero
and then on to Barra Colorado where these eight rivers merge
into a series of lagoons. Utilizing the already existing natural
channels, canals were dug during the 1970s to connect them,
thus providing a natural waterway in a region where no highway would be feasible. They extend from the transport center
of Moín to the N of Puerto Limón. Every type of craft from
dugout canoes and fishing boats to tour boats ply these waters.
The first village, 32 km upriver, is Parismina. Then, you come
to the park office, the village of Tortuguero, Jungle Lodge, and
across the river, the Mawamba Lodge. On the same side of the
river are the Ilan Ilan and, farther upriver, the Tortuga Lodge
with the research station across the river. The waterway leads
on to Barra del Colorado.

getting there, tours, and accommodations: Tour boats are the way to go if your schedule is inflexible, and they will stop for wildlife photos. Innumerable tour companies ply the canals, and all offer a variety of schedules. Costa Rican Expeditions (tel. 22–0333) will either fly or boat you in to their Tortuga Lodge. Limón's Hotel Matama (tel. 58–1123) also offers boat trips as far as Parismina where you overnight. The *Mawamba* (tel. 33–9964) will take you slowly upriver to their lodge, owned by textile magnate Mauricio Dada. Tortuguero Jungle Adventures (tel. 55–2031, 55–2262) has trips aboard their **Colorado Prince:** you stay at the Ilan Ilan Hotel. Their office is on Paseo de Colón, 30 feet W of the Hospital de Niños. "La Jungla" S.A. (tel. 58–2843, 34–1297) also has launches and tours. One of the least expensive companies, Cotur (tel. 33–0155, 33–6579, 33–0133, 33–0226) buses you to Moín where you board either the *Miss Caribe* or the *Miss America* to the Jungle Lodge, located a km N of Tortuguero village across the river. Affiliated with Río Colorado Lodge, Adventure Tours (tel. 32–4063) offers a number of packages including a trip up to the Nicaraguan border.

on your own: By far the least expensive alternative ($8 RT) is to travel up and back with *Gran Delta,* the government-run launch, which departs for Barra weekly on Thurs. and to Tortuguero on Sat., returning on Fri. and Sun. As priority is given to local passengers, you may not be able to get on. The main disadvantage of this boat is that it frightens the wildlife and it doesn't stop for photos. Call JAPDEVA (tel. 58–1106) for information. If their boat isn't running there may be a private launch running on Sat. AM. You can also try hiring a local guide with a boat, but be prepared to pay through the nose.

by air: You can also fly into Tortuguero with Costa Rica Expeditions for $60 OW; they land at the airport near the research station.

departing from Moín: The only hotel here, The Hostal Moín, has been converted into a full time brothel. Two *típico* restaurants are here. Ask permission to visit the compound of JAPDEVA, the government agency in charge of the area's economic development, where you can see the waterway and river port operations underway. Just N from Moín is the ICT-run park and farther N, at Playa Barra de Matina, is a refuge for nesting sea turtles.

the trip up: The first thing you notice is the wide expanse of the greenish-brown water flanked on both sides by tropical vegetation. Passing yellow highway signs denoting the kilometers to nearby villages at intersections, you steam upriver, the wildlife-filled greenery reflected on either side. Along the river, you might see howler or spider monkeys, caymans, turtles, white egrets, great blue herons, night herons, toucans, blue-green kingfishers, a sleeping sloth snuggling on a branch overhead, floating water hyacinths, or mud turtles jumping and splashing in the water. If you stop for a moment you can hear the intense hum of insects, which contrasts with the pounding surf in the distance. After the ranger station, the canal widens and everything save nature vanishes.

accommodation and food: One of the nicest places to stay and eat here is Costa Rica Expedition's Tortuga Lodge (tel. 22–0333). Expensive but comfortable, the lodge gives you everything you might wish for while still being in the heart of the jungle. The trail in back has a large number of poison dart frogs, and you may see other flora and fauna as well. In the front of the lodge, fishing and fruit bats fly over the docks at night while marine toads are found on the ground. Three hearty meals (ranging in price from $6.50 to $11) are served daily. Every type of excursion from fishing ($35/hr.) to turtle walks ($11 pp) are offered. None of the lodge doors have locks because there have never been any problems with theft! There's no charge for depositing you on the other side of the river where the beach and the turtle research station are. From there, it's a long but pleasant hike down to the village of Tortuguero. For information on and rates for the other lodges listed, contact the tour companies. **on a budget:** The best bet for budget travelers is clean and pleasant Sabina's Cabanas ($4 pp; more expensive with private bath). You can also stay upriver at Cabinas Tatané whose owner will come and get you in his boat. To stay at either place leave a message with Marco

Zamora at the *pulpería* (tel. 71–6716); the owners should call back and confirm. Pensión Tortuguero is grotty. Eat at Tio Leo's restaurant.

fishing lodges: This area is famous for the giant tarpon (*sábalo*) which have secured the area its reputation worldwide. Lodges are listed heading S to N. On the edge of the village of Parismina, Parismina Fishing Lodge (tel. 35–7766 in San José) features rooms in wooden cottages. Write PO Box 290190, San Antonio, TX 78280; call (800) 531–7232 or (512) 492–5517. The Tortuga Lodge is mentioned above. Three other lodges are well upriver, centered around Barra del Colorado. Río Colorado Lodge (tel. 32–8610 in San José) offers simple cabins with Jacuzzi and satellite TV. Write Hotel Corobicí, PO Box 5094, 1000 San José or call (800) 243–9777. With housing in A-frames, Isla de Pesca (tel. 23–4560 in San José) can be contacted through Fishing Travel, 2525 Nevada Ave. N, Golden Valley, MN 55427, tel. (612) 541–1088. Finally, write Casa Mar Fishing Lodge at PO Drawer 787, Islamorada, FL 33036, tel. (800) 327–2880 or (305) 664–4615.

getting around: The ideal way to experience the wonder of this park is to rent a dugout canoe (*cacuya*) from a Tortuguero villager. A guide will accompany you for about $10 pd. Park it by the river bank and take in the thousands of sounds that emerge. For those accustomed to the deafening noise of the city, it is wondrous to discover these other sounds—of a nature that exists and functions quite apart from the will or regulation of humanity. **hiking:** A hike up 328-ft. Cerro Tortuguero, the park's highest point, affords an overview of the canal system. A nice walk is down to the village of Tortuguero and on to the frequently waterlogged El Gavilan nature trail which runs in back of the park headquarters. A mixture of African Americans, white Ticos, and descendants of Mosquito tribesmen live in the village.

Green Turtle Research station: Organized in 1959 by Dr. Archie Carr, the Caribbean Conservation Corporation operates two permanent field research facilities, one in the Bahamas and the other here. Acquired in 1963, it was originally built in the 1940s as temporary quarters for land surveyors with the United Fruit Company.

egglaying: Largest of the sea turtles, leatherbacks nest on the beach in March and April, hatching from May through June; they are also occasionally found through to the start of the green turtle nesting season in July. Continuing on to Sept., up to 4,000 females lay annually in Tortuguero, the largest such colony in the Americas. Solitary and rarely encountered, the hawksbill also nests here in July through Sept. The first recorded observation of egglaying was by the Dutch in 1592. Turtles lay eggs in the middle of night. If you go out to watch on your own, be sure to minimize use of your flashlight because you may frighten a mother arriving to nest, sending her lumbering back towards the water. After searching for a spot which the high tide will not reach, the mother turtle becomes totally involved in digging the nest, shoveling out the round nest with her paddle-shaped hind legs. Crouching over the nest, which may be up to 16 inches deep, she expels an average of 100 eggs together with a lubricating fluid. Covering the nest with sand, she then returns to the sea. During the two-hour procedure, she heaves constant sighs and cries, presumably to clear her eyes of sand. Facing the world's greatest obstacle course, the hatchlings race to the sea two months later. Very few make it.

Refugio de Fauna Silvestre Barra del Colorado: At 227,332 acres Barra Colorado terminates the waterway system. Once a prosperous lumber center and cargo depot, timber depletion has led to its demise. The flora, fauna, and local cultural milieu are similar to Tortuguero. **practicalities:** Stay at inexpensive Cabinas Tarponland. Other alternatives are Río Colorado Lodge, Isla de Pesca, and Casa Mar Fishing Lodge—all mentioned under "fishing lodges" above. It may be possible to get back and forth between Tortuguero and here via coconut barges which take passengers or you can charter a boat. From this village the Río San Juan leads up the Sarapiquí to the village of Puerta Viejo where a rough road leads down to San José. SANSA flies here on Tues., Thurs., and Sat.

La Penca: This small Nicaraguan border town is a place you will want to know about. On May 30, 1984 an explosion here at a press conference called by ARDE leader Eden Pastora at his jungle camp off the San Juan River, killed three journalists and five contras, and left 26 wounded. The incident has been alleged by journalists Martha Honey and Tony Avirgan to have been set up by 29 US officials, right-wing US citizens, Costa Rican security forces, and the CIA in an attempt to discredit the Sandinistas and provoke US intervention.

PARQUE NACIONAL CAHUITA (CAHUITA NATIONAL PARK)

A relaxed and somnolent village of about 3,000, Cahuita stands next to one of the nation's most popular attractions, Cahuita National Park. **flora, fauna, and the reef:** While the most famed life is underwater, there's plenty to see on the ground as well. Thousands of coconut trees line the beaches, and it's easy to see monkeys as you walk along. The 593-acre reef is outlined by the seaward waves which form around it. It generally is less than one yard deep near the coast and in places where live coral grow, and up to 24 feet deep in several channels. There are 34 species of coral, over 100 types of seaweed, and 500 species of fish. The water is clearest from Feb. to April. There are also two old shipwrecks with cannons. Unfortunately, the reef is dying because of pesticide runoff from the banana plantations. Meanwhile Dole wants to purchase more land and expand. The fish supply is also decreasing.

Smaller fish, which used to attract the larger fish as food, have now been killed off.

getting there: From Limón, buses (one hr.) leave from Av. 4, C. ³/₄ at 5, 10, 1, and 4. Direct buses to Sixaola (bypassing Limón) leave from Av. 4, C. Central/1 at 6 and 2:30, passing both park entrances. Sixaola is about 25 min. farther down the road. Returning buses leave at 5, 8, 10, and 3 for Limón, and for San José at 6 and 2:30.

orientation: The town features wide gravel streets with cabinas and restaurants interspersed randomly at intervals. The bus stop is next to the park across from Salon Vaz. While one side of the wide gravel main street leads to Hotel Cahuita and the park entrance, Black Beach is in the other direction. The road heading towards the water leads to Cabinas Palmer and, around the corner and down to the L, to Surfside and then Edith's. The road to the Black Beach passes Miss Edith's and the Guardia Civil, then continues on down with sandy stretches punctuated by coral outcrops. A *verduras y frutas* stand is 100 yards off the Black Beach road to the L; watch for the sign. A small soda stand is across from the soccer field. This is a beautiful road to walk or cycle. On the way, you pass blooming hibiscus, birds, palms, giant green iguanas—their finned backs undulating like a pack of cards being shuffled. The pounding surf is off to the R.

history: The area's name comes from the indigenous words *kawe* (mahogany) and *ta* (point). Created in 1970, it includes 2,636 acres of land and the 1,483 acres of coral reefs 1,600 ft. offshore. Only 20% of the local farmers were reimbursed as promised after the park's creation. There have been unsettling rumors that the Calderón administration would like to eliminate the park, opening it to the wonders of free enterprise development. Let us hope these rumors are ill founded and the park will continue just as it is.

visiting the national park: Cross a bridge down past Hotel Cahuita to enter the park. Several picnic tables are near the entrance. The sandy beach stretches out in the distance as far as the eye can see. Both the beach, and the nature trail to its rear, come to a halt in front of a river which must be crossed. Along the way the trail is alive with bright blue morpho (birdwing) butterflies, land crabs, birds, and, at times, monkeys. If you're planning on continuing, you'll need a good pair of shoes or windsurfing sandals. Soon, you'll reach a shallow stream, the Río Perezoso, colored red from the tannic acid released by decomposed vegetation. The water all along this stretch is smooth and translucent because the water is breaking on the reef way offshore.

accommodation: Most of the accommodation is low-budget, giving an opportunity for even the most highbrow traveler to sample a simpler way of living. If you're game to camp, the only campgrounds are at the other park entrance at Puerto Vargas. All hotels may be reached by dialing 58–1515 and requesting the extension given. Run by a friendly Texan, dilapidated but atmospheric Hotel Cahuita (x 201) has a pool and a restaurant whose TV specializes in sports. Upstairs rooms are priced at $3.50 s and $6 d with shared bath, cold water, and no fans. Cabinas cost $8.50 s, $11 d. Write Apdo. 121, Limón. Next door, Cabinas Sol y Mar (x 237) charges $25 pn for up to six. Across the street from these two, Cabinas Vaz (x 218) charges $8.50 s, $10.50 d, and $2 per extra person. One of the very best places to stay, Cabinas Palmer (x 243) charges $3.50 pp for its room in the family's house and a bit more for the facing set of cabinas. Low-budget Cabinas Jenny is just down the road by the water. Another very nice place to stay is Surfside Cabinas (x 246, 202, 218) down the road towards the coast to the L. They charge $6 s, $10 quad; their larger cabinas on the beach are $10 d and $15 quad. Inexpensive Cabinas del Mar are across from the school and near the ocean. **Black Beach accommodation:** Out of range of the pulsating nightly *riddims* pouring out from Salon Vaz, the Black Beach area has a wide range of quiet hostelries. Near the ball field and about a km from town, Cabinas Atlántida (x 229) charges $5 s, $10 d with fans. The Taller de Artesanías (Letty's) has rooms for $3 pp. Italian-run with two-story, stone and wood structures, Cabinas Black Beach (x 251) hold up to four ($7.50 s,

$12 d, plus $3 extra pp). Advertising for surfers, Soda Ciancla charges $3.50 pp for cabinas. Next up is Cabinas Bridgitte; she charges $4 s, $6 d and $3/hr. for horse rental. Be sure to check out her collection of poison dart frogs. To her rear, attractive Apartamiento Iguana rents for $15 pn. Ask at the small soda about low-budget Cabinas Samuel. Way up at the end of the road, Cabinas Algebra charges $11 for three without kitchen and $16 for four with kitchen. Swiss-owned and managed Chalet Hibiscus has two houses facing a coral rock beach which rent for around $50/pn; two more with a pool in front are planned for across the road. For reservations call 39–4485 in San José.

food: Depending upon where you're staying, you may find yourself spending more per meal than per night. Most of the food is higher priced than that found in similar establishments in San José without a corresponding increase in quality. The least expensive place but also the best is Miss Edith's; she has some vegetarian specialties. Be prepared for a *long* wait. In addition to its restaurant, Hotel Cahuita sells Texas BBQ on Sat. and Sun. Sol y Mar and Cabinas Vaz both have restaurants as does Cabinas Surfside. A friendly lady sells baked goods and drinks at the park entrance. Screened in and attractive, El Típico is up the road and off to the L. In front of Salon Vaz, there's an old lady who sells fish ($1.75) or chicken ($1.50) dinners on Fri. and Sat. night. Out down the Black Beach road, Cabinas Black Beach features Italian dishes ($6 for lasagna). Soda Ciancla is also nearby. Bananas is the name of Cabinas Algebra's attractive porchtop restaurant. **services:** Cahuita Tours (tel 58–5515, x 232) and Moray's offer tours and rent snorkeling equipment.

entertainment: The local hot spot is Salon Vaz, a typical bar with a large "disco" in back and lots of cool dreads hanging out. Bar Hannia nearby also plays reggae.

from Cahuita: Buses to Limón run at 6:30, 10:15, 12:15, 1:30, and 5. The express bus departs at 6:50, 9:15, and 4. The buses may be either early or late so get there ahead of time.

Child in Puerto Viejo

THE TALAMANCA HIGHLANDS

An area which was virtually inaccessible until the late 1970s, Talamanca is the poorest but greenest section of the nation. Shaped like a triangle, this densely forested region remained unconquered until the end of the 19th C. Today, it still retains considerable charm and is very refreshingly unspoiled. There's not much reason to come here if you like everything first class; this is definitely the area for those who want to rough it. A locale where you can still hear such Jamaican-style English phrases as "How you keeping?" and "How de morning?," the region is a relaxing melting pot of Indian, African-American, and Spanish culture. Most of the indigenous peoples did not in fact make this their original home. After the Bribri, Guatuso, and Cabécar tribes burned down several missions and killed priests, they were forcibly resettled here and in Guanacaste. Although the impact of tourism has caused a shift away from traditional life for the largely African-American coastal dwellers, the Bribri and Cabécar peoples still maintain many of their customs and ancient beliefs side by side with their jeans and radios. The three indigenous peoples' reserves in the area are the Talamanca-Bribri, Talmanca-Cabécar, and KékoLdi.

getting there: Direct buses (four hrs. from San José at 6, 2:30, and 4:30) run via Cahuita all the way to Bribri, and on to Sixaola on the Panamanian border. To arrange a ride into Puerto Viejo from El Cruce (the crossroads) where this bus leaves you, telephone 58–3844 or 58–0854 two days in advance. Buses from San José to Puerto Limón leave hourly from the NE corner of Parque Nacional (2.5 hrs). From there, buses to Sixaola which enter Puerto Viejo (1.5 hrs) depart at 5, 10, 1, and 4.

Puerto Viejo de Limón: This "Old Harbor," surrounds a small bay with still waters and beautiful black sand beaches. The lifestyle here gives new meaning to the description "laid

Gourd tree, Puerto Viejo

back." Children play in front of the crashing surf. The capsized barge at the village entrance once was used to carry black sand for export. The inhabitants here still have an attitude of innocence toward foreigners which is no longer found in places such as Jamaica. The area is relatively compact. If someone hasn't stolen it again, there should be a map created by the progressive local alternative tourism association which shows all of the listings in this section.

accommodations: The first places you come to on the way here are also two of the best. A 49-acre private reserve with nature trails, Nature Lodge Chimuri features Indian-style cabins set 500 yards from the beach. Mauricio Salazar and his Austrian wife Colocha have three four-person units for $10/day and one four-person cabin for $20/day. Horseback rides ($25 pp) and one ($50) and three day ($140) camping trips are available. Bikes and rubber boots can be rented by visitors, and hiking trips are also available. For more information contact Mauricio Salazar, Cabinas Chimuri, Puerto Viejo de Limón, Talamanca. Featuring limited but spectacularly located facilities, Cabinas Black Sands were originally built by Mauricio Salazar. New owners Ken and Diane have preserved it intact. They charge $4.50 s, $7.50 d, and $20 for an entire three-bedroom cabina. Both of these places have communal kitchens available. If you leave a phone message with Ana or José at 58-3844 either of these two places will call you back collect. In the same area, Cabinas Playa Negra has one nine-person unit ($25) with kitchen, TV, and private bath and two four-person units ($10) with kitchen and private bath. For reservations call 56-1132 or 56-6396. Closer in to town, Mr. O'Conner has one room with private bath and fan for $10 (three persons maximum). The Hotel Maritza (tel. 58-3844) charges $4 s, $6.50 d. Cabinas Ritz, Hotel Puerto Viejo, and the friendly British-Rastafarian-run Cabinas Kaya are all less than $4 pp. More expensive, at around $9 s or d, are Cabinas Manuel, Cabinas Anselmo (only one unit), Cabinas Stanford (fans), and Cabinas Recife. Cabinas Frederico has two units (six persons maximum) for $15 with private bath and stove. Cabinas Zoyla has four units at $5 (two person maximum) with private bath.

Also try Pensión Grant and the recently remodeled Agaricia which is owned and operated by former National Park Service employee Javier Escobedo, an illustrator who designed some of their most imaginative posters. For information and reservations, call 58–4579 or write Apdo. 704, Limón.

enroute to Manzanillo: First is El Escape Caribeño, just 400 yards from El Bambú. One two-person unit is $17 and the other four-person is $22. Both have private bath and fan. In Barra Cocles, Cabinas Katty has two four-person units ($7.50/unit) with private bath. Moderately-priced Cabinas DASA at Playa Chiquita has four units ranging from around $10 to $30. For information and current rates contact Elizabeth at 20–4089 or Rosa María at 36–2631. Maracú (tel. 25–6215) has one house with kitchen. Ask Susana or Daniel at Soda Aquario about their two-unit cabina with kitchen. Next is Jardín Miraflores Lodge, a plantation raising heliconias for export, which offers modest rooms with fans for $15 pp including breakfast. For reservations call 28–4730. The final alternative is the low-budget Cabinas Maxi which has five units alongside a bar, disco, and *pulpería*.

upscale accommodation: The most expensive but nicest place to stay is definitely El Pizote which is set back from the Black Beach as you approach town. It's named after the mischievous coatis who inhabit a cage to one side near the entrance. The bungalows and cabins are set to the rear of the main lodge, separated from it by a planted forest of ornamental cane. Tastefully designed with elegant simplicity, the lodge has screened rooms with fans, mirrors, and reading lamps. They also have shared water showers with the largest shower heads you've ever seen in your life. Rates run from $22 s, $33 d to $55 s or d for the bungalows which have a private bath. Food is extra. For reservations call 29–1428.

food: If you're planning on doing your own cooking, don't miss the once-weekly vegetable truck which pulls in across from the Támara on Wed. afternoons. Probably the best place to eat overall, Soda Támara has a nice patio in the back. They're open 6:30–9 and closed on Tues. Another great place to eat is the small shop down the road which has tables set outdoors under plastic canopies. Generous fish *casados* ($2) are served here. Stanford's has a balcony overlooking the sea. They have vegetarian dishes as well as fish dinners from $1.50 and up. El Pizote has $6.50 breakfasts and $12 dinners. Next to Cabinas Kaya, Soda La Amistad features *comida criollos*. Pricey Soda Coral has a large breakfast menu and serves pizza most afternoons during tourist season. Other places to try include Bambú, Johnnie's Discotheque and Chinese Seafood Restaurant, and the Restaurant Maritza. At Playa Chiquita, Soda Aquario has both fair prices and friendly management. Out in Manzanillo, Miss Marva, Miss Alfonsina, Miss Edith, and Doña Cipriana will prepare homecooked meals if notified in advance.

baked goods: Miss Dolly, Miss Sam, and Miss Daisy sell traditional treats. Mateo sells whole wheat bread at his home near the soccer field.

entertainment: In tourist season the large disco below Stanford's features live music as does Bambú, just to the S past the dump. Outsiders are welcome to drop in on meetings of the local tourism association which are held Mon. nights at the Coral.

services: Most of the locations of the services and activities listed here can be found on the map in town. Make phone calls from Hotel Maritza and Pulpería Manuel León. The nearest banking service is in Bribri. A ministry of Health clinic here is open Mon. to Fri. from 7 to 4. In Puerto Viejo, Dr. Rosa León sees patients from 5:30 to 8 PM and on an emergency basis. To rent bicycles contact Aldo Figueroa, Jacobo Brent at Cabinas Kaya, Petra at El Escape Caribeño, and René and Priscilla in Punta Uva. For horseback riding, contact Mauricio Salazar and Antonio at "Tropical Paradise." Earl Brown can arrange snorkeling and ocean fishing expeditions. Also contact Daniel Brown at Soda Aquario, and "Papi" Hudson about snorkeling trips. Lica at Hotel Puerto Viejo repairs surf boards. Miss Dollly can take you on a walk to learn to identify medicinal plants and herbs.

Punta Uva: From Puerto Viejo, the road continues to Manzanillo, 12 km to the S. A scarcely populated area which is just starting to be developed, it is also one of the nation's most beautiful. This beach is third in line, after Playas Pirikiri and Chiquita, in the series running to the S from the village. Offshore are 650-ft. coral reefs. A $3 million 240-room bungalow development is planned here. At the end of the road is the small community of Manzanillo. Here, Juan Rocha (Spanish-speaking only!) will take you to his farm (6.5 km RT from Manzanillo). Contact Jácamo regarding horse rentals. Local resident Miss Alfonsia will share her knowledge of local plants. Bus service is planned, but right now you have to drive, hike, cycle, or hitch this stretch.

Refugio Nacional Vida Silvestre Gandoca-Manzanillo: This is a mixed-management reserve, meaning that its goal is not only preserving resources but also sustaining them through their active use by the community in the pursuit of economic development. The reserve is the only area containing mangrove swamps along the Caribbean Coast; there's also *cativo* forest, a 741-acre estuary, two *jolillo* swamps, and coral reefs. Some of the mammals here include the tapir, manatee, margay, sloth, paca, and ocelot. Birds include the falcon, hawk, pelican, chestnut-mandibled toucan, and five species of parrots. Of 358 species of birds sighted, 40% are rarely seen in neighboring Panama. **practicalities and hiking:** Boat rides and snorkeling in this area can be arranged with Willie Burton. He can also arrange trips to nine-km-long Gandoca, a turtle nesting beach. You can walk from Monkey Point to Manzanillo (5.5 km). Rubber boots are essential, and the trail can be a mite treacherous in places. Another alternative is the "government road," a 5-km route passing through dense tropical forests; it's very muddy during the wet season. Contact Florentino Gerard in Manzanillo about local guides and birdlists.

from Puerto Viejo: The bus to Limón leaves Mon. to Sat. at 6 AM, 1:30, and 4 PM and on Sun. at 6 AM and 4 PM. If you can get to the crossroads (*cruce*), the express bus from Sixaola passes by at around 6:30 AM, 9:30 AM, and 3:30 PM. The bus to Bribri leaves at 6:30 AM, 11:30, 2:30, and 5:30, returning at 12 and 3:30.

Bribri: Set 65 km (40) mi.) from Limón, this is the region's administrative center, and there's no reason to come here except to go to the bank or post office. It's also a transportation center where you can catch buses to the indigenous village of Amubri (stay at the Casa de Huespedes run by nuns there) and other indigenous villages.

FROM COSTA RICA

departing by air: To get a taxi to the airport, call 21-6865, ask at your hotel, or go out in the streets and search for an orange taxi well in advance of your departure. The Alajuela-bound microbus, which makes a stop at the airport, runs from Av. 2, Calles 12/14. Upon departing, tourists may change *colones* equal to only US$50. Since this is a bureaucratic hassle, you may wish to spend your remaining currency for the airport tax (US$7) and/or at the shops. If you expect the bank at the airport to be closed or if you just want to do it in advance, you may change money at a local bank, but you'll need to bring your airplane ticket, passport, and a photocopy to leave at the bank for its records.

for Panama: TICA bus (tel. 21-9229), Calle 9, Av. 4, runs to Panama City for about $18. It departs on Mon., Wed., Fri., and Sun. at 11 AM, arriving at 5. Leaving daily at 7:30 AM and arriving at 5, TRACOPA bus (tel. 21-4214, 23-7685), Av. 18, Calle 4, runs to David, Panama for around $7.50. There you can take another bus on to Panama City hourly (7 hrs.) or an express at noon and midnight (5.5 hrs). Other alternatives are to fly directly ($110) or fly SANSA to Coto 47 ($11) Mon. to Sat. and then take a taxi to Paso Canoas on the border. There you can catch a bus into Panama; the border closes here from 12 to 2 daily.

for Nicaragua: SIRCA (tel. 22–5541) bus has a 12-hour run ($7) to Managua, Nicaragua at 5 AM on Wed., Fri., and Sun. from Calle 11, Av. 2. TICA bus (tel. 21–9229, C. 9, Av. 4) also runs on Mon., Wed. and Fri. at 7 AM; it has better buses, costs about $1 more, and arrives about the same time. Other buses from Coca Cola run to the border at Peñas Blancas. A visa is no longer required for US citizens, but you must change $60 at the border. Call the Nicaraguan Embassy (tel. 33–8747) to check on the latest requirements.

BOOKLIST

Travel and Description

Finchley, Alan: *Costa Rica: An Alternative for Americans.* New Brunswick, NJ: 1975.

Lougheed, Vivian. *Central America by Chickenbus.* Price Geroge B.C.: Repository Press, 1988. The best available budget-oriented guide to Central Ameica.

Mayfield, Michael W. and Gallo, Rafael E. *The Rivers of Costa Rica: A Canoeing, Kayaking, and Rafting Guide.* Birmingham, AL: Menasha Ridge Press, 1988.

Nelson, Harold D. *Costa Rica: A Country Study.* Washington, D.C.: American University, 1983.

Villafranca, Richard. *Costa Rica: Gem of American Republics.* New York: 1976.

Flora and Fauna

Allen, Dorothy. *The Rainforest of Gulfo Dulce.* Sanford. CA: Sanford Press, 1977.

Allen, P. H. *The Rain Forests of Golfo Dulce.* Gainesville: University of Florida Press, 1956.

Boza, Mario A. and Rolando Mendoza. *The National Parks of Costa Rica.* Madrid: Industrias Graficas Alvi, S.A., 1981.

Boza, Mario A. *Costa Rica National Parks.* Madrid: Infaco, S.A., 1988.

Hall, Carolyn. *Costa Rica, a geographical interpretation in historical perspective.* Boulder, CO: Westview Press, 1985. Possibly the best ecological guide to any nation ever.

Carr, Archie F. *The Windward Road.* Tallahassee, FL: University Presses of Florida, 1955.

de Vries, Phillip J. *Butterflies of Costa Rica.* Princeton, NJ: Princeton University Press, 1987.

Forsyth, Adrian. *Journey through a Tropical Jungle.* Toronto: Greely de Pencier Books, 1988.

Janzen, Daniel H., ed. *Costa Rica National History.* Chicago: University of Chicago Press, 1983.

Skutch, Alexander F. A. *A Naturalist in Costa Rica.* Gainesville, FL: University of Florida Press, 1971.

Stiles, Gary and Alexandr Skutch. *A Guide to the Birds of Costa Rica.* Ithaca, NY: Cornell University Press, 1989. This superb 477-page guide lists not only everything you might want to know about the nation's birds (including description, mating calls, habits, and range) but also illustrates them in beautiful color plates. As an added bonus, descriptions of numerous avian habitats and birding localities are included.

History

Creedman, Thomas S. *Historical Dictionary of Costa Rica.* NJ: Metuchen, 1977.

Hovey, Graham and Gene Brown, eds. *Central America and the Caribbean.* New York: Arno Press, 1980. This volume of clippings from The New York Times, one of its Great Contemporary Issues series, graphically displays American activities and attitudes toward the area. A goldmine of information.

Mannix, Daniel P. and Malcolm Cooley. *Black Cargoes.* New York: Viking Press, 1982. Details the saga of the slave trade.

Politics and Economics

Ameringer, Charles D. *Don Pepe: A Political Biography of José Figueres of Costa Rica.* Albuquerque, NM: University of New Mexico Press, 1978.

Ameringer, Charles D. *Democracy in Costa Rica* New York: Praeger, 1982.

Barry, Tom. *Costa Rica: A Country Guide.* Albuquerque, NM: The Inter-Hemispheric Resource Center, 1989. One in a series, this superb book surveys the political and economic situation, taking in military, environmental and social issues, as well as foreign influences.

Barry, Tom. *The Central American Fact Book.* New York: Grove Press, 1986. A guide to the economic and political situation in each of the region's nations, together with a list of transnationals active in the region.

Bell, John P. *Crisis in Costa Rica: The 1948 Revolution.* Austin, TX: University of Texas Press, 1971.

Booth, John A. and Thomas W. Walker. *Understanding Central America.* Boulder, CO: Westview Press, 1989. A fine overview of five of its nations.

Denton, Charles F. *Patterns of Costa Rican Politics.* Allyn and Bacon: Boston, 1971.

Edelman, Marc and Joanne Kenen *The Costa Rica Reader.* New York: Grove Weidenfeld, 1989. An excellent introduction covering everything from cooperatives to contras.

English, Burt H. *Liberacion Nacional in Costa Rica.* Gainsville, FL: 1971.

Herrick, Bruce and Barclay Hudson. *Urban Poverty and Economic Development: A Case Study of Costa Rica.* NY, NY: 1980.

Interbook, Inc. *Rural Development in Costa Rica.* NY, NY: 1978.

Jones, Chester Lloyd, *Costa Rica and Civilization in the Caribbean.* New York: Russell & Russell, 1967. This rather dry account written by a University of Wisconsin economics and political science professor was first published in 1935.

Rolbein, Seth. *Noble Costa Rica.* New York: St. Martin's Press, 1989. A firsthand account of Costa Rican politics and its press during the late 1980s.

Saunders, John. *Rural Electrification & Development: Social and Economic Development in Costa Rica and Colombia.* Boulder, CO: 1978.

Seligson, Mitchell A. *Peasants of Costa Rica and the Rise of Agrarian Capitalism.* Madison, WI: 1980.

Sociology and Anthropology

Biesanz, John and Mary. *Costa Rican Life.* Westport, CT: Greenwoood Press, Inc., 1979. A portrait of sleepy Costa Rican life as it was during the laid back 1940s.

Biesanz, Richard, Karen Zumbris Biesanz and Mavis Hiltunen Biesanz. *The Costa Ricans.* Prospect Heights, IL: Waveland, 1987 (updated edition).

Art and Archaeology

Jones, Julie, (ed.), Michael Kan and Michael J. Snarkis. *Between Continents/Between Seas: Pre-Columbian Art of Costa Rica.* Detroit, MI: Abrams/Detroit Institute of the Arts, 1981.

COSTA RICA GLOSSARY

a la Tica—in the Costa Rican fashion, as Costa Ricans do it.

apartotels—an apartment hotel which has rooms with kitchen facilities. These are often suites and usually have daily, weekly and monthly rates.

buttress—You'll often hear this term used in reference to rainforest trees. Although most roots are invariably a combination there are three main varieties: often looping or undulating from side to side, serpentine buttresses extend some distance from the tree. Flying buttresses are of the stilt-root type. Resembling giant wedges, plank buttresses are the most spectacular of the three.

bocas—Costa Rican term for late afternoon hors d'oeuvres.

cabina, cabinas—literally cabin or cabins, these are sometimes similar to motels and sometimes identical with apartment hotels.

cafetaleros—the wealthy coffee growers who have commanded a dominant economic and political influence.

cantina—bar.

cantones—counties; administrative districts of a province.

carretera—a route or highway.

colón—the currency of the country; divided into 100 *céntimes*.

distritos—districts; subdivisions of a canton.

hospedaje—an inexpensive hotel usually run by a family.

iglesia—church.

jefe politico—district political chief who is appointed by the president.

marimba—a xylophone constructed with gourds traditionally found in many Latin American and African nations.

medieria—a type of land tenure in which the landlord supplies everything except labor.

mirador—a scenic lookout point.

mesa—polling place.

municipalidad—municipal council.

Nica, Nicas—nickname for Nicaraguans.

pensiŏn—an inexpensive hotel.

precarista—a squatter on agricultural land so named for his "precarious" position.

pulpería—general store.

punta guanacasteco—the national dance, performed with marimba and guitar accompaniment.

sendero—a hiking trail.

soda—small bar or snack joint.

Tico, Ticos—the nickname commonly applied to the Costa Rican people.

tugurios—urban slums, generally constucted on hills or areas subject to flooding. They are the locus of environmental contamination, ill health, prostitution, crime, and broken families.

SPANISH VOCABULARY

DAYS OF THE WEEK

domingo	Sunday
lunes	Monday
martes	Tuesday
miercoles	Wednesday
jueves	Thursday
viernes	Friday
sabado	Saturday

MONTHS OF THE YEAR

enero	January
febrero	February
marzo	March
abril	April
mayo	May
junio	June
julio	July
agosto	August
septiembre	September
octubre	October
noviembre	November
diciembre	December

NUMBERS

uno	one
dos	two
tres	three
cuatro	four
cinco	five
seis	six
siete	seven

ocho	eight
nueve	nine
diez	ten
once	eleven
doce	twelve
trece	thirteen
catorce	fourteen
quince	fifteen
dieciseis	sixteen
diecisiete	seventeen
dieceiocho	eighteen
diecinueve	nineteen
veinte	twenty
veintiuno	twenty-one
veintidos	twenty-two
treinta	thirty
cuarenta	forty
cincuenta	fifty
sesenta	sixty
setenta	seventy
ochenta	eighty
noventa	ninety
cien	one hundred
ciento uno	one hundred one
doscientos	two hundred
quinientos	five hundred
mil	one thousand
mil uno	one thousand one
dos mil	two thousand
un million	one million
mil milliones	one billion

primero	first
segundo	second
tercero	third
cuarto	fourth
quinto	fifth
sexto	sixth
septimo	seventh
octavo	eighth
noveno	ninth
decimo	tenth
undecimo	eleventh
duodecimo	twelfth
ultimo	last

CONVERSATION

¿Como esta usted?	How are you?
Bien, gracias, y usted?	Well, thanks, and you?
Buenos dias.	Good morning.
Buenas tardes.	Good afternoon.
Buenas noches.	Good (evening) night.
Hasta la vista.	See you again.
Hasta luego.	So long.
¡Buena suerte!	Good luck!
Adios.	Goodbye.
Mucho gusto de conocerle.	Glad to meet you.
Felicidades.	Congratulations.
Muchas felicidades.	Happy birthday.
Feliz Navidad.	Merry Christmas.
Feliz Ano Nuevo.	Happy New Year.
Gracias.	Thank you.
Por favor.	Please.
De nada.	You're welcome.
Perdoneme.	Pardon me.
¿Como se llama esto?	What do you call this?
Lo siento.	I'm sorry.
Permitame.	Permit me.
Quisiera...	I would like ...
Adelante.	Come in.
Permitame presentarle...	May I introduce ...
¿Como se llamo usted?	What is your name?
Me llamo...	My name is ...
No, se.	I don't know.
Tengo sed.	I'm thirsty.
Tengo hambre.	I'm hungry.
Soy norteamericano (-na).	I'm an American.
¿Donde puedo encontrar...?	Where can I find ...?
¿Que es esto?	What is this?
¿Habla usted ingles?	Do you speak English?
Hablo (entiendo) un poco espanol.	I speak (understand) a little Spanish.
¿Hay alguien aqui que hable ingles?	Is there someone here who can speak English?

Le entiendo.	I understand you.
No entiendo.	I don't understand.
Hable mas despacio, *por favor.*	Please speak more slowly.
Repita, por favor.	Please repeat.

TELLING TIME

¿ Que hora es?	What time is it?
Son las . . .	It's
. . . cinco	five o'clock
. . . ocho y diez	ten past eight
. . . seis y cuarto	a quarter past six
. . . cinco y media	half past five
. . . siete y menos cinco	five to seven
antes de ayer	the day before yesterday
anoche	yesterday evening
esta manana	this morning
a mediodia	at noon
en la noche	in the evening
de noche	at night
a medianoche	at midnight
manana en la manana	tomorrow morning
manana en la noche	tomorrow evening
pasado manana	the day after tomorrow

DIRECTIONS

¿En que direccion queda . . . ?	In which direction is . . . ?
Lleveme a . . . , por favor.	Please take me to . . .
Lleveme alla . . . , por favor.	Please take me there.
¿ Que lugar es este?	What place is this?
¿ Donde queda el pueblo?	Where is the town?
¿ Cual es el mejor camino para . . . ?	Which is the best road for . . . ?

De vuelta a la derecha.	Turn to the right.
De vuelta a la izquierda.	Turn to the left.
Siga derecho.	This way.
En esta direccion.	In this direction.
¿A que distancia estamos de . . . ?	How far is it to . . . ?
¿Es este el camino a . . . ?	Is this the road to . . . ?
¿Es . . .	Is it . . .
. . . cerca?	near?
. . . lejos?	far?
. . . norte	north
. . . sur	south
. . . este	east
. . . oeste	west
Indiqueme, por favor.	Please point.
Hagame favor de decirme donde esta . . .	Please direct me to . . .
el telephono	the telephone
el excusado	the toilet
el correo	the post office
el banco	the bank
la comisaria	the police station

INDEX

ADDITIONAL READING